W9-CBM-628

Theirs
Is The
Kingdom

Theirs Is The Kingdom

THE NEW TESTAMENT

Lowell Hagan
Jack Westerhof

Illustrations by Paul Stoub

WM. B. EERDMANS PUBLISHING COMPANY
GRAND RAPIDS, MICHIGAN

MARSHALL MORGAN & SCOTT PUBLICATIONS, LTD.
BASINGSTOKE, ENGLAND

To our special friends
whose vision, patience,
confidence, and generosity
made this project possible.

First published 1986 by Wm. B. Eerdmans Publishing Co.
255 Jefferson Ave. S.E., Grand Rapids, Mich. 49503
and
Marshall Morgan & Scott Publications, Ltd.
3 Beggarwood Lane, Basingstoke, Hants RG23 7LP, UK

The authors and publisher wish to express their gratitude to Bijbel-Kiosk-Vereniging,
the Netherlands, publishers of G. Ingwersen's *Bijbel in vertelling en beeld*

Library of Congress Cataloging-in-Publication Data

Hagan, Lowell.
Theirs is the kingdom.

Summary: Retells the stories of the New Testament with
the intention of being faithful to the Scriptures,
sensitive to the Bible's richness, and alert to children's needs.
1. Bible stories, English — N.T. [1. Bible stories —
N.T.]   I. Westerhof, Jack. II. Stoub, Paul, ill.   III. Title.
BS2401.H34   1986   225.9′505   86-11679

ISBN 0-8028-5013-8

Marshall Morgan & Scott edition 0-551-01412-1

The New Testament

I.
THE COMING OF THE CHRIST

II.
THE GOOD NEWS OF THE KINGDOM IN WORD AND DEED

III.
ARE YOU THE ONE?

IV.
THE SURPRISE OF THE KINGDOM

V.
THE FINAL CONFLICT

VI.
THE BOOK OF ACTS

VII.
THE REVELATION TO JOHN

Preface

I would not have become deeply involved in the production of *Theirs Is the Kingdom* except for a series of events which date back all the way to the middle sixties.

My own children were young then, teaching techniques were being refined, and many young parents felt the need for a fresh and honest retelling of the mighty acts of God in graphic, contemporary English.

During a three-year stay in the Netherlands my family and I used a children's story Bible written by Gezina Ingwersen. Ingwersen brought to the art of story telling a unique insight into the interplay of promise and fulfillment in the two testaments, an insight she learned from her teacher S. G. De Graaf. Her work became so popular that it was affectionately referred to by the color of its cover—the Blue Children's Story Bible. An early English edition was titled *Bible—our Guide*.

I became a serious student of children's story Bibles when the publisher of this edition asked me to prepare a new English version of Ingwersen's work. That was an enjoyable experience and one in which family and friends shared as the work progressed. Instead of the moralistic twist so often given children's Bible stories, Ingwersen's account told the captivating story of God at work—God in his majestic holiness and incredible patience, God keeping covenant with stubborn people till the fulness of time, when in the coming of Christ he broke through Satan's power and Israel's borders to let the nations taste his great salvation.

Many people were disappointed when for a variety of reasons this manuscript was, after all, not published—except for serialization in the odd church paper. I was disappointed too—until a brand new opportunity came along.

Almost playfully at first, and then quite seriously, the team responsible for *Theirs Is the Kingdom* suggested that we start from scratch. This was not to be a retranslation of an existing work, but a brand new project inspired by and in various ways indebted to the Ingwersen volume. It had to be faithful to the Scriptures, sensitive to the Bible's own movement, richness, and depth; alert to the needs of the children for whom we were writing; it had to be well told; and, last but not least, extremely well illustrated.

That was our dream.

I was the person mainly responsible for the theological tone and sensitivity of *Theirs Is the Kingdom*. Harry Fernhout—project manager, author of several Bible studies, and a teacher's teacher—worked hand in hand with me. It is absolutely true that those who first work with the Scripture receive the first blessing. It was a delight to work through the Gospels as we did, arranging the accounts of the ministry of Christ in concentric circles around the theme of the kingdom which he embodied and taught. We were astonished by the revealing structure of the Book of Acts, and our eyes were opened to the powerful encouragement that comes our way in the bold and imaginative language of the apocalypse. As we worked we learned.

Our master storyteller is Lowell Hagan. A teacher by profession, and a Bible scholar in his own right, he managed to catch our signals and translate them into the engaging story that is told on these pages.

Don Sedgwick has extensive editorial experience. To him we owe a great deal of the readability of the book. We expect that most ten-year-olds will be able to read and comprehend the story by themselves. Younger children will certainly catch on to the message as they hear the story read, and whole families should be able to enjoy a reading time "around the table." Arnold De Graaff, a theologically trained psychologist, gave valuable advice from his perspective.

Illustrations are important. They, as much as the text, interpret the action. Paul Stoub's lively artistry tells you at a glance the tone, mood, and action of this book. His own love for the Story shines in the faces of children crowding Jesus, in the awesomeness of the crucifixion, in the rich symbolism of his depictions of the apocalypse.

Bert Witvoet worked with us as a journalist and teacher at the outset of the project. To him and many others who enabled and encouraged us: our heartfelt thanks!

This is the New Testament part of *Theirs Is the Kingdom*. The Old Testament is still in preparation. It is our prayer that this volume and the next will bring to a multitude of children the great good news that theirs indeed is the wonderful kingdom of our great God and Savior Jesus Christ!

August 1985
Jack Westerhof

The New Testament

There is only one Bible, but it has two parts. The Old Testament tells us the story of how God made the world, and how he made people to take care of it for him. But people turned away from God and decided to try to take charge of the world alone. They thought their taking charge would bring them glory, but it only brought them ruin. In spite of their sin, though, God promised Adam and Eve that one day he would send a Redeemer to save them.

Many years later, God chose the children of Abram to be his special people, and he kept all his promises to them. He led them out of their slavery in Egypt, through the desert, and into the land he had promised. There he wanted them to live according to the law of his covenant, and to be an example to all the world of the blessings that would come from loving and serving him.

Again and again the people of Israel turned away from God, and each time he brought them back, even if it meant punishing them. He gave them a king, and for a while Israel under David and Solomon became a light to the nations around them. But in spite of the warnings of the prophets, the kings also deserted the Lord, and he had to send Israel's enemies to defeat them. All the while, God had his prophets remind his people that he would send the true king, born into David's family, to save his people from their sins.

The New Testament tells how God kept his promise and sent the Redeemer into the world. He lived his life obeying God, was killed as a common criminal even though he had done nothing wrong, and was raised from the grave on the third day after his death. This man, Jesus of Nazareth, was the true king God had promised. He came, not to the people of Israel only, but to all the people of the world. He was the one the prophet Isaiah spoke of, the one who would be "a light for the Gentiles, to open the eyes of the blind, to bring the captives out of prison."

Once again, God called out a special people for himself, a new Israel. He called them from every nation of the earth. All those who believed in Jesus and loved him as their Lord became members of that new Israel, the church. After Jesus went back to be with his Father, his followers traveled all over the world, bringing the good news of the kingdom of God. The church grew and spread, even though the powers of the world opposed it. It has continued to grow and will until the end of all things, when Jesus will come back to establish his kingdom forever in the new earth, where the curse of sin will finally be taken away.

All these things are part of the story of the New Testament. For this is the story of Jesus, the Christ, and the new covenant that God made with his people through the death of his son on the cross.

The Four Gospels

FOUR FOLLOWERS OF Jesus wrote down the story of his birth, life, death, and resurrection. We call these four men the Evangelists because they wrote the Evangel, the Good News of the kingdom of God. Each had his own way of telling the stories. Matthew wanted to show the Jewish people that Jesus was the Messiah, the Redeemer God had promised. He told the story to bring out the fact that in Jesus the kingdom had come and Scripture had been fulfilled.

Mark presented Jesus as the Son of God. He wanted to show his power to teach, to heal people, and to forgive sins. He did not repeat as much of what Jesus said but instead concentrated on what Jesus did.

Luke wrote the good news for the Gentiles. He therefore told the gospel story to show that Jesus came to save not only Israel but the whole world. He especially showed that Jesus came to bring good news to the poor, and he included many stories of how Jesus met the needs of lowly people.

John said he wrote his story of the gospel "so that you may believe that Jesus is the Messiah, the Son of God, and that by believing, you may have life through his name." John wanted to bring out the meaning of many of the things that Jesus did, meanings that Jesus' followers did not understand at the time.

So each of the four Gospel writers told the story of Jesus in his own way. They chose which stories to tell, which details to include, and the order in which to tell them—to bring out their individual points. None of them sat down to write a history the way we would, with all the pieces of information lined up like tin soldiers. This means that in many cases we can't know for sure the exact order of events. But then, the exact order of events is not really very important in telling the gospel story.

Some of the stories in the Gospels are told by all four of the Evangelists; but many are told by only one. In retelling the stories, we decided to tell each story only once. And we have not tried to put everything in order like a modern-day history book. Instead, we have told the stories in five main groups. Each group of stories centers on one main idea. By doing this, we have tried to bring out the different ways in which the four Gospels look at the life of Jesus. All these separate stories together are the one story of Jesus of Nazareth, God's chosen Messiah.

I.
The Coming
of the Christ

THE ANNOUNCEMENT

Zechariah

IN THE DAYS when the Romans ruled Judea, and they made Herod the king of the Jews, there was a priest named Zechariah. He and his wife Elizabeth loved God and were waiting for the Redeemer. But there was one great sorrow in their lives: Zechariah and Elizabeth had no children. For years they had prayed and asked the Lord for a child; but no child had been born yet. Now they were both old, past the age for having children.

Then there came a day when it was Zechariah's turn to go up to the temple in Jerusalem to burn incense on the altar of the Lord. There were so many priests and Levites at that time that they were not all needed in the temple at one time; so they took turns. It had been years since Zechariah had been to Jerusalem, and he was glad that he would see the city of David once more before he died. He packed his belongings, kissed Elizabeth good-bye, and set off on his donkey for Jerusalem.

The city was full of people, even though it was not a feast time. Pilgrims came from all over the Roman world to worship at the temple, Israelites who had been scattered during the times of conquest. Everywhere there were Roman soldiers, reminders that the Jews were now a conquered people. The temple had been rebuilt by King Herod. It was much more grand than the one built in the days of Ezra and Nehemiah, but it was not as glorious as the temple of Solomon.

As Zechariah walked into the temple early one morning to perform his service as a priest, people were already gathering in the courtyard to pray. Zechariah carefully washed his hands and feet at the basin in the courtyard and then went into the Holy Place, where only priests were allowed to enter. He placed the incense on the bronze altar standing there, then picked up a glowing coal with a pair of metal tongs and touched it to the incense. As the incense began to glow, the whole room was filled with a wonderful smell. Zechariah watched the thin trail of blue smoke curl up toward heaven. He turned to set down the tongs, then stopped and stared. There by the altar, half hidden by the smoke of the incense, stood a man. No, it wasn't a man. It was an angel of God! Frightened, Zechariah covered his face with his sleeve.

"Don't be afraid, Zechariah," said the angel gently. "Your prayer has been answered. Your wife Elizabeth is going to have a son. You must call him John, which means *God is merciful*. John will make you very happy, and many others will also be full of joy because of him. He will be great in the Lord's eyes, and you must dedicate him to God. He must not drink wine or strong drink, but he will be filled with the Spirit of God. He will become a

5

prophet like Elijah, and he will turn the hearts of the parents to their children. He will call God's people to obedience once again."

Zechariah shook his head. How could this be true? He and Elizabeth were too old to have children. Finally he spoke to the angel: "How can I be sure this will happen?"

The angel's voice was not so gentle now. "I am Gabriel, who stands in the presence of God," he said. "The Lord has sent me to tell you this good news. Now listen! My words will come true when it is time. But since you did not believe me, this will be the sign you asked for: until my words come true, you will not be able to speak a word." Then the angel vanished.

Outside, the people were getting restless. Why was Zechariah taking so long? Had the old man died in there? No one could go in to see, because only priests were allowed into the Holy Place. The people were still whispering to each other when the curtain opened and Zechariah walked out, pale and trembling.

"What's wrong, Zechariah?" someone asked. "You look like you've seen a ghost!" Then they saw Zechariah pointing to his mouth and shaking his head. He couldn't speak! He made signs to them, trying to tell them what had happened. Finally the people began to understand. "He *has* seen a vision," they said. "God has spoken to him!" Zechariah could only nod his head and make signs telling them to go home. The people went away, shaking their heads and wondering.

Zechariah also went home when his service in the temple was over. Using signs and gestures, it took him a long time to tell his wife what had happened. Even when he finally got the whole story out, it was hard for her to believe. After all, she was an old woman, much too old to have a baby. Then she remembered what had happened many years before to Abraham's wife, Sarah. She too was past the age for having children, but the Lord gave her a son, Isaac. Now the Lord was going to do the same thing for her!

Then a new thought came into her mind. The angel had said that many people would be made happy through him, that he would be a prophet like Elijah. She remembered something she had heard one day when Scripture was being read. The prophet Elijah must come before the Messiah, the Lord's promised Redeemer. Perhaps the day was coming closer when the Messiah would come! Elizabeth got down on her knees and praised the Lord. "After all these years you have heard me and helped me," she said. "Thank you that our family name will be carried on. Now, please keep your other promises and send the Redeemer to us soon."

Mary and the Angel

FAR TO THE north, in a town called Nazareth, lived Elizabeth's cousin, a young woman named Mary. Her parents were not rich, but they always had enough to eat. They loved the Lord and were also waiting for the day when the Messiah would come. Mary had learned to long for that day too. When he came, she was sure that he would drive out the Romans and rule over God's people in Jerusalem, just as the great King David had. Perhaps—she scarcely dared to think it—but just perhaps, God might choose her to be the mother of the Messiah. But then, all the young women of Israel treasured the same secret hope. Surely God would choose someone from a more important family.

And there were other things on Mary's mind these days. She was going to be married soon! Joseph, the young carpenter, had already asked her father. Sometimes Mary passed by the carpenter's shop to watch Joseph at work. His hands were so firm and steady on the tools, and he did such fine work. But the most important thing for Mary was the look in Joseph's eyes. He loved her, and that she knew for certain. So Mary lived quietly and happily. And then one day something happened that changed her life forever.

She didn't see the stranger at first; she was too busy with her sewing. She heard no footsteps, no rustle of clothing. But when she looked up, he was just standing there. She should have been afraid, and in a way she was, although she could tell at a glance that the stranger did not mean to harm her. He looked at her for a moment, then spoke in a firm but gentle voice.

"Hello, Mary." he said. "You have been favored above all other women. The Lord is with you."

Then Mary did start to tremble, and her heart beat faster. What could he possibly mean? Certainly this was no ordinary man.

"Don't be afraid, Mary," he went on. "God loves you very much. You are going to have a son, and you will name him Jesus. He will be very great and will be called the Son of the Most High God. The Lord will give him the throne of his ancestor David, and he will be king over Jacob's people forever. His reign will never end."

Now Mary was sure that the stranger was an angel of God. But his words confused her. "How can that be?" she asked. "How can I have a son? Joseph and I aren't married yet!"

The angel—it was Gabriel, the same one who had spoken to Zechariah—looked kindly at Mary and said, "The Holy Spirit will come upon you. The power of the Most High God will cover you. Therefore, your holy child will be called the Son of God. And here is a sign for you. Your cousin Elizabeth is old now, and they say that she will never have a child. But she is already six months pregnant and soon will have a son. Nothing is impossible with God."

It was more than Mary could understand. But she knew that what the angel had said was true: with God, nothing was impossible. So she bowed her head and said, "I am the Lord's servant. I am ready for him to do just as you have said." And when she looked up, the angel was gone.

Mary Visits Elizabeth

"I MUST GO TO see my cousin Elizabeth," Mary said to her mother on the day after the angel had visited her.

Her mother looked at her in amazement. "Go visit your cousin? What an idea, child! It takes a week to get there from here!"

"But I *must* go see her, Mother," Mary insisted. "She—" And then Mary bit her lip because she knew how foolish she would sound. "Elizabeth is going to have a baby."

Her mother's eyes went wide with surprise, and then she began to laugh. "Elizabeth have a baby! The very idea!"

Mary grabbed hold of her mother's sleeve. "But it's true, Mother! An angel of God came to me and told me!"

The laughter stopped almost as quickly as it had begun. Mary's mother looked deeply into her eyes. Then she slowly nodded her head. "You have never lied to me before," she said. "I can see that you believe what you are saying. Very well, we will prepare you for the journey. If it's true, someone should be with Elizabeth when her baby is born."

Three days later Mary was on her way to the hill country of Judea, where her cousin Elizabeth lived. A friend went with her so that she would not have to travel alone. They traveled during the day, and at night they slept in small inns along the way. At last, after days of travel, they came to the house of Zechariah and Elizabeth. Mary hurried into the house.

"Elizabeth!" she called. "Elizabeth, are you home?"

At the sound of Mary's voice, something happened deep inside Elizabeth. She felt the power of God's Holy Spirit rushing into her, and she

knew at once who had come, and why. At the same time, her unborn baby moved inside her body as if to greet the mother of the Messiah. She hurried to meet Mary, and in words that God put into her mouth, she said, "You are more blessed than all other women! The child you will bear is greatly blessed! What an honor, that the mother of my Lord should come to visit me! My unborn baby jumped for joy at the sound of your voice. The woman who believes in God is truly happy, for his promises to her will come true."

Then Mary was also filled with the words of God, and she said:

"My heart is full of praise for the Lord,
    And my soul is full of joy in God my Savior,
Because he has noticed me, his humble servant.
    From now on, all people will call me the happiest of women,
Because the Mighty One has done great things for me.
    His name is holy!
He is kind to those who honor him,
    But those who oppose him are brought down.
He has filled the hungry with good things,
    But he has sent the rich away empty-handed.
He has kept the promise he made to our ancestors
    And has shown his mercy to the children of Abraham!"

9

The Birth of John the Baptist

MARY STAYED WITH Elizabeth for three months, helping with the housework, until Elizabeth's baby was born. Then she set out on her journey back to Nazareth, knowing that in a few months her own son would be born, just as the angel Gabriel had promised.

When Elizabeth's new baby was eight days old, it was time for him to be circumcised as the sign that he belonged to God's covenant. That was also the time when baby boys were named, so friends and neighbors gathered around to find out his name. "He should be called Zechariah, after his father," they said.

"No!" Elizabeth said. "His name is going to be John."

"John? What kind of a name is that?" the neighbors objected. "You don't have any relatives named John. God gave you this baby to carry on your family name. He should be named Zechariah!"

"Everything you say is true," Elizabeth replied, "but the baby will be named John."

Now the neighbors were upset. "There's no sense in talking to you," they said to her. "Zechariah, what do you have to say about this?"

Zechariah signaled Elizabeth to bring him something he could write on. He wrote these words: "His name is John."

The neighbors looked at each other in surprise. But they were even more surprised a moment later when Zechariah began to speak! God had given him back his ability to speak, and Zechariah was filled with the power of God's Holy Spirit. Like Mary and Elizabeth, he spoke in the words God gave him:

> "Praise the Lord, the God of Israel!
> He has come to help his people, and to set them free!
> He has given us a mighty Savior,
> A true son of his servant David.
> Long ago he promised through his prophets
> That he would save us from our enemies.
> He promised to remember his holy covenant,
> Which he promised to our ancestor Abraham."

When the neighbors saw that the Holy Spirit had filled Zechariah, they were afraid. None of them had ever seen a prophet before! What was that he was saying about a Savior? What kind of child was this baby John? No sooner had the questions popped into their minds than Zechariah turned to his infant son and said:

> "You, my son, will be a prophet of God.
> You will go ahead of the Lord to prepare the road for him,

> To tell the people that they will be saved,
>   That their sins will be forgiven.
> Our God is full of love and mercy.
>   He will send the light of heaven to shine on us,
> To give light to those who are in darkness,
>   And to guide our feet into the path of peace."

As the baby grew, he became a strong child who loved God with his whole heart. When he became a young man, God called him away from the home of his parents. He lived in the desert places, away from the towns and cities, where he learned about God, and prayed, and waited for the day when the Lord would send him out to preach to the people of Israel.

Joseph and Mary

"JOSEPH, I MUST speak with you."

Mary was standing in the doorway of the carpenter's shop. She had a secret she could not keep any longer. But what would Joseph say? What would he do? She watched his strong brown hands as they planed and smoothed the wood. How she did love him! She could only trust God to help him see the truth.

Joseph laid aside his plane and the piece of wood and came to Mary's side. "What is so important, Mary?" he asked.

"Do you remember when I went to see my cousin Elizabeth?" she asked.

"How could I forget?" Joseph replied. "You were gone for three whole months. I missed you very much."

"And I missed you too, Joseph. But do you know why I went?"

"You said that Elizabeth was going to have a baby. And she did too, as old as she is. That's truly a miracle from God."

"How did I know my cousin was going to have a baby?" Mary asked him.

"You said an angel told you. And I have to believe you, because I don't know of any other way you could have found out."

"There was more to what the angel said. Much more." Joseph waited silently, and Mary went on. "He also said—he told me—he said that I was going to have a baby also!"

11

Joseph smiled at Mary. "Of course you will have a baby, Mary. We will have many children after we are married."

Mary looked at him uncertainly, then looked away again. "No, Joseph, you don't understand. I don't mean later—after we are married. I mean now. Very soon."

Mary felt him move away from her. She looked up at him, and his eyes were filled with anger and fear. "Are you trying to tell me that you are pregnant now?"

"Yes, Joseph, but it's not what you think. . ."

"Not what I think?" Joseph demanded. "Not what I think? How can it be anything but what I think?" He grabbed her roughly by the arms. "Who is it? Who is the father? Oh, I see. You go on a little trip to visit your cousin Elizabeth and you come back pregnant."

"No, Joseph, I have not loved any other man. No man has ever touched me."

Joseph drew away from her again, and there was a look almost like hatred in his eyes. "I don't believe you!" he shouted. "You have been unfaithful to me before we could even be married! Get out of here! Get out! I never want to see you again!" Roughly, he pushed her through the doorway and slammed the door behind her. Mary stared at the door for a moment, then turned and ran to her home, the tears streaming down her face.

For several days Mary did not see Joseph at all. They were sad and lonely days for her. Joseph had cast her aside. What would she do now? Then one morning there was a knock at the door. Mary held her breath as her mother went to open the door. But it was not Joseph. It was the rabbi.

"Are your husband and your daughter at home?" the rabbi asked.

"Come in, Rabbi," the mother answered. "They are both here."

The rabbi entered and shut the door behind him. He looked uncomfortably around the room, not knowing quite what to say. Finally he asked, "Has Mary told you of her condition?"

"Yes, she has told us," Mary's father answered.

"And do you believe her?"

Mary's parents looked at each other. Then her father answered slowly. "When Mary told us that an angel had spoken to her, we thought she was dreaming. But when she went to see her cousin Elizabeth, everything she had said turned out to be true. Yes, we believe her."

The rabbi thought for a moment. Then he said, "Mary promised to be faithful to Joseph, but now she is pregnant. She has broken the law of God. Joseph could have demanded that Mary be killed. That is the penalty written in our law. But Joseph is a kind man. He loves your daughter, and he does not want to see her disgraced. Therefore, he is willing to break the marriage agreement, and he will seek no punishment."

There was silence in the room, except for the sound of Mary crying softly. Just then there was another knock at the door. Mary's mother opened the door, and there stood Joseph the carpenter. His eyes were full of excitement. "May I come in?" he asked. He stepped into the room, then looked at the anxious faces of Mary and her parents. He turned to the rabbi. "Rabbi, have you already. . . ?"

"Yes, my son, I have told them."

"Then I must tell you something else," Joseph said. "A strange thing happened to me last night. I was lying in bed, asleep, when an angel of God came to me in a dream. He said to me, 'Joseph, don't be afraid to take Mary as your wife. She has not been unfaithful to you. She is going to have a baby because of the power of the Holy Spirit of God. She will have a son, and you will name him Jesus, because he will save his people from their sins.' Then I woke up. Rabbi, I believe what Mary told me. I want to go ahead with our marriage."

The rabbi frowned. "But Joseph, if you marry her, everyone will believe that you are the father of the child."

"I know that, Rabbi," Joseph answered. "But what will they think if I do not marry her?"

"Yes, I see what you mean," the rabbi said thoughtfully. "Very well, I will perform the ceremony."

And he did. The people of the town wondered why Mary and Joseph were married in such a hurry. When they discovered that Mary was going to have a baby, they thought they knew the answer. But Joseph remembered something he had read in Scripture. Isaiah the prophet had said, "A young woman who has never been with any man will have a son, and his name will be Immanuel." And Immanuel means *God with us.*

THE ARRIVAL

The Birth of Jesus

IN THE GREAT city of Rome, far away from Nazareth, the home of Mary and Joseph, lived the Roman emperor, whose name was Augustus. His armies ruled over many lands, including Palestine, where the Hebrew people lived. The armies of Rome were powerful, and they were also very expensive. It took a lot of money to feed and pay the soldiers. The emperor Augustus decided that not enough people in his empire were paying taxes. "We've lost track of where all the people are," he said one day. "We can't tell whether everyone is paying taxes or not. We must find a way to get the name of everyone in the empire."

Some of the emperor's advisors had an idea. "Caesar," they said—for that is what the Romans called their emperor—"Caesar, perhaps it would be best to take a census, a count of all the people you rule."

"An excellent suggestion," replied the great Augustus. "See to it. All my subjects are to be counted, so that I can be sure they're paying their taxes."

So his officers sent out orders to all the people who lived under the rule of Rome. "Before this year ends," the orders said, "every man must take his wife and children and return to the place where his ancestors came from. There he and his family will be counted, and their names will be placed on the tax records."

For Joseph and Mary, the Caesar's order meant a long journey, down through Samaria, past Jerusalem, and on to the little town of Bethlehem, the birthplace of Joseph's ancestor, King David. It was a hard journey for Mary, who was expecting her baby any time. But Caesar did not care about those who were old, or sick, or pregnant. He only cared about his taxes. So, even though it was the worst time for Mary to travel, Joseph had to pack food for the journey and saddle the donkey. They stopped often to rest, but there was plenty of company because the roads were crowded with other families traveling to their home towns to be registered. The journey was slow and very uncomfortable for Mary, who rode on the donkey's bony back. Sometimes they stayed with relatives, like Zechariah and Elizabeth, but more often they had to find an inn or sleep under the stars.

Days later, when they arrived in Bethlehem, they found the streets crowded with people. Bethlehem was only a small town, but there were hundreds of families returning to be counted. It seemed that every house had at least one visiting family. As Joseph and Mary made their weary way through the streets of Bethlehem toward the town's only inn, Joseph heard his wife draw in her breath sharply, as if she were in pain. Quickly he turned to her. "Is something wrong, Mary?" he asked.

"No, it's nothing," she answered. But a few minutes later he heard the same sound. Once again he turned to ask Mary if she was all right. This time he could see the signs of pain on her face. Then her frown disappeared, and she smiled. "Joseph, perhaps we should hurry to the inn," she said. "I think the baby is going to come soon."

Joseph smiled back at her and said, "Mary, it's only a little way now." He tried not to think what would happen if the inn were too crowded for them. But when he led the donkey into the courtyard of the inn, his heart sank. Travelers were setting up tents in every open space. Slowly they made their way to the door of the inn, and Joseph knocked; but he had little hope. Shortly, the door opened and the bald, sweating little innkeeper, his face flushed from the bustle and hurry, stared at them.

"Sorry, I have no room left at all. You'll have to go elsewhere," he barked, starting to shut the door.

"But we must find a place for tonight," Joseph pleaded. "My wife is going to have a baby."

"You're not alone, mister," the innkeeper replied. "If you look out there in the courtyard, I'll bet you'll find half a dozen pregnant women sleeping on the ground tonight. It's those blasted Romans, that's who it is. It's their fault. If we had our own king, we wouldn't have to put up with this. But the law is the law, and we just have to make the best of it. I'm sorry you didn't get here earlier. Now I really have to get busy." And he started to shut the door again.

"But you don't understand!" Joseph protested. "My wife is going to have her baby now—tonight! She's having labor pains right now."

The innkeeper frowned—and hesitated. "Just a minute," he said. "Let me talk to my wife."

Joseph and Mary stood in the courtyard, surrounded by the sounds of the families setting up camp. The donkey lazily brushed away flies with its bristly tail. The setting sun cast a reddish glow over the mud walls of the town. Twice Joseph saw the little frown of pain cross Mary's face, the frown that showed that her body was preparing for the birth of the baby. At last the innkeeper returned and motioned to Joseph to bend closer.

"There is only one place where you can spend the night," he

whispered. "Do you see that hillside behind the inn? Cut into the bottom of the hill is a cave that we use as a stable for the animals. It isn't much, but then, neither is the inn, crowded as it is. At least you'll be out of the cold and wind. There's plenty of hay there you can use for bedding. Go back into town and come around the back way. My wife will come out later to see if you need anything." Then he raised his voice and said, "I'm sorry I can't do anything for you. You'll just have to go back into the town and see what you can find." Then he winked and hurried on about his duties.

And that is how it happened that Jesus, the baby sent to be the Savior of the world, was born in a stable. Besides Joseph and Mary, it was the goats and the donkeys who were the first to see the newborn king. Mary wrapped her baby boy in strips of linen cloth and laid him down to sleep in the clean, sweet hay of the manger.

The Shepherds and the Angels

IT WAS COLD that night on the hillsides around Bethlehem. Darkness came quickly when the sun went down, taking with it the warmth of the day. The stars shone brightly in the night sky. Flocks of sheep and goats lay down for the night and huddled together to keep warm. The shepherds ate their evening meal together and talked a while of home and family. As the night grew colder, they rubbed their hands together to keep them warm and pulled their cloaks more tightly around them.

One by one the shepherds stretched out on the hard ground and drifted off to sleep. Only two still sat silently watching, watching for the wolves who might sneak into the flocks in the darkness and carry away the lambs. But there were no wolves or thieves stirring tonight. Three hours later, the two shepherds woke two others and then lay down themselves to sleep.

But they did not sleep long. All at once they sat up, startled, rubbing their eyes in the glare of a light that nearly blinded them. It could not be the sun; it was still too early. Shivering more with fear than with cold, the shepherds stared up toward the light. And there, at the center of the light, standing in the air, was a man! No, not a man, it had to be an angel! Some of the shepherds threw themselves on their faces on the ground, afraid that they might see God and die. But the angel said to them, "Don't be afraid! I am here to bring you good news, news of great joy for all people. This very day, in David's town, Bethlehem, your Savior was born. He is the Christ, the Messiah. He is the Lord. And this is how you will know him: you will find him wrapped in strips of cloth, lying in a manger."

Suddenly the light grew even brighter, blotting out the whole sky. And the angel was no longer alone. The whole sky seemed to be filled with angels, like a heavenly army, and they were all singing praises to God. "Glory to God in the highest heaven," they said, "and peace upon earth to those who find favor with God." The song seemed to go on and on, and it was so beautiful that it made the shepherds' hearts ache with joy. And then, as suddenly as they had come, the angels were gone.

The shepherds, still dazzled by the light, sat or lay in silence on the ground. Then they found their voices and began to talk all at once. "Did you see them too?" "Was I dreaming?" "What was that about a Savior being born?" "Did you ever see such a sight?"

"Quiet! Quiet!" ordered a voice. The voice belonged to the oldest of the shepherds, the one who always settled things whenever there was an argument. "Something happened tonight, that's for sure," he said. "Either that light was the glory of God, or we've all gone crazy. Now, what did you hear the angel say?"

"He said something about a Savior being born in David's town," one of the shepherds offered.

The chief shepherd nodded. "That must mean Bethlehem, there at the bottom of the hill," he said. "At least, we've always called it David's town. There's only one thing to do. We'll have to go down to Bethlehem and find out what this great thing is that the Lord has done tonight."

"But what about the flocks?" one of the shepherds asked.

"We'll leave a couple of men here to guard them, and the rest of us will go down to Bethlehem to find out about this."

A few minutes later, a little band of shepherds hurried down the hill into Bethlehem. Quickly they moved through the silent streets, looking into every barn and shed, looking for a baby in a manger. But they found nothing but goats and donkeys and chickens, until at last they came to the little cave behind the inn.

Inside the stable, a knot of people crowded around the manger where a little baby lay, all wrapped in strips of linen.

"Was this baby born tonight?" the chief shepherd asked.

"Yes. Isn't it marvelous?" said the innkeeper's wife, who loved children.

"It is," the shepherd answered, as he stepped forward for a closer look. Then he turned to his companions and said, "It is just as the angel said."

"Angel? What angel?" asked the innkeeper's wife. "Why are you here?"

"We are only poor shepherds," he answered. "Tonight we were guarding our flocks on the hillside when an angel came to us from God. He said, 'I have good news for you. A Savior was born tonight in David's town. He is the Christ, the Lord. You will find him wrapped in strips of cloth, lying in a manger.' So we came here, and we found this baby, lying here just as the angel said."

Then the others watched in amazement as the shepherds bowed down on their faces in front of the baby. None of them understood the shepherd's story. But Mary remembered every word, and she thought of what the angel Gabriel had said to her almost a year before in Nazareth. The shepherds got up again and went back to their flocks. All the way they sang praises to God, and they told everyone they met of the wonderful things that had happened that night.

A week later, when the baby was eight days old, the time came for him to be circumcised, the sign of God's covenant with his people. Just as the angel had instructed Mary, she and Joseph named him Jesus, which means *Savior*.

Jesus and the Two Servants of God

IN JERUSALEM THERE lived a man named Simeon, who loved God and was waiting for the day when God would send the Redeemer he had promised. Simeon knew that the day was coming near, because God had told him that he would not die until he had seen the Messiah. One morning Simeon woke up with only one thought on his mind: he had to go to the temple. He was not sure why, but he knew that the Lord was telling him to go.

An old woman named Anna lived in the temple. As a young woman she had married, but her husband had lived for only seven years after the wedding. When he died, Anna did not marry again. Instead, she went to the temple in Jerusalem, and she worked there every day, sweeping the floors and cleaning, and all the while fasting and praying for her people. On this morning she awoke with the feeling that something special was going to happen, that somehow her prayers were about to be answered.

Simeon stood nervously in the temple courtyard. Was this to be the day? He watched the face of each pilgrim who arrived in the courtyard. Then he saw them, a young man and a young woman with a small child in her arms. The man was carrying two small birds to offer as a sacrifice to the Lord. Quickly Simeon walked up to them. "Why have you come to the temple this morning?" he asked.

"To dedicate this child to the Lord," Joseph answered.

A look of joy passed over Simeon's face. He reached for Jesus, and Mary was happy to have the kindly old man hold her child. Then Simeon lifted his face up toward heaven and said, "Now, Lord, you have kept your promise. Now I can die in peace. I have seen your promised salvation with my own eyes."

"What are you saying?" Joseph demanded. "What does this mean?"

Simeon looked again at Joseph and Mary and smiled. "God has chosen

19

this child," he said. "Many will be saved through him, and many will stumble and fall. He will be a sign from God, but many people will speak against him. When they do that, they will show on the outside what they are really like on the inside." Then he turned to Mary and said, very quietly, "Sorrow will pierce your heart like a sharp sword because of him."

While Joseph and Mary were still wondering at what Simeon had said, the old woman Anna hurried up to them. She took one look at Jesus in Simeon's arms and raised her hands to heaven. "Thank you, O Lord," she said, "that you have allowed me to live to see your Redeemer with my own eyes." Then she turned to Mary and said, "God has blessed you more than any other woman that you should be the mother of his Redeemer. Now I must go and tell my friends. Oh, there are many more in Jerusalem who have waited long for this day." She hurried away, praising the Lord, leaving Mary and Joseph staring at each other in wonder.

Strange Visitors

FAR FROM JERUSALEM lived people who had never heard of Abraham or of the promises God had made to him. They did not have the Bible to tell them about God. But they did have the world around them. Everywhere they looked they could see the power of God. Most of them did not pay any attention to that power, just as many of the people of Israel did not listen to Moses. But some of them wanted to hear, and God taught them. They learned that there is only one God, and that he made heaven and earth. They watched the plants and the animals, and they watched the stars, because they thought they might find some new word from God there. Even though he had forbidden his own people to practice astrology, God chose to speak through the stars to those who did not know him.

On a housetop in a country, far to the east of Judea, a group of men stood watching the stars. Suddenly one of them pointed to a far corner of the sky. "Look!" he said excitedly, "what is that bright star rising over the horizon? I don't remember it from any of our charts." The others looked in wonder for a while, then hurried into the building below. By the light of an oil lamp they consulted their maps of the heavens. Then they looked at each other in amazement. "It's a new star!" they exclaimed. "Not many people live long enough to see such a great thing. It must mean that some great event has taken place."

For weeks they watched eagerly each night to see the new star rise. Each night it rose farther to the west. During the day they read their old books to find out what the star might mean. "It is written in the ancient books," one of them said at last, "that a star like this arises only when a great new king has been born."

"And the star is moving westward," another said. "That must mean that the new king has been born in a land to the west of us."

At this, the oldest of the astrologers stood up. "I have studied the stars all my life, hoping for a moment such as this," he said. "I could not go to my grave in peace if I did not see for myself what God is telling us through this star. I will follow it wherever it leads and see the new king with my own eyes."

"So will I," said another of the astrologers. "Don't forget us!" others joined in. And so they all agreed to set out on a journey to try to discover what wonder the star had announced.

The long caravan moved slowly westward, over rivers and through forests—until it came to the edge of the great desert of Arabia. Each night the star rose farther in the west. Day after day the camels plodded through the desert sands until they had brought the astrologers into the ancient land of Canaan, now the Roman province of Judea. Since they were seeking a new king, they went directly to the palace of King Herod in Jerusalem. Their long journey was nearly over.

Herod and the Wise Men

"YOUR MAJESTY, THERE are visitors from the East who wish to see you."

King Herod stirred from his half-sleep. "Huh? What's that you say? What visitors?"

"Your Majesty," his secretary said, "there are some very strange men outside in the courtyard who wish to see you. They appear to be very wealthy. They say that they are learned men from far to the east, and they have come to pay their respects to you and to your new son."

"My new son? Where did they get that idea? You say they seem to be well-educated men?"

"Yes, Your Majesty, and very rich. They have come a long way to see you."

"Very well, show them in."

The foreign men came slowly into the throne room, dressed in their finest robes. They bowed in respect to King Herod and waited for him to speak to them.

"They tell me you have come a long way to see me," the king said. "I welcome you to my kingdom."

"We have come bringing gifts to the newborn king of the Jews," the oldest of the wise men said.

"I fear your wisdom has misled you," Herod replied, his eyes darting back and forth. "I am king of the Jews. And I have a son, but he is not newborn. What made you think you would find a new baby here?"

"We read it in the ancient books, Your Majesty, after we saw his star."

"Star? What is this about a star?"

"We have learned a great deal in our study of the stars. We saw a new star rise in the east, and each day it moved farther to the west. We knew that the star announced some great event, probably the birth of a king. And in some ancient prophecies we found it written that a new king of the Jews would be born, one who would rise like the morning star. So we came here, King Herod, to the city where the great King David once sat on the throne. We have come to honor the one who is born king of the Jews."

By this time there was a deep scowl on Herod's face. He did not like this talk about a new king of the Jews. He was old and ill, but he was not dead yet. He turned to his own advisors. "Send for the priests and the teachers of the law," he ordered. "Perhaps they can tell us something about this. In the meantime, my friends," he said to his visitors, "how do you like my capital city, Jerusalem? Isn't it magnificent?"

The wise men spoke politely about the city, but the conversation did not last long. Three of the chief priests and half a dozen rabbis from the temple hurried into the throne room and bowed before King Herod. They looked very worried, as if they did not know what to expect from the king.

"My friends from the East have a question for you," the king said. "Is it written in the law and the prophets that a new king shall be born in Israel?"

The priests and teachers looked at each other, each waiting for the other to speak first. Finally one of the priests spoke up. "Yes, Your Majesty, many of the prophets have spoken about this.

"And where and when is this new king to be born?"

Now it was the turn of one of the teachers of the law to speak. "Your Majesty, these words are written in the book of the prophet Micah:

> Bethlehem in the land of Judah,
>   You are small, but you shall be great,
> For from you shall come a leader
>   To guide my people Israel.

It is our judgment, therefore, that some day a king shall be born in the city of Bethlehem. As to when, Your Majesty, no one knows. The prophecy is very old. And you and your son have many years still to reign over Israel."

"You have told me what I wanted to know. Now back to your service in the temple. All of you—leave me! I wish to speak with my learned friends alone." Herod was thinking fast. What if the prophecy were true? After all, he was not a true king of Israel. He was not even a Jew, really. The Romans had made him king. But he intended to stay king. If a baby had been born who might claim to be king of the Jews, there would be only one thing to do: kill him! But how was he to know for sure? Perhaps these wise men could find out for him.

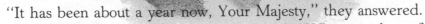

"You have been on a long journey," he said to them. "How long ago did you first see this star?"

"It has been about a year now, Your Majesty," they answered.

"Then go to Bethlehem," the king replied. "When you have found the child, come back and tell me. I too would like to go and worship him."

Night fell as the wise men continued their journey toward Bethlehem. Anxiously they watched for the star. Then they saw with wonder and delight that that star had stopped over the city of David. "Bethlehem is the place!" they said. "In the morning we will find him!" It was hard for them to fall asleep that night, knowing what awaited them in Bethlehem.

They made a strange procession as they came into the city the next morning, dressed in their strange clothes, asking questions everywhere. Yes, there had been many babies born. Oh yes, there were many descendants of King David living in Bethlehem, but none of them was a king. Anything unusual? Well, there was that business with the shepherds. They saw an angel or something. Why don't you ask one of them? Who, me? Yes, I was there. Yes, we saw an angel from God. He said that a Savior was born in Bethlehem who was Christ the Lord. What's that? Yes, they still live here—in a house not far away. Mary and Joseph are their names. The baby's name is Jesus. Follow me, and I'll take you there.

A crowd of curious people followed the wise men as they made their way to the house where Joseph and Mary lived. They went into the house carrying the gifts they had brought for the new king. And when they saw

Jesus with his mother, their hearts were filled with joy. "God has blessed our journey," they said, "for we have seen with our own eyes the child he has sent to be both King and Savior." Then they bowed low on the floor and worshiped the baby, putting their gifts in front of him. There was gold, the precious metal of kings; there was frankincense, which the priests burned as a sweet-smelling offering to God; and there was myrrh, the sweet medicine spice that was also used to wrap the bodies of the dead for burial. Gold, frankincense, and myrrh for the King and Priest who would die for the sins of the world. It was just as the prophet Isaiah had written:

> *The nations will walk in your light,*
> *And kings in the brightness of your shining.*
> *Look up and see them come to you,*
> *Your sons and daughters, babes in arms.*
> *Caravans of camels will fill the city,*
> *Bearing gold and frankincense,*
> *Declaring the praises of the Lord.*

After the wise men from the East had blessed the child, they left the house and went back to the place where they had camped. All over Bethlehem people were buzzing with the news of the strange visitors from the East. Mary remembered everything that had been said and wondered what it all meant. Some day, some day she would understand it all.

Herod Tries to Kill Jesus

"**I** HAD THE STRANGEST dream last night," said one of the Eastern wise men in their camp outside Bethlehem.

"I also dreamed a terrible dream," said another. "What did *you* see?"

"I dreamed that an angel of God came to me and said, 'Go back to your own land, but don't travel the same road you came here on. Do not go back to Jerusalem, for King Herod wants to do only evil to the child Jesus.' Then I woke up. But it seemed so real."

"That was my dream exactly," said the other.

"God led us here," the oldest of them said. "He will lead us back. We must do as the angel said. Hurry now, before Herod sends his soldiers after *us.*" So the wise men returned to their own land. And everywhere they went they told the story of the star and how it led them to the house where the new King and Savior lived.

Not long after that, Joseph also had a dream. An angel came to him in the night and said, "King Herod wants to kill the child. You must take him and Mary and escape into Egypt. The Lord will take care of you there. You must stay until the Lord tells you to leave again." Then the angel was gone, and Joseph woke up. He shook Mary awake.

"Quick, Mary! We must leave now. The Lord has told me that we must go into Egypt to be safe from King Herod. Herod will be sending soldiers here soon to find Jesus and kill him. We must leave now, while it is still dark, so no one will see which way we have gone."

So they got up and quickly packed the few belongings they had brought with them from Nazareth. Mary picked up the baby Jesus, who was still sleeping, and Joseph helped them onto the donkey. Then they stole away into the night, heading toward Egypt. As they traveled, Mary remembered a line from one of the prophets: "I called my Son out of Egypt."

Day after day in his palace in Jerusalem, King Herod waited anxiously for the Eastern wise men to return from Bethlehem. A week went by, then two weeks. Certainly that was enough time for them to travel to Bethlehem, find the baby, and return. After all, Bethlehem was only a day's trip from Jerusalem. Finally, he could stand the suspense no longer. "Send some men to Bethlehem," he ordered the captain of his palace guard. "Find the visitors who came here from the East and bring them back to me."

The next day, the captain of the guard returned to Herod. "We went to Bethlehem, Your Majesty, but there was no sign of the strangers."

"No sign of them?" Herod roared. "You mean you didn't bring them back?"

"The local people said they left more than a week ago, Your Majesty."

"A week ago? I've been tricked!" Herod's face was white with rage, and he could hardly speak. "Take your soldiers back to Bethlehem," he ordered, "and kill every male child under a year old. No, make that two years old."

The captain of the guard turned pale. "Your Majesty, I can't order my men to do such a thing," he said.

"Can't!" Herod roared. "What do you mean, 'Can't'? Who is the king here anyway?"

"But, Your Majesty, they are soldiers. They are trained to fight men, not to kill little children," the captain protested.

"They are trained to obey me! And my orders are to kill every boy under two years of age in Bethlehem and all the villages around. And if you do not obey me now, you will go to the grave with them!"

The people of Bethlehem had no idea of the terrible thing that was about to happen to them. Herod's soldiers drove down on them like

25

lightning from a clear sky, snatching children from their mother's arms, storming into houses and pulling infants from their cradles. It was all over in an hour, and the soldiers thundered away again on their horses. Then the sound of a great crying came from Bethlehem, the weeping of the parents whose children had been killed. It was just as the prophet Jeremiah had written long before:

"A sound is heard in Ramah,
 the sound of great mourning.
It is Rachel, weeping for her children
 and she will not be comforted,
 because they are no more. . . ."

The wicked king Herod did all this to try to kill the new king who had been born. But Jesus was safe in Egypt with Mary and Joseph.

After Herod had died, the angel once again came to Joseph in a dream. "Go back now to Nazareth," he said. "Those who tried to kill the child are dead." So Mary and Joseph took the baby Jesus and returned to the town where they had been married, Nazareth in the land around Lake Galilee. And so the words that were written by one of the old prophets came true, that the Messiah would be called a Nazarene.

Jesus in the Temple

JOSEPH AND MARY settled down in Nazareth, and Joseph returned to his work as a carpenter. Mary's son Jesus grew up like all the other boys in Nazareth, and everyone thought that Joseph was his real father. As a little boy, he went along with Joseph to the carpenter's shop and played with the little blocks and scraps of wood. He watched Joseph craft the wood into boards for houses or legs for tables and chairs.

Joseph and Jesus would often walk through the countryside watching the farmers as they planted and harvested their crops and the fishermen as they sailed out in their little boats on Lake Galilee. As he grew older, Jesus began to learn how to be a carpenter himself, and he learned the ways of his people as well.

Every Sabbath day he went with his father and mother to the synagogue, where he heard the reading of Scripture. He learned the history of his people, how God called Abraham out of the land of Chaldea and promised him the land of Canaan. He learned how God used Moses to lead his people out of Egypt and through the wilderness to the land of promise. He learned about Jacob and Esau, about Joshua and Gideon and Samson, about David and Solomon. And again and again he heard the promise that God would send the Messiah, the one who would save his people from their sins. The rabbi noticed how bright and thoughtful the young Jesus was, and he took a special liking to him. He taught him how to read and write so that he would be able to read Scripture in the synagogue himself when he became a man.

Each year, Joseph and Mary went to Jerusalem to celebrate the Passover feast. When Jesus was twelve years old, they took him with them for the first time. At twelve, by Jewish custom, he was considered a man. It was time for him to go to the temple to worship the Lord. Like every boy visiting the city for the first time, Jesus was fascinated by the crowds of people, the merchants peddling their goods in the streets, the noise and the bustle. He saw the Roman troops as they rode through the streets on horseback, their swords and armor sparkling in the bright sun. He saw the rich and powerful in their expensive clothes.

But these things did not hold his attention. More than anything else, he loved to be in the temple. He was there every day of the feast, watching the pilgrims as they washed their feet in the great brass basin that stood in the courtyard, watching them as they brought their offerings to the priests. He smelled the sweet incense being burned on the altar and saw the smoke from the many sacrifices rising into the sky. This was his Father's house.

What he liked best was to sit and listen to the teachers of the law. He had a hunger to know Scripture of which he had already memorized long sections. He was so fascinated by what he heard that even when the seven days of the feast were over, he went back to the temple on the day his family was to leave for Nazareth. There were so many people in the caravan that Mary and Joseph did not even notice that Jesus was missing. They thought he was with some of the other boys or one of his aunts or uncles.

That evening, after the caravan had camped for the night, Mary started looking for Jesus. He was nowhere to be found. Worried, she went back to Joseph. "Have you seen Jesus anywhere?" she asked. "I've looked through the whole camp for him."

"No, I haven't seen him since we left Jerusalem. Have you asked all our relatives?"

"Yes, every one. No one has seen him. In fact, no one remembers seeing him since we left the city."

Joseph frowned deeply. "Do you suppose he wandered away to look at something, and we left without him?"

Now Mary was really frightened. "Oh Joseph, Jerusalem is such a big city. If he's lost there, where will he spend the night? Anything could happen to him! We should go back and look for him—right now!"

Joseph took Mary in his arms to comfort her. "We can't travel by ourselves at night," he said. "Besides, the city gates are locked by now. We'll go first thing in the morning. I just can't understand what has gotten into that boy. It isn't like him to disappear like that."

Mary hardly slept that night. Before dawn she and Joseph were on their way back to Jerusalem. Alone, they could travel faster than the caravan. Even so, it was afternoon before they reached the gates of the city. They went at once to the place where they had stayed; but Jesus was not there. They asked everyone they saw, but no one had seen a lost twelve-year-old boy. They searched the streets and shops until nightfall, but they still did not find Jesus.

They slept that night in a small inn, then began their search again early the next morning. By noon, they were about ready to give up hope. Then Mary said, "There is one place we haven't looked yet, Joseph."

"Yes, I know—the temple," Joseph answered. "He did love to spend time there. It's our last hope."

They were tired from the long search and nearly frantic with worry when they finally got to the temple. And there was Jesus; but he was not lost and lonely and hungry, as they expected to find him. He was sitting in the circle of elders and teachers, listening to them and asking them questions. Everything he said showed that he was much wiser than any twelve-year-old ever is. To their astonishment, the teachers found that talking with him was like talking with a grown man. Jesus didn't even notice his mother as she came closer. After all she had gone through, worrying about Jesus, the sight of him sitting there so calmly made her angry.

"Child, why did you do this to us?" she cried. "Your father and I have been worried sick about you. We've been looking for you everywhere."

Jesus looked at his mother in surprise. "Why did you have to search for me?" he asked. "Didn't you know that I would have to be in my Father's house?"

Mary hardly knew what to say. What did he mean, his Father's house? Who was he, really? She could see that he had not abandoned them on purpose. And when he saw how upset they were, Jesus left the teachers and went with them.

They returned to Nazareth, where Jesus continued to grow—both in physical size and in understanding. Everyone who knew him liked him; and he pleased God in everything he did. He became a carpenter like Joseph, and no one in town thought he would ever be anything else. But Mary remembered the message of the angels, and the words of Simeon and Anna, and the gifts of the wise men from the East. And she never forgot what Jesus said that day in the temple. Someday . . . somehow, she would understand it all.

PREPARE YE THE WAY OF THE LORD!

The Ministry of John the Baptist

WHILE JESUS WAS growing up in a carpenter's home in Nazareth, another young man was growing up in a hill town in Judea. From the time he was a child, his mother Elizabeth had told him of the angel who had appeared to his father Zechariah and told him that they would have a baby, even though they were old. "The angel said that you would be a prophet like Elijah," his mother told him. "It will be a hard and lonely life for you, and few will listen. But your father and I have given you to the Lord, so that he may use you as he wishes."

Like his cousin Jesus, John learned the history of his people. He heard how God had kept his promises to Abraham and Isaac and Jacob. He listened in the synagogue as Scripture was read, and he heard again and again about the redeemer God had promised to send. He had learned from his mother that the Messiah had already been born, would soon show himself to the people of Israel. He listened as the words of the prophet Isaiah were read: "Listen! The voice of one crying in the desert, 'Make a straight road for the Lord!' " John knew that he would be that voice.

Even when he was a child, John was already filled with the power of God's Holy Spirit. He burned with a desire to serve the Lord. As he grew older, he spent more and more of his time in the desert, praying and asking

God for strength to do his work. At last, when he was thirty years old, he was ready. He dressed like the prophets before him, in a rough coat of camel hair with a leather belt around the waist. He ate the food of the poor people of the desert, a kind of bread made of ground-up, dried grasshoppers and wild honey.

John went to the banks of the Jordan River. Many people came there to dip their hands in the water. It was a holy place, because there God had opened the waters to let Joshua and the people of Israel cross over into the land of promise. But now, when pilgrims came to the river, they were greeted by a fiery prophet in a camel's hair robe who shouted at them, "Do you think you can make yourselves holy by dipping your hands in the Jordan? Change your hearts! Turn away from your sins, for the kingdom of heaven is near! You have to go all the way! Don't just touch what is holy. Be bathed in it! Be baptized to show that you have turned away from your sins, that you are beginning a new life. Messiah's reign is about to begin!"

The people at the river were astonished. Who was this man? Was he a prophet, or just a crazy man? They went back to the city and spread the word about a prophet at the Jordan who cried out that the Messiah was coming. And many people in Jerusalem listened. They had heard in Scripture that terrible times would come before the Messiah would appear, and life under the rule of the Romans was terrible. Hundreds of people, rich and poor, farmers and merchants, flocked to the Jordan to hear the prophet. Many of them confessed their sins, and John baptized them in the river.

Some of those who came were Pharisees and Sadducees, religious people who thought they were already good. They came to be baptized by

30

John because everyone else was doing it. But when John saw them coming, he pointed his finger at them and shouted, "You snakes in the grass! Who told you that you could escape from the punishment that is coming? You must change your lives! Do things that show you have turned away from your sins!"

That was more than they could take. What right did he have to call them sinners? "We are children of Abraham," they answered angrily. "We are the chosen people of God!"

"So what?" John demanded. "Do you think that will save you? Children of Abraham are a dime a dozen. God can take these rocks and turn them into children of Abraham! You are not true children of Abraham unless you obey God and keep his covenant. If a tree bears rotten fruit, God will chop it down. And I tell you, the axe is swinging already!"

"Who can be saved then?" some of the people around asked. "What shall we do?"

"Do what is right! Do justice! If you have two shirts, give one to a person who has none. If you have food, give it to someone who is starving."

"I am a tax collector, Rabbi," one man asked. "What shall I do?"

"Don't collect more than is due you," John answered. "Stop making yourself rich when it hurts someone who is poor."

Even some Roman soldiers came to be baptized by John. "What shall we do now?" they asked him.

"You get paid for your service," he replied. "Be content with that, and don't steal more from the people. And don't bring false charges against anyone."

One day even the great King Herod came down to the river to hear the Baptizer preach. "I should find out what this madman is up to," he said to his wife Herodias. "You can never tell what kind of rebellion he might have up his sleeve. Besides, it might be amusing."

Herodias was not so sure she wanted to go. She had divorced Herod's brother Philip in order to marry Herod. If the Baptizer was going to talk about sin, he might decide to talk about her. But she went, just to please her husband. As it turned out, she had good reason to be afraid of John.

King Herod traveled in a carriage, not pulled by horses but carried on the shoulders of servants, as was customary in those days. As soon as John the Baptist saw the king and queen being carried toward the Jordan, he began to shout, "King Herod, you have sinned against God! You have stolen your brother's wife! Turn away from your sins, and turn to God! If you reject him, he will surely reject you as king!"

"How dare he talk that way to you?" Herodias hissed in anger. "Are you going to let him get away with that? And what about me? He's saying terrible things about me."

"Now, now, don't get upset," Herod said to her. "We have to let these prophets scream and shout. It's much better to have them out in the open where we can watch them. If these people didn't complain, they might revolt, and that would be much worse. I think we have heard enough. Let's go back to the palace now."

But Herodias couldn't get the words of John out of her mind. How dare he call her a sinner! She was the queen! From that day on, she began to plot to have John arrested and killed. And after a while, King Herod did begin to see John as a threat to his throne. In the end, he had John arrested and thrown into prison.

In the meantime, John kept right on preaching. So many people were coming to the river to see him, and he was causing such a stir throughout the whole countryside, that the Jewish rulers in Jerusalem also decided to find out what he had to say for himself. They sent some messengers out to talk with him.

"Who are you?" they demanded.

"I'm not the Messiah, if that's what you mean," John answered.

"Then are you Elijah?"

"No, I am not Elijah."

"Well, who are you then? We have to take an answer back to Jerusalem."

"I am a voice crying out in the desert, 'Make a straight path for the Lord!' "

"If you aren't the Messiah, and you aren't Elijah the prophet, what right do you have to baptize people?"

"Ah, but I only baptize people with water," John answered them. "There is another one coming after me. He is among you right now, but you don't know him yet. I don't even deserve to be the servant who unties the laces on his sandals. He will baptize people with the Holy Spirit and with fire. He will clean out sin the way a farmer blows the hulls away from the grain."

The messengers went back to Jerusalem and reported what John had said, but none of the rulers understood it. Later, when they began to hear of Jesus, they would remember the words of John the Baptist.

The Baptism of Jesus

As SOON AS John saw him on the other shore, he recognized him. Still, he could scarcely believe that it was true. Crowds of people were pressing around him, begging him to baptize them. But he could only watch in amazement as Jesus stepped into the water and made his way to where John was standing. The crowd fell silent as Jesus approached.

"Baptize me, John," Jesus said.

John's mind was in confusion. Did Jesus have sins that needed to be washed away? Was this the person God had chosen to redeem his people? Or could his mother have been wrong? Was Jesus only an ordinary man after all?

"I am the one who needs to be baptized by you," John said. "Why should you come to me to be baptized?"

"Let it be this way, John," Jesus answered him. "It is right that we should do all that God requires."

Still wondering, John lowered Jesus into the waters of the Jordan. After baptism, Jesus stood and walked slowly back toward the shore. Suddenly he stopped and looked up. John looked up too, and what he saw he would never forget as long as he lived. It seemed as if the sky itself opened up, and the Holy Spirit came down on Jesus from heaven, like a dove swooping down and landing on him. Then a voice thundered from heaven: "This is my own dear Son. I am well pleased with him."

The sight faded away, and John saw only Jesus standing alone on the bank. The people around John were looking up at the sky, wondering where the storm clouds were, because they thought they had heard thunder. John walked slowly to the shore and stood there watching Jesus disappear in the distance, as his own followers gathered around him.

"Why are you looking at him like that?" they asked.

"Look!" he said. "There is the Lamb of God, who takes away the sin of the world!"

"Lamb of God?" his followers echoed in amazement. "What are you talking about, John?"

"I told you that I was only preparing the way for someone greater than

I. I didn't know who he would be, but the Lord sent me to baptize people with water to prepare the way for him. And he told me, 'When you see the Spirit of God come down, that person will be the one you are waiting for. He will baptize with the Holy Spirit.' That is what I saw just now. I saw the Holy Spirit come down from heaven in the form of a dove and remain on him. I tell you, he is the Son of God!''

The Temptation in the Wilderness

IT WAS TIME for Jesus to begin his work. But first he had to pass the test that Adam had failed. He came out of the Jordan River filled with the Holy Spirit, and the Spirit led him away into the desert. There he would come up against Satan, that same old serpent who had come to Adam and Eve in the garden of Eden.

Jesus looked at the land around him. As far as the eye could see, there was only dry, dusty earth with rough stones scattered everywhere. Everything about it suggested a place where God didn't belong, a place where Jesus would be left all alone. It was the very opposite of the garden where God had once walked with Adam and Eve.

Jesus spent forty days and nights in that desert. And all that time he faced the temptations of Satan. Wild animals surrounded him, but angels came to his aid. The whole time, Satan just kept after him, questioning him, needling him, tempting him.

After the first few days without food, Jesus' hunger went away. As he continued to fast, his body began to use the food energy stored in the thin layers of fat under the skin. But after forty days that was gone too, and the hunger returned. This time it was a hunger that told Jesus he was beginning to starve. Now Satan moved in for the kill.

"If you are really the Son of God," Satan said, "you can take some of these stones and make bread out of them." Would Jesus set himself up as a creator himself who would turn stone into bread? Or would he accept being a creature and place himself under the conditions of the law God had established?

"No," Jesus answered him. "Scripture says, 'Man cannot live on bread alone, but on every word that God speaks.' There is more to human life than hunger and thirst. Obedience to God comes first."

But Satan was never one to take no for an answer very easily. He carried Jesus away to the top of a very high mountain. There he had all the nations of the world pass before Jesus' eyes in a moment of time, with all their power, their strong kings, and their mighty armies.

"Isn't it beautiful?" Satan asked. "All that power, just waiting to be used. Do you think it will be easy to take control over the creation? I can save you all that struggle. All this power is mine, and I can give it to you right now. You only have to do one small thing. Bow down to me. Surely that's not too much to ask in return for all that power! Think how much good you could do with it!"

It was a lie and Jesus knew it. All that power did not belong to Satan, but to God. Because people have often turned power to evil uses, Satan thought it belonged to him. Jesus had come into the world to reclaim what was already his by right. In the end, he would rule the world in God's way, by dying on a cross. He would not take the shortcut Satan offered. "No!" Jesus said. "Scripture says, 'You shall worship the Lord your God, and serve him alone!' "

Satan was defeated for the second time. But he still had one more trick up his sleeve. Did Jesus like to quote the Bible? Satan could do that too. He took Jesus to the temple in Jerusalem, to the very peak of the roof. Far below lay the stony pavement. "You say you are God's Son," Satan taunted him. "Then prove it. It should be easy for you. All you have to do is jump off. If you are God's Son, he'll save you, won't he? At least, that's what it says in the Bible. It says, 'God will order his angels to protect you. They will hold you up with their hands so that you won't even stub your toe on a rock.' So jump, and prove that you are the Son of God!"

Make something of yourself, Satan was saying. Draw attention to yourself. Do something spectacular and amaze the folks down there in the street; make them see that you are someone special. Forget about suffering. Do it the easy way. Make God keep his promises."

"No!" Jesus said for the third time. "There is more to Scripture than you have said. This is also written: 'You shall not put the Lord your God to the test.' "

Satan had played his last card and had lost. Defeated, he left Jesus alone at last. "For now," he said to himself. "I'll quit for now. But I'll think of something. There has to be a way to stop him!"

Jesus slumped to the dusty ground of the desert, exhausted from hunger and the struggle with the devil. God's angels came to him, bringing him food and drink. His strength returned, and he began the walk back toward Nazareth. He was ready to begin his work.

Jesus and John

THERE WERE MANY teachers in Jesus' day, and each one would gather around him a group of followers who wanted to learn from him. Some of the teachers had studied in faraway Athens or Rome and came to Judea to teach the wisdom of the Greeks and Romans. Others knew the Scriptures and taught their own ways of understanding them. Still others, like John the Baptist, claimed to be prophets who spoke the Word of God.

Many people came to be baptized by John, and a few stayed to learn from him. These disciples, or followers, followed him everywhere and listened carefully to every word he said. Some time after John had baptized Jesus, two of John's followers were standing with him by the Jordan River, when Jesus again came walking by.

"Look!" John said, pointing to Jesus. "There is the Lamb of God."

The two disciples looked at each other for a moment, then back at John, with an unspoken question in their eyes. John nodded slowly in agreement. Silently they reached out and gripped John's hand in farewell. Then, without a word, they turned and followed Jesus.

When Jesus saw them walking up to join him, he turned to them and asked, "What are you looking for?"

"Where do you live, Rabbi?" they asked in return.

Jesus understood at once what they meant. They wanted to follow him, live with him, and learn from him. "Come and see," he answered. So they went with him and stayed with him as he traveled through the countryside around Lake Galilee, the land of the Hebrew tribes of Zebulun and Naphtali. In every town Jesus would go into the synagogue to speak, and always his message was the same: "The time has come! God is fulfilling his promises. Turn away from your sins, because the kingdom of God has come."

From Galilee Jesus and his followers moved back into the region of Judea, where John was still preaching. Jesus began to baptize many people, and when some of John's disciples saw it, they became very upset. They went to John and said, "Do you remember that fellow who was with you before, the one you were talking about? He's going around baptizing people now, and everyone is following him instead of you."

This news did not upset John at all. "Don't be concerned for me," he said. "I didn't come out here to make a name for myself. God gave me a job to do, and I am doing it. God has given Jesus a job to do also. Don't you remember what I said when you first came to me? 'I am not the Messiah,' I said. 'I have been sent ahead to announce him.' You know that when there's a wedding, the groom's best friend arranges everything—but he doesn't expect to marry the bride! When he hears the bridegroom coming for her, it makes him very happy. That is how I feel right now. When I hear what Jesus is doing, it makes me very happy."

"But Rabbi," John's disciples objected, "what will happen now?"

"Now? I will tell you. My work is nearly finished. I am an ordinary man, and I speak about the things I understand. But he is no ordinary man. He comes from God, and he can tell you what he has seen and heard from God himself. God sent his Holy Spirit upon him. I saw that, you know. The Spirit of God came down on Jesus in the form of a dove, and he speaks the words of God. The Father loves his Son and has put everything in his power. So everyone who believes in him has eternal life. But those who disobey him deserve God's punishment. So, you see, from now on he must grow more important, and I must become less important."

John smiled then, a smile that his followers had seldom seen before, and they were silent at last. But they continued to listen for every bit of news about Jesus. And what news they heard! In every town there were people who were sick, people who were racked with pain, people who were paralyzed, people who were enslaved by the evil angels of Satan. Jesus cured their diseases, healed their broken bodies, and commanded the demons to set their victims free. Crowds of people gathered to hear him, bringing their sick to be healed. Word spread throughout the countryside that a great new prophet had come, and the crowds that followed him grew larger. Some of the people were reminded of the words spoken long before by the prophet Isaiah:

Land of Zebulun, land of Naphtali,
    land of Galilee, beyond the Jordan!
The people who walked in darkness
    have seen a great light.
On those in a land shadowed by death
    the light has dawned.

II.
The Good News
of the Kingdom
in Word and Deed

The news of a prophet who healed the sick and cast out demons spread through Galilee and Judea like wildfire, and people flocked to see him. The time had come for Jesus to declare far and wide the good news of the kingdom. The time spoken of by the ancient prophets had come at last. The kingdom of God was here and now, present among them. Good news was being proclaimed to the poor, freedom to the captives, sight to the blind.

And Jesus would not stop with words. His actions also showed that God was indeed making all things new. Lame people would walk, blind people would see, captives to Satan's power would be set free. In both word and deed Jesus would now, for the first time, openly declare who he truly was.

The honor of hearing that message for the first time belonged to Nazareth, the city of Jesus' youth. But would Nazareth feel honored?

JESUS DECLARES HIS MISSION

The Prophecies Are Fulfilled

THE NEWS OF Jesus' miracles spread quickly from town to town. His message did not always travel as quickly. So it happened that before Jesus came to town, the people of Nazareth had already heard about the things he had done in other places. "At last he's coming here," some of them said when they heard that Jesus was returning. "He's been off doing miracles everywhere else, and he's become famous. Now we'll get to see him right here in Nazareth." But even though they had heard news of his miracles, they had not heard the message that God's kingdom had come. Even now, were they ready to hear it?

The synagogue was more crowded than usual that first Sabbath morning after Jesus returned. People had heard that he was a powerful preacher, and they had no doubt that he would exercise his right to speak in the synagogue. Now they waited to hear what he would say. The usual prayers were said, and the sacred scrolls of the Scriptures were brought from their place of safekeeping. As Jesus stood and walked to the front of the synagogue, a whisper of anticipation passed through the crowd. Carefully, Jesus turned the scroll until he came to the book of the prophet Isaiah, and in his clear, strong voice he read these words:

> The Spirit of the Lord is upon me,
>> because he has chosen me to preach good news to the poor.
> He has sent me to proclaim freedom to the captives,
>> and recovering of sight to those who are blind;
> To set free those who are oppressed,
>> and to announce that the day of God's help has come.

His old neighbors looked at one another and nodded knowingly and

39

proudly. "He reads vey well," they seemed to be saying. Then a hush fell over the crowd as they waited expectantly to hear what Jesus would say. He looked at them in silence for a long moment. Finally he spoke: "Today, even as you heard it read, this word of the prophet has come true."

A buzz of conversation went through the synagogue as if it were a hive of disturbed bees. What was this? Who would dare to say that the words of the prophet had come true? Jesus did not wait for them to be quiet before he went on. "I am the one the prophet is talking about," he said. "The Lord has chosen me to bring good news. I have come to set the captive free, to give sight to the blind, to announce that the day of the Lord's forgiveness is here."

Now the buzz was becoming angry. "Who does he think he is?" people asked each other. "What makes him think he can say such things? He's nothing but a carpenter. He grew up right here with the rest of us. We know his parents, Joseph and Mary." One man leaped to his feet and shouted, "You have no right to talk that way! No one can claim to fulfill the prophecies—except the Messiah himself!"

"Then why did you come here today?" Jesus asked. "You have a saying: 'Doctor, heal yourself.' You came because you said to yourselves, 'He performed miracles in other cities; now he can do some here.' But there is no faith here. In every other town people have believed in me. But here in Nazareth no one believes. It is just as they say: 'A prophet is honored everywhere except in his own home town.' "

This only made the crowd angrier. "Who made you a prophet?" some of the men demanded. And others said, "We are sons of Abraham! How dare you say we have no faith?"

Jesus did not shout back at them, but he raised his hand and waited for them to quiet down. "God did not send me to call those who already think they are good people," he said. "He sent me to find those who know that they are sinners. In the days of Elijah the prophet, when no rain fell for three and a half years, there were many widows in Israel. But God sent Elijah to only one widow, and she was a heathen. In the days of Elisha the prophet, there were many people with leprosy in Israel, but the only one who was cured was Naaman, the Syrian."

Now the synagogue was in an uproar. Men were shouting, waving their fists, tearing their robes in anger and disgust. "He's a carpenter, not a prophet!" some of them shouted. Others howled, "Nobody can say that a Gentile is better than a Jew and get away with it!" Still others said, "Only the Messiah can fulfill prophecy! Blasphemy!" The angry mob surged to the front of the synagogue. Strong arms grabbed Jesus and dragged him out of the building, down the street, and through the gates of the city—out to the top of a cliff. "The man has spoken against Israel and against God," the people shouted. "Throw him off the cliff! Kill him!"

Then Jesus turned and faced the mob. Wherever he looked, people turned their eyes away from him. The shouts died on their lips and they became strangely quiet. There was something about him as he stood there, something powerful and full of majesty, something that made them step aside as he walked slowly forward. No one said a word, and no one stopped him as he walked through the center of the crowd and back to his parents' home. Finally, muttering to themselves and wondering what had happened, the people of Nazareth went back to their own homes. But they did not turn to Jesus or accept him as their Lord. And Jesus did not heal many people there, because they had no faith.

Jesus did not stay long in Nazareth, nor did he often return to his boyhood home. For the rest of his life on earth he became a man without a home who wandered from place to place, bringing the good news of the kingdom.

Fishers of Men

NIGHT TIME WAS the best time for fishing on Lake Galilee. For the fishermen it was a hard life. They set out for their work when other men were just returning to their homes and families. All night they sailed the lake, stopping often to throw their nets over the side and pull them in again. When the sun finally rose, they came ashore and began the long chore of sorting the catch, folding and storing the nets, and getting things

41

ready for the next night's work. When they went home to sleep, the town was noisy with the activities of those who worked during the day.

Simon the fisherman was bone weary. He and his brother Andrew had fished all night, but their nets had nothing to show for it. All they could do now was fold the nets and hope for a catch the next night. Looking up from the nets, Simon wiped the sweat from his forehead. In the distance he saw a crowd of people walking along the shore of the lake. They seemed to be surrounding one man—questioning, arguing, listening. Simon shaded his eyes with his hand, then drew in his breath sharply. He knew this man! How could he ever forget the day his brother Andrew had come to him, his eyes shining with excitement? He could see it all over again in his memory.

"Come quickly, Simon," Andrew had said breathlessly. "We have found the Messiah!"

"The Messiah?" Simon shot back scornfully. "Which one? The woods are full of messiahs these days. Who is it now, this baptizer you've been listening to?"

"Just come and see for yourself," Andrew had insisted. Grudgingly, Simon had gone with his brother. The man Andrew led him to took Simon by surprise. He was bronzed by the sun and dressed in the simple robe of the Judean countryside, but there was a look of quiet strength about him. As Simon approached, Jesus stood and clasped his arm in greeting. This is no proud scholar, Simon thought; he has the hands of a working man.

"Your name is Simon, son of John," Jesus said. "But you will be called Peter."

Simon could only stare at Jesus in surprise. People had called him many names, some of them not very nice, but no one had ever called him "the Rock," for that is what the name Peter means. Everyone who knew Simon knew that he had a hot temper, and that he often acted first and thought about the consequences later. His moods were as shifting as sand, but Jesus said he would be called "the Rock." No one had ever shown such confidence in him before. Whether he was the Messiah or not, Simon wasn't ready to say; but he certainly was a remarkable man.

Standing by the lakeshore, watching this same man, Simon again remembered his touch, his look, and those few words he had spoken. Jesus came closer, still with the crowd pressing around him. He turned to speak to them, but there were so many that they pressed him closer and closer to the water's edge. Suddenly Jesus turned to the fisherman and said, "Simon, row out into the lake a little way." With that, he stepped into Simon's small boat. His voice was quiet, but there was something in his tone that made Simon hurry to push the boat away from the shore.

Now with the boat as his pulpit, Jesus was able to speak to the crowd. He told them the good news of the kingdom of God. He spoke to them of

God's love and how God wanted them to love and obey him. When he had finished speaking, the fishermen and farmers who stood on the shore went away to their own homes. Then Jesus turned to Simon and said, "Row out where it is a little deeper, and throw out your nets."

Simon didn't move. "Master, we have been fishing all night and we haven't caught a thing." Jesus said nothing. "The fish are too deep to catch during the daytime," Simon added. Jesus still said nothing; he just looked at Simon. They stared at each other, but it was Simon who finally looked away. "Oh, all right," he grumbled, "since you say so." He rowed out into deeper water, and he and Andrew carefully placed their fish nets. They waited and then began to pull on their nets to trap any fish that might be swimming by.

Andrew started to pull in his net, but he could not lift it. "Simon, help me," he called. "This net is heavy." Peter came to his side and grabbed hold of the net. The veins in his arms stood out as he pulled and tugged at the net. At last the net began to come up, but ever so slowly.

"Simon, the net is full of fish," Andrew gasped. "I've never seen so many!"

"Don't talk! Pull!" Simon shouted. But the net was so heavy with fish that as they tried to bring it into the boat it began to tear.

"John! James!" they called to the men in the other boat on shore. "Hurry up and lend a hand! We can't pull in all these fish!" Quickly the two brothers, with their father Zebedee and their hired men, jumped into the boat and rowed out to help Simon and Andrew. They pulled with all their might, but still they could not lift the nets out of the water.

"It's no good!" James panted. "We'll have to empty the fish into the boats." While some of the men held the nets, the rest began to scoop fish into boats. They pulled the nets and scooped the fish, and the boats began to fill with fish, and still they could not lift out the nets.

"Stop! Stop! The boats are going to sink!" shouted one of the men.

"Drop one side of the net!" James and John dropped their side of the net, and Simon and Andrew pulled the net out from under the squirming fish. And as they watched, more fish than they had taken into the boat swam from the net and back into the depths of the lake.

Simon sat breathing heavily at the rear of the boat, trying to ignore the fish that wiggled against his legs. Suddenly he caught sight of Jesus. He had been too busy with the net to think about what was happening. But now his jaw dropped open as he realized the truth. Jesus had brought all those fish into their nets. He was even the master of the fish! And Simon had tried to argue with him!

Simon Peter struggled through the mass of fish in the boat until he stood in front of Jesus. Then he dropped down on his knees. "Lord, you don't want to have anything to do with me," he said. "I am a sinful man."

"Don't be afraid, Peter," Jesus said kindly. "Come with me, and I will teach you how to catch men." Peter could hardly believe his ears. Jesus still wanted him to be his disciple.

"I'll come, Lord," he said. He grabbed the oars and began to row the boat to shore. He beached the boat, and he and Andrew jumped out, ready to go with Jesus. But Jesus looked back at the other boat. "James! John!" he called. "Will you come with me?"

The brothers looked at each other in amazement, and then broke into wide grins. As quickly as they could, they rowed to shore and left their boats to go with Jesus. "Father, will you take care of the boats?" they called back to Zebedee. Their father nodded silently and watched them as they turned and walked away with Jesus. "If only I were younger," he said to himself, "I would go along." Then with a sigh he turned back to his nets.

Jesus Calls His Disciples

IN EVERY TOWN, crowds of people came out to hear Jesus and to see the miracles he did. Some followed him for a few days, others came back again and again. But there were a few he chose to be his disciples. First there were the fishermen, Simon and Andrew and their friends James and John, the sons of Zebedee. Soon they met Philip, a friend of Simon and Andrew. "Come with me," Jesus said to him. "Be my disciple." Philip had been waiting all his life for the Messiah to appear. Everything he had seen and heard told him that his search was over. He thought at once of his friend Nathanael and hurried to tell him the good news.

He found Nathanael sitting under a fig tree, shading himself from the hot afternoon sun. "Nathanael, you must come with me," Philip said breathlessly. "We have found the one Moses and the prophets wrote about. We have found the Messiah! He is Jesus, the son of Joseph from Nazareth."

"Slow down, Philip, don't get so excited," Nathanael said lazily. "Nobody expects the Messiah to come from Nazareth. You know what the prophets said."

"Just come with me and see for yourself," Philip pleaded.

"You really believe this, don't you?"

"Yes, I do. Come with me, please," Philip said.

So Philip brought Nathanael to Jesus. Jesus took one look at him and said, "Ah, here is a true Israelite. There is nothing false in him."

Nathanael stared in surprise. How could a man he had never met make such a statement about him? "How do you know me?" he asked.

"Are you surprised that I know you?" Jesus asked in return. "I saw you when you were under the fig tree, even before Philip called you."

Nathanael was dumbfounded. Philip must be right! "Teacher," Nathanael cried out, "you are the Son of God! You are the king of Israel!"

Jesus smiled at him. "Do you believe in me just because I told you that I saw you under the fig tree? You will see much greater things than that." How could there be anything greater? Nathanael wondered. But Jesus' face was serious now, and as if he knew Nathanael's every thought he said, "I am telling you the truth. You will see the heavens opened and the angels of God coming down upon the Son of Man and going back up again."

Although this was more than Nathanael could take in in a moment, he gladly joined the others who were becoming Jesus' disciples. But he was no more prepared than were the others for the next one to join the group. His name was Matthew, and he was a tax collector.

Everyone in Israel hated the tax collectors because they worked for the Romans. They took money from their own people to give to the conquerors. Most of them were even worse than that. They not only collected the taxes, but they collected more for their own pockets. Many of the tax collectors had become rich by stealing from their own people.

But one day by the shore of the Jordan River, Matthew the tax collector had listened to a man named John the Baptist. "Don't collect more than is due you," the Baptist had said. "Stop making yourself rich at the expense of the poor." Ever since that day, Matthew had tried to be fair in collecting the taxes. In spite of that, he still felt like a sinner.

On this day, Matthew looked up from his work to see some men walking toward him. Who was the one leading them? Matthew was sure he had seen him before. Of course! That was the man John the Baptist had pointed to and said, "There is the Lamb of God, who takes away the sin of the world." And he was coming straight toward Matthew! Jesus walked steadily forward until he stood in front of the tax collector.

"Follow me," Jesus said. Only two words, but they were enough. Matthew left his collection table, left the money for the other tax collectors to count, left his job, and followed Jesus.

A few nights later, Matthew invited Jesus and his disciples to dinner. All of Matthew's friends were there—tax collectors and others who were hated and avoided by most people. Some of the Pharisees, men who were proud of how good they were, saw Jesus dining there and said, "Why does he eat with these worthless people?"

"People who are well don't need a doctor," Jesus responded. "Only the sick do. I did not come to call people who already think they are good enough. I came for those who know that they are sinners."

So from among the many people who followed him, Jesus chose twelve to be his own disciples. There were Simon Peter and his brother Andrew; James and John, the two sons of Zebedee; Philip and his friend Nathanael, whose other name was Bartholomew; Matthew the tax collector, who was also called Levi; another James, the son of Alphaeus; there was Thomas, who was a twin, and a man named Thaddaeus, and another Simon, who had been a Zealot, one of those who plotted to overthrow the Romans. Finally there was Judas Iscariot, the one who later betrayed Jesus. These twelve Jesus chose to be with him always. He taught them carefully about the kingdom of God. They followed Jesus everywhere, watching and listening and slowly learning from him.

The disciples were ordinary men, and they lived with Jesus among the common people. This made some people angry, and they said to Jesus: "John's disciples fast and pray a great deal. So do the disciples of the Pharisees. So why do your disciples go around eating and drinking like ordinary people?"

Jesus answered: "Do the guests at a wedding fast? Of course not! As long as the bridegroom is with them, they feast and have a good time. Some day the bridegroom will be taken away from them, and then they will fast.

"If your old coat has a hole in it, do you try to patch it with a new piece of cloth?" Jesus went on. "If you do, the new piece will shrink and the patch will be worse than the hole was. You have to throw away the old coat and put on a new one. You don't pour new wine into an old wineskin, or the skin will break and spill all the wine. New wine needs new wineskins!"

The people who asked the question did not understand the answer.

Even the disciples took a long time before they began to understand. Jesus had not come to patch up the old system of things. He had come to bring something new. The kingdom of God had come. He had not chosen twelve disciples to show how holy they could be. He had chosen them to be eyewitnesses of what he said and did, so that they could carry the good news of the kingdom far beyond Israel, to all the peoples of the world.

RELEASE TO
THE CAPTIVES

Jesus Brings Joy to a Wedding

THE FAMILY OF Joseph the carpenter was well known in the region of Galilee. There were many people who had known Jesus since he was a small boy. The other boys Jesus had grown up with had reached manhood themselves, and many of them were getting married. One day a friend of the family who lived in the town of Cana invited Jesus and his mother to his wedding. Knowing that Jesus was some kind of a wandering rabbi, he invited the disciples also.

Like all weddings among the people of Israel, it was a joyous time, a time for feasting and celebration. The house was packed with people, many more than had been expected. The feast went on for hours, and the wine flowed freely—so freely, in fact, that the servants began to fear that it might run out. One of them whispered quietly into the bridegroom's ear, and he glanced at the dwindling supply of wine, frowning deeply. It was too late to buy more now, for the wine sellers were all home with their own families.

What a disgrace it would be to run out of wine! Did he dare have the servants thin the wine with water to make it go further? No, watering the wine would be too noticeable and would make him look like a miser who couldn't even buy good wine for his guests on his wedding day. The worry began to destroy his enjoyment of his own wedding feast.

Mary noticed the worried looks on the servants' faces, and she soon learned the reason for them. What a shame it would be if the wine ran out, she thought. It would certainly ruin the day for the bride and bridegroom, who were already beginning to give each other anxious looks. What would their guests think if they ran out of wine? She knew there was one person at the party who might be able to do something about the problem. Mary called Jesus aside and said to him, "They have run out of wine."

"Dear woman," Jesus answered her, "why do you want to bring me into this? My time has not yet come."

Mary knew that Jesus had not come into the world just to satisfy some thirsty wedding guests. But she also knew his great love, and she was sure he would care about the feelings of the bride and bridegroom. He would do something, of that she was sure. So she went to the servants and said quietly, "Do whatever my son Jesus tells you to do, no matter how strange it may seem."

It was a good thing Mary warned them, because what Jesus asked them to do was very strange indeed. Standing in the entry hall of the house were six stone jugs, each as big as a barrel. The water that was in the jugs had been used to wash all the plates and utensils, as well as the hands of all the guests, in accordance with the law of Moses. Now the jugs stood empty and forgotten. Jesus called the servants aside and said, "Take these jugs out to the well and fill them with water."

"We're running out of wine, and he tells us to fill the water jugs!" one of the servants complained on the way to the well. "If they're going to water the wine, they ought to start when there's still plenty left! I've been sent on some crazy errands in my time, but this one beats all!"

But they managed to carry the heavy jugs to the well and stagger back with them full of water. "We have done as you said," they said to Jesus.

"Very well. Now dip some out and take it to the master of ceremonies to taste."

This was really getting strange! Did he seriously think the master of ceremonies would serve the guests water instead of wine? Still, they had heard some unusual things about this Jesus. And they had promised his mother. So they dipped a goblet of water out of the jug and took it to the master of ceremonies. Without even looking it over, he took the goblet and tasted the water. His eyebrows shot up in surprise. The servants stood back and waited for the angry outburst that was sure to follow. But there was no outburst. There wasn't even a scowl. Instead, he smiled. "Excellent,

excellent!" he said with satisfaction. "The best yet!" He beckoned to the
bridegroom. "Come here, my boy, come here."

Still worried about the lack of wine, the bridegroom hurried over to the
master of ceremonies. "You pulled a good one on us this time, Son," the
master said.

"I'm not sure I know what you mean," said the young groom.

"The wine, my boy, the wine!"

"Oh, yes, you mean that. Well, you see, we didn't realize there would
be so many guests," he began, but the master of ceremonies wasn't
listening.

"Everyone else serves the best wine first. Then, once the guests have a
few under their belts, they bring out the cheap stuff and no one even
notices. But you saved the best wine for last!"

"The best wine? I don't understand," stammered the groom.

"Taste it yourself," said the host, holding out the goblet. The groom
took the goblet and tasted the wine. Then he smiled too.

"It really is good!" he said.

"Congratulations, Son," said the master of ceremonies heartily. "This is
the best wedding in years!" Then he turned to the servants, who were still
standing in confusion nearby. "Well, go on, serve our guests some more
wine!"

49

The servants hurried back to the water jugs and looked in. "That doesn't look like water to me," the first one said. The second put his finger into the jug and licked it off. "It's wine!" he exclaimed. "And really good wine too, just like the master said."

"It's a miracle," the third servant said. "A miracle, I tell you!" And they looked at Jesus with a new kind of respect. Who was he really? they wondered. But there was no time for wondering now. They had to get back to the guests—with more of the best wine anyone in Cana had ever tasted.

The bride and groom, the master of ceremonies, and most of the guests still did not know what had happened. But the servants would soon spread the news all over town. And the twelve disciples, who had watched it all in amazement, were more certain than ever that Jesus was no ordinary man. With this miracle Jesus showed that he had come to bring joy back into human lives.

Healing the Sick and Freeing the Captives

SOON AFTER THE wedding in Cana, Jesus and his disciples went into the synagogue in Capernaum. When it came time for the Scriptures to be read, Jesus stepped to the front, opened the scroll, and began to read. Then he taught the people what the prophet meant when he wrote about the Messiah. "No one ever preached like that before," the people said to each other. "He doesn't say 'I think' or 'I believe' or 'the great Rabbi So-and-so once wrote.' He speaks like someone who knows!"

But there was one man in the synagogue who hated every word that Jesus said. Many years before this, a demon, an evil angel who served Satan, had entered into this man. The demon sometimes took control of him, using his arms and legs and voice. Now the man with the demon stood up in the synagogue and shouted, "We don't want anything to do with you, Jesus! Did you come here to destroy us? I know who you are. You are the Holy One from God!"

"Be quiet!" Jesus commanded the demon. "Come out of that man and leave him alone!"

The man screamed in terrible pain and thrashed around with his arms and legs, kicking and scratching at the people around him. Then suddenly the man fell on the floor and lay still. Jesus walked to his side, stooped down, and helped him to sit up. The man looked up into Jesus' face and smiled. The people in the synagogue were amazed. "He speaks with such power!" they said to each other. "Even the evil spirits obey him!"

After the service in the synagogue was over, Jesus and his disciples went to the house of Peter and Andrew. A neighbor, looking very worried, met them at the door. "I'm glad you've come home, Simon," she said. "Your

mother-in-law is sick in bed with a high fever. Nothing seems to help. She really is very ill."

"Take me to her," Jesus said. So they took him upstairs to the room where Peter's mother-in-law was lying. Jesus stood beside her and placed his hand on her forehead as if to feel how high the fever was. But as soon as his hand touched her, she opened her eyes and looked into his face. Then she looked beyond him and saw Peter standing there.

"Oh, Simon, I'm so sorry," she said. "You have brought guests home, and here I am lying in bed. I should get up and fix you something to eat."

"No, Mother, you're sick," Peter protested.

His mother-in-law sat up straight in bed. "Sick? I've never felt better in my life! Excuse me, I'm going to the kitchen." And before anyone thought to stop her, she was out of bed and down the stairs, leaving Peter and the other disciples staring after her in surprise and wonder.

Soon the whole town had heard about the man in the synagogue and about Simon's mother-in-law. By evening there was a line of people a block long outside Simon Peter's door. It seemed that the whole city was there, bringing those who were blind and lame and sick, and some who were controlled by evil spirits. Jesus healed all those who were sick, and he commanded the evil spirits to leave the people they were using. The demons recognized him, but he would not allow them to speak, because he was not yet ready.

It was very late before Jesus and the others were able to get some sleep. But early the next morning, when the disciples awoke, Jesus was already gone. They quickly left the house and went out into the desert, where Jesus sometimes went to pray. They found him there, talking with his Father. "Won't you come back to Capernaum with us?" they asked. "There are many people there who need you."

"I know," Jesus answered, "but there are many more towns in Israel. I came into the world to preach the good news of the kingdom of God. I cannot spend all my time in one city. We will stay here a while to rest and pray. Then we will go into as many towns as we can, and I will preach there also." So Jesus rested in the desert and spent time praying to his Father.

A Leper Is Healed

JESUS WAS EXHAUSTED from his work of healing the sick and casting out demons in Capernaum. He needed time away from the crowds, time to rest, time to pray. He spent several days in the desert with his disciples, resting and seeking God's strength to continue his work. When he was ready, he went with his disciples back into the towns of Galilee. There he healed those who were sick, set free those who were controlled by demons, made lame people walk and blind people see again. Wherever he went he told people that God's kingdom had come. Soon he was again being followed by great crowds of people.

One day, as Jesus was walking on a hillside surrounded by people who were talking, asking questions, and trying to get close to him, the crowd suddenly began to scatter. "Look out! A leper!" they cried.

Jesus turned and looked behind him. There, stumbling down the hill on his crutch, was a man with a terrible skin disease called leprosy. He had been standing far back from the crowd, listening to the words of Jesus. Because of his disease, he was not allowed to come close to other people. But as he listened to Jesus, he felt the love Jesus had for all people. He felt that here was one man who would not turn him away. And there was something else about Jesus. There was power in him, the power of the Spirit of God. If anyone could help him, it was Jesus.

Painfully he hobbled toward Jesus. He was a terrible sight: he was dirty, his clothes were ragged, and his skin was covered with open sores. People turned away their faces and moved as far as possible from the leper. But Jesus stayed where he was. Closer and closer the leper came, until he could kneel on the ground a few feet in front of Jesus. "Lord," he said, "if you want to, you can make me clean."

Of all the people who heard Jesus speak that day, only one decided to do something about what he had heard. That one was the leper. He believed in Jesus, and he came to him to be cured. Jesus stepped forward and reached out his hand to touch the sick man. The crowd gave out a gasp. No one was allowed to touch a man with leprosy. But Jesus had come into the world to take all its sin and sickness and misery onto himself. So he touched the man and said, "I do want to. Be clean."

There was no puff of smoke, no flash of light, no thunder from the sky. But when the leper looked down at his arm, he saw that the sores were gone. He grabbed Jesus' hand and kissed it, then stood up and began to

run and jump for joy. "I'm well!" he began to shout. "Praise God, I'm clean again!" Now he could live among his fellow men once again. And best of all, now he could go into the temple and worship God.

Jesus called to the man again. "Don't tell anyone what has happened," he said. "There are already too many people who come to see me just for the miracles. But go to the priest now and make the offering that Moses has commanded in the law. The priest must first see that you are healed from your sickness. Then you will be able to live among other men. And the priest will see that we have obeyed the law."

But the man couldn't keep quiet. He couldn't wait to tell his friends and neighbors what had happened. Soon there were so many people coming to see Jesus that he could hardly move. He could not go into the towns any longer, because the crowds of people nearly crushed him. So he had to go out into the desert, and those who wanted to see him had to come to him there.

Jesus Heals the Nobleman's Son

IN THE TOWN of Cana lived a rich nobleman. He was not only rich, but he was also very powerful, for he served King Herod. But he had no time to enjoy his riches or his power. He had a son who lived at Capernaum, and his son was very sick. He had had the best doctors in the land come to the boy's bedside, but they all shook their heads sadly and said that there was no hope for him. His parents would have done anything for him;

unfortunately, all their money could not buy his health.

But now there was news that brought hope to the nobleman and his family. The nobleman knew about Jesus. He had heard that Jesus was making sick people well again. So he set out to find Jesus, who was his son's last hope. When he found Jesus, the rich man begged him, "Please come down with me to Capernaum. My son is sick there. The doctors have given up hope, and he is dying. I believe that you can make him well."

Jesus looked at the rich man and at the crowd around him. Some, he knew, were there because they believed in him; others were there because they hoped to see him perform a miracle. So many loved to see him do impossible things, but so few would listen to what he said. "You won't believe unless you see signs and wonders, will you?" Jesus said to them.

The nobleman looked at Jesus in confusion. What was this about signs and wonders? All he knew was that he had a sick son and that Jesus could make him well. He did not know what else to say, so he simply repeated, "Please, sir, come to Capernaum before my son dies."

Jesus saw that the man really believed in him, but he was not there to put on a show for the crowd. Quietly he said to the man, "Go back now to Capernaum. From this moment your son is alive and well."

The nobleman looked up at Jesus again, and there were tears of joy in his eyes. He turned away, smiling, and hurried back to Capernaum. It was a long way, and he did not arrive there until the next day. But even before he reached the outskirts of the city the following morning, he saw some of his servants hurrying down the road to meet him, their faces bright with joy. "Your son is well! Your son lives!" they shouted as soon as they saw their master.

"I knew it! I knew it!" he cried. "Tell me. When did my son start to get better?"

"It was yesterday afternoon, about one o'clock," they replied.

"The exact moment!" he exclaimed. "That was the very time when I talked with Jesus of Nazareth, and he said my son would get well. Praise God, my son is healed! Quickly, we must hurry home to see him. On the way, I can tell you all about what Jesus has done."

When the nobleman had finished his story, everyone in his household, including his wife and children, even all his servants, believed in Jesus. The house was filled with joy, and it is hard to say which joy was greater—the joy that the son had been made well or the joy that the Son of God had come to earth at last. And there was joy back in Cana too, the joy of the Lord Jesus over the faith of the nobleman and his family. The good news of the kingdom was not only for the poor, and not only for the rich, but for all those who had faith in him.

A Hole in the Roof

SEVERAL MONTHS AFTER Jesus had healed the nobleman's son, he was in Capernaum again. As soon as word got around that he was there, people again came from all over the countryside. Some were Pharisees, who believed that a man could be holy only if he obeyed every command of Moses' law to the letter. Some were teachers of the law, who were supposed to know and interpret everything about the ancient Hebrew laws. But most were ordinary men and women, farmers and fishermen, housewives, carpenters, and shopkeepers. They brought along friends and relatives who were sick or lame or blind, and Jesus healed them all.

Late that day, four men came to find Jesus. They were carrying a stretcher, and on the stretcher lay a man who could not use his arms or his legs. He had been paralyzed for many years. But he had four good friends who had heard of Jesus, and now they were bringing him to be healed. When they arrived at the house where Jesus was teaching, however, they found a large crowd outside the door. Jesus was inside, and everyone was trying to hear his words by pushing in close. They shuffled and elbowed and squeezed together so that they made a solid wall. No one would step aside to make a path for the paralyzed man.

"What are we going to do?" one of the men asked.

"We could go back and wait for another day," another one suggested.

"No," said the third. "We came to find Jesus of Nazareth, and we'll find him if we have to dig a tunnel into the house."

"Wait a minute," the fourth man suggested. "That gives me an idea. There's just a flat roof made of tiles on this house. And there's a stairway going up the outside to the roof. If we pull some tiles off the roof, I'll bet we can make a hole big enough for us to lower the stretcher right down in front of Jesus!"

"We'll need some ropes," one of the men said. "Nathan and John, see if you can find some, and Joshua and I will carry the stretcher up onto the roof."

Inside the house the crowd was listening intently as Jesus spoke. Suddenly several people looked up toward the ceiling. What was that noise up there? It sounded like someone was scraping something on the roof—a stick maybe, or even a knife. All at once, some dust and mortar fell from the ceiling onto the heads of the people in front. They too looked up at the ceiling, just in time to see one of the big tiles disappear, leaving nothing but a hole. A murmur ran through the crowd. Soon three more tiles were gone, and the people below could see blue sky and men's faces on the roof above.

"My roof! They're tearing up my roof!" cried the owner of the house. "I have to go up there and stop them. Let me through! Please, let me through!" But the people were squeezed into the room so tight that no one could step aside to let him out. He watched helplessly as the hole in his roof grew bigger.

It was hard to see against the bright light now streaming through the hole in the roof. Then the hole was suddenly covered by a dark shape coming slowly down through the roof and into the room. Lower and lower came the stretcher, held with ropes by the four men on the roof. "Look at that!" someone shouted. "It's a man on a stretcher!" At last the paralyzed man lay directly in front of Jesus, and the crowd waited to see what Jesus would do. He raised his hand to quiet their murmuring. "It took a great deal of faith for those men to do this," he said. Then he knelt down beside the paralyzed man, and everyone in the crowd strained to hear what he would say. "Cheer up, my son," Jesus said to him. "Your sins are forgiven."

Immediately the room was a buzz of excited conversation. The people had hoped to see the man healed of his sickness, but what was this about forgiving sins? The Pharisees and the law teachers who were there thought to themselves, "Only God can forgive sins. If Jesus claims to forgive sins, he is making himself God. That's a crime, and he deserves to die!"

Then Jesus stood up and looked straight at the Pharisees. "I know what you are thinking," he said. "You think that I can't heal this man, so I covered up by telling him his sins are forgiven. After all, who can see

56

inside the man to know whether or not that is true?" The Pharisees were
startled. That was exactly what they had been thinking. But how did Jesus
know? "If I had only healed the man," Jesus went on, "you would not have
said I was acting against God, even though you know that only God can
heal. But if I can heal him, then I should be able to forgive his sins also,

57

because both are God's work. Now I am going to show you that God has given me the power to do that." He turned to the paralyzed man and said, "Stand up! Pick up your bed, and carry it back to your own house."

The man on the stretcher cried out as if in pain. His arms and legs began to tingle, and nerves that had felt nothing for years began to send their messages to his brain once again. He felt strength flowing into his body, and to his amazement he found that he could move his fingers. He opened and closed his fists, bent his elbows, wiggled his toes, while the smile on his face grew wider and wider. He heard the gasp of the crowd as he sat up on his bed, then stood on his own feet. He bent down, rolled up his sleeping mat and lifted it to his shoulder. "Take your bed home," Jesus had said. So he moved in the direction of the door. The crowd inside pulled back to make room, and those outside moved to let him pass. And then, for the first time all afternoon, he opened his mouth and spoke for himself.

"Praise the Lord! He has made me walk again!" he cried out, and all the way home he shouted praises to God. The crowd around Jesus took up the cry, and men and women began praising God for the great work he had done that day.

GOOD NEWS TO THE POOR

Lord of the Sabbath

JESUS AND HIS disciples seldom stayed long in one place. They walked from town to town all over Galilee. Sometimes they would spend the night in a friendly home, but often they slept under the stars. Wherever they were, they rested on the Sabbath day, as God had commanded in Moses' law. These were quiet times, times when the disciples could walk slowly through the fields listening to Jesus and talking with each other along the way.

One Sabbath afternoon as they were walking through the fields, Peter began to complain that he was hungry. "I wish we'd brought some food along with us," he said.

"Look at all this grain growing in the field," Andrew answered him. "We could pick some and eat it for lunch."

"Don't you think the farmer might be upset?" Peter asked.

"Why should he be?" Andrew said. "You know the law Moses gave us. If anyone is hungry, he can eat his fill from any field or orchard, as long as he doesn't try to take any home with him."

"Well then, let's eat!" Peter said, and they all began to pick the heads of grain. They rubbed the grain between their hands to break off the hulls, and they ate the ripening grain inside.

There were some Pharisees standing nearby who immediately came up

to Jesus. These days, wherever Jesus went there seemed to be some Pharisees nearby. They were hoping to catch him breaking one of their many religious laws so that they would have good reason to turn him over to the authorities. "Why do you let your disciples do that on the Sabbath?" they demanded. "You know it is against our law to do any work on the Sabbath. And if harvesting and threshing aren't work, we don't know what is!"

"Perhaps you don't know Scripture as well as you think," Jesus replied. "Do you remember what David did when he and his men were escaping from King Saul and they didn't have any food? He went to the house of God and asked the high priest Abiathar for some bread. So the high priest gave him some of the holy bread that was set out on the table before the Lord. No one but the priests were supposed to eat it. But David was doing God's work, so Abiathar gave him the bread. Tell me, was David wrong to eat it?"

The Pharisees said nothing. They didn't dare say that David had sinned by eating the temple bread. But they didn't want to admit that Jesus was right either.

"If what you say is true," Jesus went on, "then none of the priests would be able to do any work in the temple on the Sabbath. But they offer sacrifices there every Sabbath, and that's pretty hard work. Are they breaking the law?"

Once again the Pharisees were silent.

"You don't understand Scripture at all. It is written, 'I want mercy from you, not sacrifice.' If it is good to offer sacrifices on the Sabbath, isn't it much better to do mercy on the Sabbath? Doing good on the Sabbath can never be against the law of God. God did not make men to obey the rules of the Sabbath; he made the Sabbath for the good of man. I am telling you this because I, the Son of Man, am Lord of the Sabbath."

The Pharisees were outraged, but they had no answer to give him. And that angered them even more. They still did not have enough evidence to have him arrested, but later, when Jesus did go on trial, they would remember that he had said he was the Lord of the Sabbath. For the present they would continue to follow him to see what he would do next.

Jesus Heals on the Sabbath

THE SAME AFTERNOON that Jesus claimed to be Lord of the Sabbath, the Pharisees followed him and the disciples into the synagogue of the nearby town. Standing in the synagogue praying was a man who could only use one hand. The other one had shriveled up to half the size it should have been. "Now we'll see!" the Pharisees said to each other. "If he heals that man on the Sabbath day, everyone will have to say that he worked—and therefore broke the law!"

Jesus knew what they were saying. So he called the man from his prayers. He put his arm around the man's shoulders and said to the Pharisees, "If you had a sheep, and it fell into a pit on the Sabbath day, would you pull it out?" They did not answer. "And what's worth more, a sheep or a man?" They still said nothing. "Is it right according to law to do good on the Sabbath? Or should we do evil instead? Is it lawful to save life on the Sabbath? Or is it better to do nothing, and let someone die?"

After all this, the Pharisees still said nothing at all. They really did not care what Jesus said. Their minds were already made up. The law was the law, and whoever broke it deserved to die. There was no room in their hearts for mercy or love. Jesus knew this, and he knew what they were up to. He also knew that God's work was more important than anyone's opinion.

Jesus turned to the man with the withered hand. "Hold out your hand," he said. The man held out his withered hand—but it wasn't withered at all! It was just like his other one, a healthy, working hand. The man looked at his own hand in astonishment, wiggled his fingers, balled up his fist, and swung his arm around in a circle. Then  he looked back at Jesus, and there were tears in his eyes.

The Pharisees were furious. What made them angriest was that they had no answer for Jesus. When someone insists on being wrong, nothing will make him angrier than the truth. From that day on, the Pharisees began to plot ways they could use to successfully get rid of Jesus.

Jesus and his disciples left that place and went back to Lake Galilee. Crowds of people came to see him there. They were coming from far and wide now, from Galilee, from Jerusalem, from Judea, from the east side of the Jordan, even from the far-off seacoast cities of Tyre and Sidon. There were so many that Jesus had to speak to them from a boat out on the water so that the crowds would not crush him. They continued to bring people who were sick and blind and lame, and some who were under the control of evil spirits, and he healed them all. Some of the evil spirits cried out,

"You are the Son of God!" But Jesus commanded them to be silent. It was just the way the prophet Isaiah had described him:

> The servant I have chosen
> > will have my Spirit upon him.
> He will not argue or shout
> > or raise his voice in the streets.
> He will not brag about himself.
> > He will not destroy those who hate him,
> Until the day when he comes in victory.
> > His name will be the hope of the world.

The Sermon on the Mount: Hope for the Poor

THE CROWD ON the shore of Lake Galilee grew so large that most of the people there could not see Jesus. "Let's go up on the hill," Jesus said to his disciples. "Then the people will be below me, and those in back will be able to see over the heads of those in front. I want them all to be able to hear my words."

So the disciples gathered around Jesus to protect him from the crushing crowd, and they struggled through the throngs of people. When the crowd saw where Jesus was going, they broke up and began to follow him up the long hillside. At the top Jesus sat down on a large flat stone. He looked out over the crowd, and what he saw nearly broke his heart. Out there were poor people dressed in rags, even though God had commanded his people always to take care of the poor among them. There were men with faces creased with worry and women grown old before their time, even though God had promised to bless them if only they would remain true to him. There were people for whom every day was an agony of fear and oppression, people who had been cheated out of their family properties by rich landlords from among their countrymen, and people who suffered under the crushing rule of Rome. These were the people Jesus had come to set free, those who were not too blinded by riches and their own sense of goodness to see their need for God, those who knew they were sinners and only wanted to know the peace of being forgiven.

He stood, and a hush fell over the crowd. "How happy are you poor," he said, "for the kingdom of God belongs to you. How happy are you who are hungry now, for you will be satisfied. How happy are you who weep and mourn now, for you will laugh with joy." A stir went through the crowd. No one had ever spoken to them like this before. Was this what the kingdom meant, that everything would be set right, that justice would be done at last?

62

"How happy are those who claim nothing for themselves," Jesus said. "The whole earth will belong to them. How happy are those who do mercy, for mercy will be shown to them. How happy are those who make peace, for they will be called sons of God. How happy are those who suffer because they do what is right. The kingdom of God belongs to them."

There were tears in some eyes now. These were the first words of real hope they had ever heard. Here was a man who understood their hurt and their longing, a man who promised them God's justice. This man they could follow anywhere.

"And how happy you will be when people blame you and mistreat you and say evil things about you because of me," Jesus went on. "You should jump for joy then, because your reward in heaven will be great. They treated the prophets in the same way."

Then Jesus looked out over the crowd again and saw others: the rich, who had come for amusement; the Pharisees, who believed they already knew everything that God required; the scribes, who hoped to catch Jesus in some error. His face hardened as he spoke. "But woe to you rich," he said, "because you have already taken all the comfort you are going to get. Woe to you who are well-fed now, for the day of your hunger is yet to come. Woe to you who are laughing now, for you shall yet weep in your grief." Some in the crowd turned and stalked away toward their homes; others lowered their eyes in shame; still others crossed their arms and stared defiantly at Jesus.

63

But Jesus also saw many expectant faces, and his look softened again. "You are the salt of the earth," he said. "You give it flavor and keep it from becoming completely rotten. But if salt loses its flavor, people throw it away; it is good for nothing.

"You are the light of the world. You can't hide a town that is built on the top of a hill. So don't hide the light. Let it shine where people can see it. Light their way to the kingdom of God by loving your neighbor and doing what is right, that they may come and praise God too."

For those who heard him, it was as if the world itself were being turned upside down. All their lives people had told them that things were meant to be as they were. But here was a man who told them what they knew to be the truth. God's justice was not being carried out by those who ruled them. Things were not as they ought to be. But he told them also that God had not forgotten them. The day would yet come when things would be set right again.

The Sermon on the Mount: The Real Meaning of the Law

THE PHARISEES AND the scribes stood watching Jesus, listening to his words. They were not all his enemies. Some of them were still waiting to hear him teach, hoping that he might help bring the people closer to God. What if he really was a prophet of God? But how would they be able to tell? Surely, if God had really sent him, he would tell the people to obey the law of Moses down to the last detail.

Jesus knew what they were thinking, knew what they were waiting to hear. Once more he turned to the crowd and said, "Everything you do should bring glory to God. It isn't enough just to obey some rules. The law of Moses is good, but it means much more than the Pharisees and the teachers of the law will tell you. I did not come to do away with the law. I came to give the law its full meaning."

Once again there was a rustling and stirring among the people and the sound of sharp intakes of breath from those who hated him. How dare he presume to teach them the law! But Jesus was not yet finished.

"The law says, 'Do not commit murder.' And the Pharisees say you have obeyed God if you have never killed anyone. But I tell you that the real sin is hating another man. If you come to God's temple to bring a sacrifice, but you remember that you did something to harm your neighbor, put your offering down and leave it there. First go and make things right with your neighbor. Then you can come back and give your offering to God. Loving your neighbor is more important than bringing sacrifices to the temple.

"The law says, 'Do not take another man's wife.' And the Pharisees say you have obeyed God if you have left other women alone. But I tell you that the real sin happens in your heart. If you wish you could have another man's wife, and spend your time thinking about what you would do with other women, you are just as guilty as if you had taken her."

There were a few among the listening Pharisees who recognized the truth of Jesus' words. But most grew more and more angry as he spoke. One thing especially made them angry. He was putting himself on the same level with the law of Moses itself! He kept saying, "The law tells you this, but I tell you that." He talked as if the law came from him!

"The teachers of the law," Jesus went on, "tell you, 'If you use God's name when you make a promise, then you must keep your word.' But I tell you that you must always keep your word. When you say yes, that should mean yes without using God's name to swear by. If you have to swear to something before people will believe you, it means that you are a liar most of the time.

"The law says, 'You may not punish a man more than the amount of wrong he did to you. If he knocks out your tooth, you may not knock out two of his.' But I say to you that you should never try to pay anyone back. If he hits you twice, it should never be because you hit him back the first time.

"The law says, 'Love your neighbor.' But I tell you that you should love all people, even your enemies. They are also made in God's own image. If you love God, you will love other people, because God made them and loves them. If you want to be true children of your Father in heaven, you will love those whom he loves. If you only love the people who love you back, what is so great about that? Even wicked people do that. But you should do good to those who hate you and pray for them. God is merciful. If you are his children, you should be merciful too.

"So don't think that you can obey God just by keeping all the rules. You have to love God from your heart."

The Sermon on the Mount: The True Meaning of Prayer

As JESUS SAT on a large rock on the top of the hill, with the huge crowd of people taking in his every word, what he said was so different from what they had heard before. He seemed so sure of himself, and his words had such power. He brought hope where there had been only despair before.

He had just finished telling them that they could never please God by their own efforts but only by turning themselves over to God completely. But he knew that there were some in the crowd who were very proud of their obedience to the law. They loved to pray long and eloquent prayers so that people would see how faithful they were. When they gave money to the beggars who crowded around the gates of the temple, they made sure that people saw every coin, and they loved the praise this brought them. To these people Jesus spoke about the true meaning of prayer.

"If you do the things that please God," he said, "don't go around bragging about it. Whom are you trying to please? If you give money to the poor, don't advertise it. If you pray, don't make a big show. If you get your praise from other people, why should God reward you? You don't have to make your prayers long and complicated just to impress people. Just pray this way:

Our Father in heaven,
    may your name be made holy;
    may your kingdom come;
    may you be obeyed on earth
    just as you are in heaven.
Give us what we need for today.
Forgive us what we owe you,
    just as we forgive what others owe us.
Keep us out of temptation,
    and save us from evil.
The kingdom, the power, and the glory
    are yours, O Lord, forever.
Amen.

A puzzled look came over the faces of some of his listeners. "What do you mean about forgiving others what they owe us?" one of them asked.

"If you forgive others," Jesus answered, "your heavenly Father will forgive you too. But if you refuse to forgive people, your heavenly Father will not forgive you either. God wants more than fine words. He wants to see you putting your words into practice.

"So don't try to impress God with your long prayers. And if you go without food so you can spend more time in prayer, don't be like those phony fellows who go around looking like they are starving to death. Wash your face and go out in public looking cheerful. God is the only one who needs to know you are fasting."

The Sermon on the Mount:
You Can't Have It Both Ways

By THIS TIME, almost every rich or powerful person in the audience had taken offense at something Jesus had said. He had promised the kingdom of God to the poor and the hungry and the wretched; he had spoken out against the way the Pharisees and the scribes interpreted the law; and now he had shown up their public fasts and their long prayers for the sham they really were. But he was not finished with them yet.

"Those people who pray long prayers and look half-starved to impress other people are looking for a reward here on earth," Jesus said. "Well, that's the only reward they will get. They are not going to get one from God as well. Don't build up your riches here. The moths will eat the clothes, the metal will rust, and thieves will take the rest. Worst of all, your whole life will be spent protecting those things. If you have your heart set on such things, you will waste your life on them.

"And don't think you can have it both ways! You can't obey two sets of orders at the same time. You can't serve God and money both. So don't spend your time worrying about how much food and clothing you have. Look at the birds: they have never farmed a day, but they eat well because God feeds them. Or look at the flowers: they have never worked a spinning wheel, but King Solomon never dressed as well as they do. If God can do all that, can't he find enough clothing for you? The people of this world spend their time worrying about the things of this world. You don't need to put those things first. Look instead for the things that belong to God's kingdom. Follow what is right; do what is just. Set your heart on these things. Then everything else will fall into place.

"And don't be too quick to judge other people. Remember, the same yardstick you use to measure others will be used to measure you. It's so easy to pick out all the little things that someone else does wrong and to miss the big things you are doing wrong yourself. That's how the Pharisees spend their time. They watch everyone else and forget to watch themselves. You shouldn't be like them."

The anger of the Pharisees could be felt in the air now. They glared at him; but when Jesus looked back at them, there was no hatred in his eyes. "You don't have to earn the right to come to God," he said. "All you have to do is come. Ask, and God will give you what you seek. Knock on God's door, and he will open it. After all, if your child asks you for a loaf of bread, would you give him a rock? Of course not! You know how to take care of your children. Don't you think God knows even better how to treat his children? He knows how to give good things to those who ask him. Then you will know how to treat others as you would like them to deal with you. That's what Scripture is all about."

There was no change in the hard, unyielding stare of the Pharisees who opposed Jesus. He sighed deeply, and a sadness came into his voice. "It is not as hard as you think to keep the letter of the law, and even to make a great show of it. There is plenty of room on that road, and many will go that way, but it will lead them to destruction. The gate that leads to life is a narrow one. You must obey God from your heart by loving him, and by loving your neighbor as you love yourself.

"Pious talk and religious show doesn't lead through that narrow gate. Don't be fooled by what people say. Watch what they do. Did you ever see grapes growing on a bramble bush? No, nor figs growing on a thistle bush! Neither will you see any real goodness coming from a bad person, no matter how religious he is. And a good person will always bring forth good deeds. You will know what the root is like when you see the fruit. Even calling me 'Lord, Lord' is not enough. Only those who do what my Father in heaven wants will have a place in the kingdom.

"Let me explain one more time. Everyone who listens to me and puts my words into practice is like the wise man who built his house on solid rock. When the rains and the flood came, they couldn't knock that house down. But everyone who hears me but doesn't practice what I say, is like the foolish man who built his house on sand. The rains and the flood came and washed away the sand and the house—and the man inside. So build your life on a solid foundation. Then you will be safe forever."

There was silence on the hillside as Jesus turned to go. The sheer power of his words had amazed them all. Never once had he said, "The great Rabbi So-and-so says this." He simply said, "I tell you the truth."

Jesus Heals the Officer's Slave

THE ROMANS WHO ruled Israel were not better or worse than other people. They could be hard and cruel, and they could be tender and loving. Most of them had no use for God. They were very proud, and they thought that Romans were the best people in the world. The people of Israel, as far as they were concerned, were not good for much.

But there were a few Romans who saw something different among the people they ruled, something in the life of the Jewish people that they wished they had themselves. They began to learn about Abraham and Moses and the God who had led them. The more they learned about the God of Israel, the more they realized that their Roman gods were worthless. Some of these Romans became friends of the Jewish people, and some even provided help to Jews who needed it.

Just such a man, an officer in the Roman army, lived in Capernaum. He had given up his Roman gods long before. Whenever he could, he went to the synagogue on the Sabbath. It had been a poor, shabby building, because the Romans had taken everything of any value. So the Roman officer had used his own money to build a beautiful new synagogue for the Jews of Capernaum.

No one could live in Capernaum in those days without hearing about Jesus. Of course, the Roman officer had also heard about him and about the wonderful things he had done. His Jewish friends discussed the things Jesus did, and they argued about whether he might be the Messiah. The Roman officer kept out of the arguments, but he wondered too. "Wouldn't it be wonderful," he thought, "if someone would come who would bring God's message not just to the Jews but to the whole world?"

Now it happened one day that one of the officer's slaves got sick, so sick that he was near death. The officer had learned something about God's love, and he treated his slaves almost like members of the family. But he especially liked the young Hebrew slave who carried his armor and looked after his horse—and who now lay dying. He brought the best of doctors to his house, but they all said the same thing: there was nothing they could do.

The officer had no idea where to turn. If Roman doctors couldn't help, who could? Then he remembered Jesus and the stories he had heard about how sick people were healed. He could feel hope beginning to shine through, like a small candle on a dark night. He hurried to the synagogue to find some of his Jewish friends. "Would you ask Jesus to do what he can for my servant?" he asked.

"We will ask him," they answered, and they set out to find Jesus. "Rabbi," they said when they had found him, "we have a friend who is a Roman officer. He has a servant who is very sick and near death. Will you

69

come and make the servant well? Our friend is a Roman, but he has been very good to our people. He even built us a synagogue with his own money. Will you come?"

"I will come," Jesus answered and set out at once for the officer's house.

When the officer heard that Jesus was coming, he sent friends with a message for Jesus. "Please, don't trouble yourself to come to my house," he said. "I am not worthy to have you under my roof. But I know you have the power to heal my servant. I know what it is like to be in authority. In the army I have men who do as I tell them. I say to a man, 'Go do this,' and he does it. So I know that you only have to say the word and my servant will be healed."

Jesus stopped in the street, a look of surprise on his face. The Jews who had heard him on the mountain recognized that he spoke like a man with authority. But this Roman believed he had authority. Jesus looked at the people around him and said, "That Roman officer has more faith than I have found anywhere in Israel!"

Some of the people in the crowd began to mutter among themselves. It was one thing for Jesus to help a Gentile, but now he was insulting the people of Israel! "Does it surprise you to hear me say that?" Jesus asked. "I tell you, there is a day coming when many will come from all the nations of the Gentiles, and they will sit down with Abraham, Isaac, and Jacob in the kingdom of God. And many Israelites, who should be children of the kingdom, will not be there.

"But I want you to know that what he believes about me is true," Jesus went on. He turned to the officer's friends and said, "Go to your friend and tell him this: 'Because of your great faith, your servant will get well.' " And by the time they arrived at the home of the Roman officer, the servant was already well again and out of bed.

Jesus Raises a Dead Man to Life

ONE DAY JESUS and his disciples came to the town of Nain. As they came close to the city, they met a long line of people on their way to a funeral. In front were four men carrying the body of the dead man on a stretcher. Behind them came many people from the town, crying aloud and tearing their robes, which is how the Jewish people showed their sorrow.

But there was one woman who caught Jesus' eye. She was walking alone behind the dead man. Her head was lowered, and tears were streaming down her cheeks. "I know that woman," Jesus said to his disciples. "Last year she lost her husband. Now her only son has died, and she is all alone. How sad she must be!"

70

Jesus walked forward and signaled the pallbearers to stop. He turned to the woman and said, "You don't have to cry any longer." The disciples were astonished that he would stop and talk to a woman in the middle of the street. The Jewish people were not used to that. The widow looked on in amazement as Jesus reached out and put his hand on the stretcher. His disciples moved away from him. According to the law of Moses, anyone who touched a dead body had to stay away from everyone else for seven days. Then Jesus spoke in a strong voice. "Young man, I tell you, get up!"

The people looked at each other in surprise and began to whisper among themselves. But their whispers died away and their mouths dropped open in wonder when they saw the dead man slowly begin to sit up. Some of the women screamed in fear and hid their faces. Then the young man spoke. "What happened?" he asked. "What am I doing here?" When he saw the men carrying him on the stretcher, it suddenly dawned on him. It was a funeral. *His* funeral! Now it was his turn to be frightened. But Jesus took his hand and said gently to the woman, "Mother, you have your son back." Then there were tears again; but this time they were tears of joy as mother and son hugged each other for dear life.

"What kind of man is this?" the people asked each other. "God has sent his people a prophet!" And the story of what Jesus had done spread throughout the countryside.

71

The Mission of the Twelve

WHEREVER THEY WENT in Galilee, great crowds of people followed Jesus and his disciples. For months the disciples watched, listened, and learned. And then one day, Jesus shook off the crowds and went into the hills, where he could be alone with his disciples.

"You have been with me for more than a year now," Jesus said to the twelve when they were alone at last. "You have heard my words, you have seen what I have done. But you have also seen the crowds. There are so many of them, and I cannot see them all myself. The time has come for you to go out and take the good news of the kingdom to the people yourselves, just as I have done. Come here and let me lay my hands on you."

The disciples gathered around Jesus, and he laid his hands on them and said, "I am giving you power to cast out evil spirits and to heal all kinds of diseases in my name. This first time, don't go to the Gentiles or to the Samaritans; just go to the people of Israel for now, because they are lost as sheep without a shepherd. Go out to them and preach the message that the kingdom of God is near. Heal the sick, raise the dead, cleanse the lepers, and cast out evil spirits. Give as freely as you have received."

Then Jesus sat down with his disciples and gave them instructions for their mission. "Don't take any money with you," he said. "Don't even take a change of clothing or an extra pair of sandals. Go out in different directions, two of you together. When you go into a town, find those who will listen. They will give you food and clothing and a place to stay. If no one will listen to you, then shake the dust of that town from your feet and go on to the next one."

Jesus looked beyond them at the distant horizon, and a look of sadness came across his face. He saw what would happen in the future when the message of the kingdom would go out into the world. He said: "It will not be easy, my friends. I'm sending you out like sheep into a pack of wolves. So be careful. Don't put your trust in people, but in God. People will turn you over to the authorities, and you will be whipped in the synagogues. Some day you may even be brought to trial for your lives. When that happens, don't worry about how you will defend yourselves. God will give you the right words to say when you need them."

When they heard these words, the disciples began to be discouraged. But Jesus knew what they were feeling, so he said: "You have seen how some people have treated me. They even said I was in league with the devil! Don't think they will treat you any better. A servant is no greater than his master. But don't be afraid of them. I have taught you many things in private. Now go out and shout them from the housetops! Don't be afraid of those who can't do anything worse to you than put you to death. Rather fear God, who can send you to eternal death in hell. He will never forget you. God knows when one little sparrow falls to the ground, and you are worth more than many sparrows. He even knows how many hairs there are on your head. So you don't need to be afraid of anything.

"And remember this: if someone accepts you, he is accepting me. If he throws you out, he is throwing me out. If all he has to give is a cup of cold water, but he gives it for me, he will not lose out on his reward."

So the disciples went out, two by two, preaching the good news of the kingdom. To the small towns and villages of Galilee and Judea they went, healing the sick, raising the dead, freeing people who were controlled by evil spirits—even more than Jesus had healed. And everywhere they went, they passed on this message: Turn away from your sins, because the kingdom of God is near! People talked about these things in the marketplaces and the shops, as they traveled, and as they sat at meals with their families. What would he be like, this new king? Would he raise an army? Would he fight the Romans and defeat them?"

Weeks later, the disciples came back to Jesus and began to tell him all that had happened. They were so excited and full of joy that they all tried to talk at once, the words tumbling out so fast that Jesus had to throw back his head and laugh. It was true . . . it was really true, they said over and over. The power of God had come over them, and they had done things no one had done since the days of Elijah and Elisha. Blind people could see again, lame people walked, the dead were raised to life, and even the evil spirits obeyed the disciples and came out of the people they had tormented. Yes, there had been hard times as well. They had been hungry and tired. In some towns they had been thrown out of the synagogues, and sometimes people had thrown rocks at them. But it had been an exciting time, a joyous time, because they had felt the power of God in their own lives. They believed more than ever that Jesus was God's chosen Messiah.

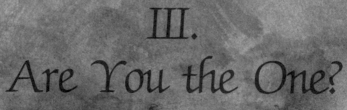

III.
Are You the One?

Now all of Israel was buzzing with the question: Who is this man who makes sick people well and raises dead people to life? Who is this man who exposed the phony Pharisees and the scribes, and speaks kind words to the poor and the oppressed? Who is this man who claims to forgive sins? Could he be the One? Had the Messiah come at last? The question reached even into the dungeon of King Herod, where John the Baptist lay in chains. It was a question that would not be answered until Simon Peter bowed before Jesus and said, "You are the Christ, the Son of the living God!"

JESUS AND JOHN

A Question from John the Baptist

JOHN THE BAPTIST had lain in Herod's prison for months. His disciples came to see him now and then, and always he had the same questions for them: "What is Jesus doing now? Have they made him king yet?"

"No," his disciples always answered. "He goes around preaching, and he has made many sick people well. But whenever anyone says, 'You must be the Messiah,' he tells them not to say anything about it."

Discouraged, John slumped back into the corner of his cell. Nothing had worked out the way he had expected. He still remembered the day when Jesus had come to him to be baptized. He had been so sure then that his cousin was the Messiah. But if Jesus was a king, why was he still wandering the hills with his disciples? Why did the Romans still hold their deathly grip on the city of God, Jerusalem? Why was John himself still in prison? The Messiah was the one who was supposed to free God's people from the Romans, just as Moses had freed them from the Egyptians, wasn't he? It was enough to make a man doubt what he knew in his heart to be true. "Oh, why doesn't he tell them?" John cried aloud. "Why doesn't he *do* something? If he is the Messiah, he should be made king of Israel!"

"Shall we ask him, Rabbi?" his disciples wanted to know.

"Yes. Go and ask him whether or not he is truly the Messiah."

So the disciples of John came to Jesus with their master's question. They had to wait to see him, because there were so many sick people crowding around him. He laid his hands on them, and they went away well. Finally, John's disciples got close enough to say, "Rabbi, John has sent this question from prison: Are you truly the Messiah, or are we waiting for someone else?"

"Go back and tell John what you have seen," Jesus answered. "The blind can see; cripples can walk again; the deaf can hear; the lepers are clean; the dead have come to life again; and the good news is being preached to the poor. Happy is the one who never loses his faith in me."

So John's disciples took Jesus' answer back to him. But as soon as they had gone, Jesus' own disciples began to grumble and complain. "Who does John think he is, asking a question like that? He was supposed to be the big prophet, and now he doubts Jesus!"

But Jesus knew what they were saying to each other. He turned to them and the crowd and said: "When you went out into the desert to see John, what did you expect to see, a piece of grass blowing in the wind? Of course not! John was not weak like that. Don't think he asked this question because he was weak. Well, when you went out into the desert to see John, did you expect to see a man wearing fine soft clothing? No, of course not! Men who live in the courts of kings wear clothes like that.

"Now, tell me honestly, when you went into the desert to see John, what did you expect to see? A prophet? Yes, you saw a prophet all right—and no ordinary prophet either. John is the one Scripture is talking about when it says, 'I will send my messenger in front of me, to prepare the way for the Coming One.'

"Believe me, there has never been a greater man than John. Yet, even the least important member of God's kingdom is greater than he is. John was only a herald of what was to come. But you are witnesses of everything he pointed to. All the people—even the tax collectors—who listened to John believed in God, and they were baptized. But the Pharisees and the teachers of the law would not listen to him and would not let him baptize them. So they turned away from God's message.

"Let me tell you what they are like. They are like little children who sit in the marketplace playing games. One of them shouts, 'If you won't play by my rules, I'll take my ball and go home!' John came, and he lived in the desert, wore rough clothes, and ate very little, and they said, 'The man is crazy!' Then the Son of man came, and he went to weddings and feasts and ate good food and drank good wine, and they said, 'He's a glutton and a drunk, and he makes friends with tax collectors and wicked people.' The way they received John already showed how they would receive me, because John was God's messenger who came to prepare the way for the Son of man. This may be more than you can take, but I tell you that John is the Elijah whom the prophet spoke about, the one who would come before the Chosen One of God." Then Jesus looked up toward the heavens and said, "Thank you, Father, that you hid these things from the people who think they are wise and showed them to the simple."

By Whose Power Do You Work?

DAY AFTER DAY Jesus and his disciples traveled through the Galilee country, and everywhere they went crowds of people pressed in on Jesus. Often he didn't even stop to eat, and each day he grew more and more tired. Even his mother and his brothers heard how he was driving himself. "He's so exhausted he doesn't know what he's doing anymore," Mary said. "We have to find him and make him come home to rest."

When they found Jesus, things seemed to be as bad as they had heard. It was only the middle of the morning, but he already looked tired. There was no end to the lines of sick people who came to him. Off to one side was a group of law experts from Jerusalem who watched everything he did, hoping to find a reason to turn him in to the authorities.

In the line of sick people was a man who was blind and mute. But when he came to the man, Jesus said, "This man is controlled by an evil spirit, which made him blind and mute." Then Jesus said in a loud voice, "Evil spirit, I command you to come out of him, and do not harm the man!" Suddenly the man screamed and fell to the ground. But when he stood up again, he could see and speak.

"He is the Messiah!" someone in the crowd cried out. "He is our new David!"

"No!" shouted the Pharisees. "You think he's the Messiah just because he cast out an evil spirit? He's in league with the Devil! His power comes from Beelzebub, the prince of demons!"

"How can that be?" Jesus demanded. "How long can a kingdom last if its rulers are fighting each other? If Satan's power is used to destroy Satan's servants, his power will end. But if I cast out demons by the power of God, then the kingdom of God has already overtaken you!

"You can't steal anything from a strong man's house unless you tie him up first. I can command the evil spirits because Satan has been tied up by the power of God. Therefore I tell you, anyone who is not with me is against me. As for you, you snakes, the things that just came out of your mouths prove how rotten you are inside! Be careful what you say. You'll have to account to God for every word!"

"If you are from God, then show us a sign!" they demanded.

"Only evil people who are far from God need a sign," Jesus answered. "Here is the only sign you will get. Jonah the prophet lived for three days and nights inside a whale. The Son of man will be in the dark heart of the earth for three days and nights. But the people of Ninevah believed Jonah, and you will not believe me. On the judgment day they will stand up to accuse you!"

The Pharisees began to shout back at Jesus, and soon the whole crowd was in an uproar. This was more than Jesus' family could take. "Let's get him out of here," said one of his brothers. "He's gone mad from overwork!" But the crowd was so great that they could not get through to him; so they passed a message to the front.

"Your mother and your brothers are here," someone said to Jesus. "They want to take you home." The people around him grew quiet to see what his response would be.

"My mother and my brothers?" Jesus asked. "Who are my mother and my brothers?" The crowd murmured their astonishment at his question. Then Jesus stretched out his hand toward them. "Here are my mother and my brothers," he said. "Everyone who does what pleases God is my mother, and my sister, and my brother." And the crowd was amazed, because they could not understand what he meant. But there were a few among them who understood. Jesus was telling them outright that all who followed him were part of a new family, the family of God. Only he had the power to bring this about.

Who Gave You the Right to Forgive Sins?

IN A TOWN in Galilee lived a Pharisee named Simon. He had heard of the new rabbi who was traveling the countryside with his disciples. People told him stories of the remarkable things Jesus said and did. They also reported that Jesus said rude things about the Pharisees. But being a hospitable man, Simon decided to invite Jesus for lunch.

Now it must be said that Simon was not exactly rude to Jesus. But he didn't treat him like an honored guest either. He would have greeted an honored guest by kissing him on the cheek, as was the custom among the Pharisees; and he would have had water brought so that the guest could wash his feet. And if the guest had been a prince or a king, he would have washed the man's feet himself, and put some drops of oil on his head. But Simon did none of these things. In fact, the way Simon looked at it, Jesus should have been grateful to have such an important man invite him to dinner.

The meal was served in an open courtyard, where people of the town could listen in on the conversation. The guests all lay on couches around the tables, leaning on their left elbows, with their feet pointing away from the table. They ate slowly while they talked about many things. Simon wanted to know what Jesus taught about the law, about sacrifices, about the Sabbath, and about many other things. Jesus answered his questions patiently, while others from the town listened to his every word. Some of them hoped that Jesus would give Simon a real lecture and put him in his place, but they were disappointed.

Suddenly there was a disturbance in the crowd, a scuffle, and a woman's voice shouting, "No! Let me through!" Then the woman who was shouting broke through the crowd and stood there panting, searching the faces of the people lying at the table. There was a gasp from the crowd as they recognized her. She was a prostitute from the town. How dare she break into a gathering of respectable people! Just then the woman saw Jesus and ran forward, tears streaming down her face. She fell on her knees at the foot of his couch and held his feet.

For a long time the woman just knelt there, crying and kissing Jesus'

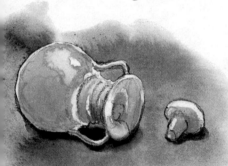

feet over and over. Then she picked up a lock of her long hair and began to wipe Jesus' feet dry with it. From under her robe she took a little bottle that was carved out of beautiful stone. She broke off the top of the bottle and poured the contents over Jesus' feet. Suddenly the whole room was filled with the most wonderful smell. The bottle was filled with sweet oil of myrrh, a very expensive perfume.

Simon watched all this with disgust. "Just like that woman to use too much perfume," he thought. "And Jesus is a phony if I ever saw one. He doesn't even realize what kind of a woman she is. If he did, he wouldn't pay any attention to her. Some prophet!" Simon didn't say a word, but from the look on his face it was clear that he was scandalized.

"Simon." The Pharisee looked up, startled. Jesus was talking to him. "Simon, I have something to say to you."

"Go ahead, Rabbi," Simon answered. No one could ever say he was impolite.

"Once upon a time there were two men, and they both owed some money to the same man. One owed him fifty dollars, and the other owed him five hundred. Neither one of them could pay his debt, and the man said to each of them, 'I forgive you the debt. You don't have to pay me a cent.' You can imagine how happy they both were. They really loved him for that. Now, Simon, which one of them do you think will love him more?"

"Well," Simon answered, "I suppose the one who was forgiven more."

"A good answer," Jesus said. "Now, Simon, I suppose you have noticed this woman here." Simon merely sniffed. "When I came to your house, you didn't bring any water for my feet. But she has washed my feet with her own tears and dried them with her hair. You didn't greet me with a kiss, Simon, but since she came in she has not stopped kissing my feet. You didn't give me any oil for my head, but she has poured precious oil on my feet." Simon shifted uncomfortably on his couch.

"You are right about one thing, Simon," Jesus went on. "She is a very sinful woman. But her sins have been forgiven because of her great love. There isn't much love in the man who thinks he doesn't need to be forgiven, is there, Simon?" Then Jesus turned to the woman. "Your sins are forgiven," he said.

The crowd listening outside began to talk excitedly among themselves. How could he claim to forgive sins? What kind of man was he? Simon the Pharisee was outraged. But Jesus turned to the woman and gently said, "Go on your way in peace. Your faith has saved you."

The Death of John the Baptist

JOHN LAY IN Herod's prison, a happy man. Was it possible? he wondered. How could he be happy in that stinking cell? He knew now that his work was truly done. His disciples had come to him and given him Jesus' answer to his question. "He told us to tell you what we saw and heard," they reported. "The blind go away seeing, cripples go away walking, the sick go away well, and the good news of the kingdom of God is being preached to the poor."

"Then I am content," John had answered them. "God is keeping his promises. Jesus is doing just what the prophets said the Messiah would do. So my work is done. Now I can go to be with God. Herod can't keep me locked up here forever. But when I am dead, you must join Jesus and his disciples. Will you do that?"

They all promised that they would. Then they were gone, and John was again alone in his cell. But now he was a happy man.

John was right about Herod. He couldn't keep John locked up forever. He was afraid to kill John because of John's popularity with the people, and he was afraid to set him free. Herod didn't know it, but his wife, Herodias, who was even more evil than her husband, had some plans of her own. She had hated John ever since that day at the river when he had called her a sinful woman. How did he dare speak that way to the queen! He would pay for that—and pay with his life. If her husband was too cowardly to get rid of John, then she would force him to do it. She would find a way.

Herodias knew her husband. She knew that he was weak and cruel. She also knew that he could not keep his eyes off other women. And there was none more beautiful than her own daughter Salome, and none more hardhearted or cruel. With Herod's birthday coming up, Herodias figured she could find a way to use Salome's beauty to destroy John the Baptist. She would speak to Salome about it at once.

When Herod's birthday came, the royal palace was filled with guests. Roman officers, court officials, Jewish leaders—all had come to join the king's banquet. The wine flowed freely, and soon no one was very sober anymore. King Herod was laughing too loud at jokes that weren't very funny. Herodias knew that the time had come to put her plan into action. She raised one finger in signal to a watching servant, who quietly left to do his mistress' bidding.

A few minutes later Salome came through the curtains into the banquet hall. She was dressed more like a belly dancer than a princess, and Herod could not hide the way he stared at her. "Ah, Salome, my darling," he said heartily. "We have spoken of nothing but your beauty all evening. Will you dance for us, Salome? Please say that you will."

Salome smiled and nodded, and the musicians began to play. Salome began to dance, slowly at first, gracefully. Gradually the music became faster, and Salome's dancing became more wild as she whirled and spun around the room. Herodias watched the king's face, and a cruel smile touched the corners of her lips. The man was wild with desire for Salome. He would give her anything she asked for now, anything at all.

With a crash of cymbals and drums the dance came to an end, with Salome bowed at the feet of King Herod. The guests applauded and cheered loudly. Herod himself had eyes for no one but Salome. "Ask me anything you wish," he said, "and I will give it to you."

Salome only smiled. "Will you swear it?" she asked.

"I swear it," Herod answered. "I will give you anything you ask, even if you ask to share my kingdom."

"There is only one thing I desire, my lord," said Salome sweetly.

"Only one thing, my dear? Surely that would be small reward for such pleasure as you have given us tonight. What is it, Salome?"

She smiled again, but this time all the sweetness was gone. "I want you to deliver to me on a platter the head of John the Baptist!"

The king turned pale and gasped for breath. "No, you can't mean that! Anything but that! Ask me for gold, jewels, power. You can even share my throne. Name anything, but don't ask me to kill that man!"

"Why not, Father?" she asked, and the way she said it showed how much she hated him. "You let that horrible man call my mother a sinner! He shamed both of you in front of your whole kingdom, and you let him get away with it. Well, I am not as weak as you. You promised me anything I asked, and I have asked. Now keep your promise!"

Herod was trapped. Everyone in the room had heard him swear to give Salome whatever she asked. He could not deny her. Herod broke out in a cold sweat. John was a prophet. If he killed God's prophet, he could only wait for God's judgment to fall on him. Almost groaning in his agony,

Herod gave the order. "Call the executioner. He is to cut off the head of John the Baptist and bring it here to Salome, on a platter."

The guests were horrified. They would never forget the gruesome sight that greeted them when the executioner brought to Salome, on a silver platter, the severed head of John the Baptist. And they would never forget the evil gleam in the eyes of Salome and her mother Herodias.

So they had won. Their enemy was dead. His voice would never again warn them, nor would his eyes accuse them.

When John's disciples heard the terrible news, they came to the prison and took the body away to be buried. Then they went to Jesus and told him what had happened. They watched Jesus' shoulders slump in sorrow as he thought of the death of his cousin John. For a while he and John had shared the privilege and the danger of bringing the good news of the kingdom. Now John was gone. The burden lay on his shoulders alone. And for him too, it would end in death.

Then Jesus squared his shoulders. Herod, that proud and cruel and evil king, had not won at all. It was John who had won. His life and his death had served one great purpose: the coming of God's kingdom. It was Herod and Herodias and Salome, with all their wealth and power, who had really lost.

For the rest of his life, Herod was filled with fear of God's judgment because he had killed John. His fear grew worse when he heard stories of a prophet who was going around the countryside healing the sick and raising the dead to life. He asked his advisors who this Jesus was, but in his heart he thought he already knew. "The people are saying that Elijah the prophet has come," his advisers said.

"No!" Herod shouted in his fear. "It's John the Baptist! He has come back to life to punish me for killing him!" But frightened as he was, Herod did not give up his evil ways. Until the end of his life, he was tormented by his own sins.

JESUS TEACHES IN PARABLES

The Farmer and the Soil

THE CROWD AT the shore of Lake Galilee was once again so great that the people crowded in on Jesus, almost pushing him into the lake. But Simon Peter's boat was waiting there. Jesus stepped in, and Peter anchored the boat a little way from shore so that all the people could hear. The people sat down on the shore, hundreds of them, waiting for Jesus to speak. At last they saw him raise his hand, and a hush fell over the crowd.

"Once upon a time," Jesus said, "there was a farmer who went out into his field to plant some seeds. The ground was plowed and ready, and he carried the seeds in a bag hanging from his shoulder. Carefully he walked, and with each step he threw a handful of seeds—first to the right, then to the left.

"There was a hard-beaten path running through the field, and some of the seeds fell on the path. As soon as they saw those lovely seeds, the birds swooped down and gobbled them up. There were also some rocky patches in the field, and some of the seeds fell there. When the rain came, those seeds sprouted up just like the rest. But there were too many rocks there, and their roots couldn't go down deep enough to keep the plants alive. So when the sun shone hot one day, the plants all withered up and died.

"At the edges of the field the earth was covered with weeds. Some of the farmer's seeds fell there, too. The seeds sprouted and started to grow, but the weeds grew even faster and choked out the grain plants. Even the few plants that managed to stay alive didn't bring the farmer any grain at harvest time.

"But there was also plenty of good plowed soil in the field. And the seeds that fell there sprouted up, and their roots grew deep. They drank in the rain and the sun and grew tall. At harvest time the heads of grain were strong and full. Some of the seeds grew into plants with thirty grains apiece on their stalks; some had sixty; and some had multiplied by a hundred times."

Later, when the crowds had gone home, the disciples asked him about the story. "Lord, why did you tell that story?" they asked. "It's very hard to understand you when you use parables like that. Those people on the shore may not have understood anything."

"Did they understand me when I said plainly why I had come?" Jesus asked. "Did they believe the signs and wonders I performed? No. So now I am going to hide my message in stories. Those who truly listen, those who truly belong to the kingdom, will understand me. Those who do not will think I am talking nonsense, or just telling stories. Do you remember what Isaiah the prophet said? 'You will listen and listen, and not understand,' he said. 'You will look and look, and not see at all.' That is the way it will be with these people when they hear my parables.

"But you are my disciples. You should be able to understand what I am saying about the kingdom of God. I tell you, many prophets longed to hear what you have been hearing. But if you don't understand the story about the farmer, how will you understand the rest of my parables? Listen now, and I will explain it to you."

The disciples sat down on the grass and waited for Jesus to explain his story to them. "In the story, I am the farmer, and the seeds are the word of God. The crowd by the lake, and all the people I speak to, are the farmer's field. Some of them are like the hard-beaten path. Their hearts are hard, and they won't accept what I say. So Satan sneaks in and takes the seeds away again; they will never even take root.

"The rocky soil shows people who listen to what I say and think it's wonderful because they think I will solve all their problems. They sing and praise God all day—for a while. But the word of God never really gets hold of them, never sends down strong roots. So the first time they run into some trouble, they begin to doubt. And when it turns out that following me may cost them something, they decide it isn't such a good idea. So the tiny plant of new life that sprouted in their hearts withers and dies.

"And what about the soil where the weeds grow? The soil there has never been properly prepared. These are people who have never really turned away from their old lives. The seeds start to sprout, but soon the weeds begin to grow: the worries of this world, and too much money, and all the other things they want. The weeds choke the plants, so they don't bear any grain. Those people will never be of any value in the kingdom.

"Then there is the good soil. These are people who listen to the message and believe it. They turn to God, and the word of God gets hold of them and puts down deep roots. Then God can use them to do many wonderful things for him, and they produce a good harvest.

"Now do you understand? The message will produce a harvest. So when you go out to scatter the seed of God's word, don't be discouraged by those who oppose you. God will give the harvest. Only make sure that you truly listen—hear the Word and do it."

How Does the Kingdom Come?

"LET ME TELL you what the kingdom of God is like," Jesus said. He was again standing in Peter's boat just off the shore of Lake Galilee, telling stories to the crowds. "After a farmer plants some seed, he goes back home and goes to bed. There is nothing more he can do. The seed will sprout and grow by itself. The farmer has no idea how it happens. First it comes up like blades of grass, then heads start to form, and at last there is grain ready for the harvest. Then the farmer gets out his sickle and cuts down the grain.

"Then again, you might say that the kingdom of God is like this. Once upon a time, a farmer went out and planted good seed in his field. Then he went home to rest. But while he was asleep, his enemy sneaked in and planted weeds in with the wheat. At first the wheat and the weeds looked alike. But when the wheat began to form heads of grain, the farmer's servants could see the difference. They came to him and said, 'Sir, didn't you plant good wheat seed in the field? It's all full of weeds now. Where did they come from?'

" 'Someone who hates me has done this,' the farmer answered.

" 'Shall we go out and pull up the weeds?' the servants asked.

" 'No, it's too late in the season now. If you pull up the weeds, the wheat will come up with them. Wait until harvest time. Then you can pull out the weeds, and we'll bundle them up and burn them. But the grain will go into my barns.' "

Jesus looked out at the faces in the crowd. People sat with puzzled looks, trying to understand what Jesus said. "How can I explain the kingdom of God to you?" he asked. "What story will make you understand? Listen. The kingdom of God is like a tiny seed from the mustard tree. It's the tiniest seed in the world. But if you plant it, it grows up and becomes a tree, big enough so that the birds can come and build their nests in its branches.

"Listen again. The kingdom is like yeast. A woman took it and mixed it with a batch of bread dough. Soon the whole batch of dough was full of yeast, and it started to rise."

Later, when Jesus was alone with the disciples, they asked him about the stories of the seeds and the yeast. "Are they like that other one about the farmer and the soil?" they asked.

"Listen, and I will explain the stories to you," Jesus answered. "In the first story, I told you of a man who sowed the seed, and it sprouted and grew overnight. I am the farmer who sows the good seed, and the field is the world. The seed is the word of God, and it grows because it is alive and powerful. No one can see how it grows, or why, but it grows without help and brings forth a bountiful harvest.

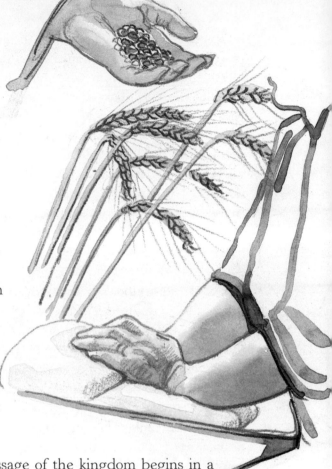

"Not even the efforts of Satan can keep it from growing. The enemy who plants the weeds in the second story is the devil. He is the one who led Adam and Eve into sin; and ever since that time, good and evil have been mixed together in the world, in people, in everything people do. It will be that way until the end. But in the final judgment, sin will finally be rooted out forever and cast into the fire like the weeds.

"So don't be discouraged. The message of the kingdom begins in a small way, like the seed of the mustard tree in the third story. But the seed is growing into a great tree, one that cannot be uprooted. You are so few, and the world is so large; but the message is more powerful than it seems, like the yeast the woman mixed with the dough in the last story. No one saw the yeast growing, just as no one will be able to watch the kingdom grow. It will happen quietly as you go out into the world with the message of the kingdom. But when the woman awoke in the morning, the whole loaf had risen. So it will be with the gospel of the kingdom. It will spread quietly in the night, and when the dawn breaks, everything will be changed!"

Is the Kingdom Worth It All?

WHEN JESUS WAS alone with his disciples, he told them three more stories about the kingdom of God. "The kingdom is like buried treasure," he said. "One day a man was digging in a field when his shovel hit something hard. It was a box, a metal treasure box. Inside was enough treasure to make him rich for the rest of his life. He quickly closed the box and buried it again. Then he found the owner of the field and asked him how much it would cost to buy the land. The price was so high that the man had to sell everything he had to pay for it. But the treasure he got was worth much more than what he paid to get it.''

The disciples looked at one another in consternation. It was all right for Jesus to talk about the kingdom growing by itself in the night. But what was this about cost? The man in the story sold everything he had to pay for the treasure. Would that be expected of them as well?

Jesus understood their frowning looks and went on to drive his point home. "The kingdom of heaven is like this," he said. "Once upon a time, there was a man who was a pearl merchant. Many beautiful pearls passed through his hands as he engaged in this trade. But one day, he came upon the most beautiful pearl in all the world. It was whiter than milk, yet it shone with the colors of the rainbow. It seemed to glow as if it had its own light deep inside. The merchant knew at once that he had to have that pearl, no matter what the cost. So he sold every pearl in his possession, and everything else he owned, in order to buy that one precious pearl."

Jesus' meaning was unmistakable now, but he was not finished with the disciples yet. He wanted to be sure they understood that commitment to the cause of the kingdom was not easy. "Listen again to a picture of the kingdom," he said. "The kingdom of heaven is like a net thrown into the sea. When the fishermen pulled it out, it was full of all kinds of fish. Some of them were good, and some of them were worthless. So they sat down on the beach and sorted them out: they kept the good ones and threw the worthless ones away. That is the way it will be at the end of the world. There are many people who will say that they belong to the kingdom, people who have never listened to me or obeyed me. But the angels of God will sort them out, and they will not make any mistakes. They will separate the evil from the good, and the wicked will be thrown into the place of torment, where they will mourn and grind their teeth.

"Have you understood all this?" Jesus asked when he had finished the stories.

"Yes, we understand," the disciples answered. And they thought they did. It was only much later that they discovered just how much the kingdom would really cost. But Jesus said to them, "Then perhaps you understand why a teacher of the law must become a learner in the kingdom of heaven. If he does, he will have both what is old and what is new."

WHO IS
THIS MAN?

Jesus Quiets the Storm

ONE EVENING JESUS stood again at the shore of Lake Galilee. For hours he had stood in the hot sun talking to the crowds, telling them stories of the kingdom. Now he was finished, but the crowd showed no sign of leaving. "This crowd will never let us get away," Jesus said to his disciples. "We'll have to sail back to the other side of the lake."

So Peter and Andrew pulled up the anchor while James and John set the sail. The sun was low in the west as they set out, and the clouds of an approaching storm were building up over the hills to the north. Silence settled over the little ship as the disciples realized how tired Jesus really was. In the stern of the boat was a seat with a cushion on it. Jesus lay down, put a pillow under his head, and fell fast asleep. The only sound now was the flap of the sail when the wind shifted a bit, and the slap of small waves against the bow of the boat.

The storm struck them almost without warning. The wind came roaring down from the cliffs at the north end of the lake and churned the quiet water into a raging sea. Rain pelted down on the men in the boat as they sprang to the sail, trying to roll it up before it could capsize the boat. Almost instantly they were soaked to the skin, but they scarcely noticed. Every muscle strained as they pulled against the ropes, finally managing to haul in the sail. It took two men to hold the rudder against the force of the waves. They stood in the stern, pulling and hauling, and they noticed with surprise that Jesus was still asleep.

Now they were at the mercy of the winds. The waves tossed and battered the boat, and the men clung for dear life to the sides. A great wave crashed over the bow of the boat, sweeping away everything that was loose and leaving the boat half filled with water. Real fear overtook them now. A few more minutes of this and the boat would go to the bottom of the lake. One of the disciples standing near Jesus grabbed him by the shoulder and shook him awake. "How can you sleep through this?" he shouted. "We're sinking! Don't you care if we all go to the bottom? We're going to drown, don't you understand? Can't you do something?"

Jesus sat up in the boat. A flash of lightning revealed a nightmare sea of boiling waves and blowing spray. Jesus lifted his face into the wind and shouted, "Be still!" At the sound of his voice, the wind stopped blowing. It didn't die away slowly, like a storm passing over; one second there was a

roaring gale, and the next second there was not a breath of breeze. Still the waves leapt furiously about the boat, but Jesus turned toward the water and said, "Waves, be calm!" Suddenly, there was a great stillness. The waves stopped pounding against the boat, dwindled away, and the sea became completely calm, as smooth as glass.

The disciples sank down in the boat and sighed with relief. Then the realization of what had happened began to dawn on them. They looked at Jesus, and there was a new kind of fear in their eyes—a holy awe. What kind of man was this, they wondered, who could command the wind and the sea?

"Where is your faith?" Jesus asked them. "Are you afraid of me now, because I am stronger than the storm? Don't you trust me even yet?"

But the disciples had nothing to say. They were still too full of wonder that a man could still the storm by the sound of his voice.

Demons and Pigs

ON THE FAR side of Lake Galilee, on a hillside above the town of Gerasa, a man stood looking out toward the lake. It was hard to tell that he was a man. He was dirty and naked; his beard was long and infested with lice, and his skin was covered with cuts and sores. From his wrists and ankles dangled pieces of rotting rope and rusting chain that had once been used to tie him down. His face was dull and lifeless, but his eyes gleamed with a look of evil. For many years he had been under the control of evil spirits—first one, then two, then a dozen, then hundreds. The spirits made him violent, a danger to everyone around him. At first the men of Gerasa had tried to tie him up. But the demons gave him such strength that he broke every rope or chain they used. Now he lived among the tombs on the hillside, stealing whatever food he could, beating and murdering people who were so foolish as to come alone to that hill. When there was no one else to beat, he beat himself, cutting his body with sharp rocks.

On the shore below the disciples were pulling their storm-ravaged boat up onto the beach. Suddenly, they heard a furious scream, and it chilled their blood to hear it—a sound that was only partly human. They looked up to see a terrible sight, a naked man screaming as he ran toward Jesus. But instead of springing at Jesus' throat, the possessed man fell to the ground at his feet. "What do you want with us, Jesus?" he cried. "Why would the Son of God bother with us? It isn't time yet! You haven't won yet! You can't come here and torture us yet!"

"What is your name?" Jesus demanded.

"My name is Legion," wailed the man, "for there are many of us."

"I command you to come out of him!" Jesus said sternly.

"No! Please, no!" the demons screamed. "Don't send us to the bottomless pit! There are some pigs there on the mountainside. Allow us to go into them."

What were pigs doing near a Jewish village? God had told his people not to use pigs for meat. But there were some people in Israel who raised pigs for the Romans and the other Gentiles who lived in the country. To them, if there was money to be made, God's law took second place. Yes, the pigs would be a good place for a flock of evil spirits to go. "Come out of him and go into the pigs," Jesus commanded.

Suddenly the man screamed one final long, loud scream and collapsed again in front of Jesus. Seconds later, there was a disturbance on the hillside. The pigs were starting to run, squealing loudly and foaming at the mouth. It was a terrible sight to behold as they ran headlong down the hillside and straight into the lake, where they drowned.

The men who were tending the pigs were scared to death. They ran into the city and found the men who owned the herd. "Your pigs have all drowned!" they cried. "They ran down the hillside and into the lake, all two thousand of them! It was a terrible thing, just terrible! It had something to do with that maniac from the tombs and this Jesus of Nazareth."

"Slow down, slow down," said the owners. "What are you talking about, a maniac and Jesus and drowning pigs? What is this all about?"

Finally the men managed to tell the story of what they had heard and seen that evening. Quite a crowd gathered to hear them tell it, and they all followed along when the owners went to see about their pigs.

As they came close to the shore, they saw Jesus talking quietly with someone. They could scarcely believe their eyes. It was the man from the tombs, the one who ran around naked and cut himself and attacked people. But he wasn't violent now. The ropes and chains had been cut off his wrists and ankles. Someone had loaned him a robe to wear, and he was talking with Jesus as clearly and calmly as anyone else. But the sight stopped them only for a moment. They had come to protect their property.

"Rabbi, I am sure this is a very wonderful thing that has happened here today," the oldest of the owners began, gesturing toward the former madman. "But do you know what those pigs cost? You can't just go around driving pigs into the lake, demons or no demons. It's not good for business! Please, don't do us any more favors. Just leave, and don't come back."

Jesus said nothing. He did not scold them for rejecting him. But he was very sad that these men thought more of their pigs than they did of the poor man who had been healed. No wonder they couldn't hear the message of the kingdom! So Jesus and his disciples turned back toward their boat.

The man Jesus had healed ran up behind him and begged him, with tears in his eyes, "Please, don't go away. You gave me my life back today. Let me go with you, please!"

"No, my son," Jesus answered kindly. "It is more important for you to stay here in Gerasa. Go back home, go back to the friends you used to know. Tell them about the great things the Lord has done for you." Then Jesus embraced him and sent him on his way.

Soon everyone in all the towns around had heard about the man from Gerasa, the man who was controlled by a whole troop of evil spirits. Everywhere he went, he told about Jesus and the wonderful things that had happened that morning on the shore of Lake Galilee.

Jesus Heals the Rich and the Poor

IT DIDN'T TAKE long for the word to spread that Jesus was back on the west shore of Lake Galilee. Once more the crowds began to gather at the shore to hear him teach, jostling and crowding each other so much that some could scarcely breathe. But when they saw an elder of the synagogue approaching, the people respectfully opened a path for him as he tried to make his way to Jesus. He walked slowly and sadly, his eyes brimming with tears. Why is he here? the people wondered. Why would a leader of the synagogue come here? Does he want to ask Jesus questions? And why does he look so sad?

The elder, whose name was Jairus, continued his way through the crowd until he stood in front of Jesus. I have heard so much, he thought. I hope it isn't all a lot of wild rumors. Please, God, let it be true that he can heal the sick. Then he looked into Jesus' face, and he knelt down on the wet sand of the lakeshore.

"Please, Rabbi," he wept, "I have a little daughter, only twelve years old. She is my only child and the joy of my heart. She is dying, Rabbi. She may have even died in the time it took me to come to you. Will you come and lay your hands on her and make her well again? Please, please come!"

"I will come," Jesus said. A look of hope came into Jairus' eyes for the first time as he stood to walk with Jesus back toward the town. The whole crowd of people followed, whispering among themselves. "Did you hear? He's going to heal a little girl! Do you think we'll get close enough to see? I've never seen a healing before." They talked and chattered away, and they pushed and shoved so much that Jesus and Jairus could hardly walk. They were all trying to get a look or touch his sleeve so that they could go home and say, "I saw the holy man today. I even touched him!"

There was one woman in the crowd who wanted to reach Jesus for a different reason. For twelve years she had been very sick, and she had spent every penny she had on doctors. They had made her take all kinds of medicines and had tried everything they knew. But she was still sick, and now she was poor as well. Then she heard about Jesus, how he spoke of the love of God, and how he made sick people well. "He must be the one God has sent," she thought. "How else could he do these wonderful things? If only I could see him—get close to him; if only I could touch him, I know he could heal me."

And so, weak and sick as she was, she made her way into the streets of Capernaum and down to the lakeshore. She tried to get close enough to Jesus so he could see her, but the crowd was too large. When Jairus came and Jesus started back for town, she was able to get closer to them. The crowd pushed and shoved, and she pushed and squirmed, until she got to within an arm's length of Jesus. She stretched out her arm and pushed forward with all her strength. There! She had done it! Her fingers had touched the hem of his sleeve, and even before she drew back her hand, she could feel in her own body that her sickness had been healed.

All at once, Jesus stopped and looked around. The woman was suddenly frightened. What if he was angry with her?

94

"Who touched me?" Jesus demanded.

His disciples looked at him curiously. "Rabbi," they said, "there are a hundred people pushing and shoving you. How can you ask who touched you?"

"No, Jesus said, "this was different. Someone touched me in faith." And he looked the woman straight in the eye.

"Yes, Rabbi, I touched you," she said in a shaky voice. At the sound of her voice, people made way for her to come closer to Jesus. She knelt in front of him and said, "I have been sick for twelve years, and no doctor could help me. But then I heard about you, and I knew you had come from God. I thought, 'If only I could touch him, I would be healed.' And now I am well again!"

"Daughter," Jesus said, "your faith has made you whole again. Go in peace."

The woman went on her way happy. She did not need to follow the crowd to see more miracles. She knew who Jesus was.

Jesus Raises a Dead Girl to Life

WHILE JESUS WAS still talking to the woman, Jairus caught sight of two of his servants coming to meet him. Their faces were sad, and he went cold with fear. When they came near, they said, "You don't have to bother the rabbi any longer, Master. You daughter has died."

Jairus turned to face Jesus, his eyes brimming with tears. If only that woman hadn't slowed us down, he thought. But Jesus saw the accusing look on his face. "Don't be afraid, Jairus," he said. "Don't give up your faith now. Your daughter will be well again."

So they walked on and after a while came to Jairus' home. The people inside the house were already wailing at the tops of their voices, and some were singing sad funeral songs. It was the custom in that land to show sadness by crying out loud. In fact, the one who cried the loudest was thought to be the saddest. So there was a great deal of weeping and wailing coming from inside the house. Jesus stopped in front of the house and turned to face the crowd. "There is sadness in this house," he said, "and no one is to go in." There was a groan of disappointment from the crowd, but Jesus said, "Only Jairus and I will go in, and Peter, James, and John, my disciples."

The five of them walked slowly through the door. Inside the house, the noise was deafening. "Why are you making all this noise?" Jesus shouted. The people in the room fell into a shocked silence. "The child isn't dead. She is only sleeping."

There were some people in the room who didn't even know the girl; they were simply hired to cry loudly at funerals so that everyone would know how sad the family was. When they heard what Jesus said, they began to laugh. "Well, that's some doctor for you—he can tell you about the patient before he's even seen her," they said. "Go on up. You'll find out soon enough. Only sleeping! Hah!"

"Leave us!" Jesus ordered. They looked at Jairus, who nodded his head. Still laughing scornfully, they left the house to tell their story to the crowd outside. "Now, where is the child?" Jesus asked. Jairus led him to the couch where she lay, cold and still. But Jesus knew that death could never have the last word. He took the dead child's hand and said, "Little girl, get up!"

There was a moment of silence. Then the girl took a deep breath, and her eyes fluttered open. When she saw Jesus, she smiled and sat up. "Get her something to eat," Jesus said to the astonished parents. "She must be hungry." Jairus and his wife stood there in confusion, not knowing what to do first. Then the little girl laughed, and suddenly her parents were laughing too, and crying at the same time, and hugging her and each other and Jesus and the disciples. The crowd outside must have been surprised to hear laughter coming from the house. But Jesus said to Jairus, "Don't go out and brag about what has happened here today. There are already too many people who only want to see miracles but don't want to listen to my message." Nevertheless, word spread throughout the countryside of what Jesus had done that day. And everywhere people were asking themselves whether Jesus was the one sent by God to bring hope and new life to the world.

Jesus Feeds Five Thousand

"WE MUST TALK together of what comes next," Jesus said to his disciples. "Let us go out into the desert where we can be alone. There we can rest and pray and talk together." But the people of the nearby towns saw which way they went—and followed them. They were joined by thousands of people who had come from all over Israel, hoping to see the man who might be their new king. Around the shore of Lake Galilee they walked, into the hill country on the other side, until they caught up with Jesus and his disciples.

When Jesus saw the crowds, he felt very sorry for them. "They are like sheep without a shepherd," he thought. "They know they need something, but they don't know what it is, and they don't know how to find it." So he spent the whole day with them, telling them stories about the kingdom of God and teaching them. He healed all those who were sick, or blind, or crippled.

It was late in the day—the sun was already low in the west—when the disciples came to Jesus. "Rabbi, it's getting late," Philip said. "There is no food out here in the desert. You should let the people go now, so they will have time to walk to the villages around and buy food for their supper."

But Jesus had something else in mind. He intended to feed the people gathered in this lonely place, to give them a sign that he really was the Son of God. They would see that he was the same God who had fed his people in the desert with manna after they came up out of Egypt. So Jesus said, "Philip, why don't you give them something to eat?"

"You must be kidding!" Philip answered. "There are five thousand families out there. How many of them could we feed on ten dollars worth of bread? That's all the money we have among us!"

"How much food do we have here?" Jesus asked.

"I already checked, Rabbi," Andrew answered. "I found one little boy who still has his lunch—five rolls and two dried fish. That isn't much."

"Bring the boy to me," Jesus said to him. "And in the meantime go out and have the people sit down in groups of about fifty people or so. And borrow some empty baskets from the people." The disciples didn't understand, but they did as Jesus told them.

Then Jesus knelt down to talk with the boy. "Your lunch is all the food we have," he said. "May I use it to feed these hungry people?"

The boy looked longingly at his lunch, then back at Jesus. He was hungry himself. But there was something about the way Jesus asked him that made him feel this was a man he could trust. Without a word, he held out his lunch to Jesus. Jesus smiled and touched him for a moment on the head. Then he stood and faced the crowd. Picking up one of the rolls of bread, he broke it in his hands and said, "We praise you, O God, King of the universe, who gives us bread from the earth." Then he broke pieces of bread and dried fish into each of the baskets the twelve disciples had brought back with them. "Now, I have broken the bread among you," he said to them. "You go out and share it with the people."

The disciples looked at one another and shook their heads in disbelief. But they had learned one thing in their months with Jesus: you never knew what might happen next. So they took the baskets out into the crowd, wondering if they would be killed by a hungry mob. Half a roll and one little piece of fish in each basket! Nathanael couldn't bear to look. He held the basket out toward the first group of people he came to. "I'm sorry there isn't more," he apologized.

"More?" the man cried. "It's a feast!" Nathanael opened his eyes and looked down. The basket was filled with bread and fish! Hungry hands were reaching, people were laughing, and some were asking, "Where did they get all that food?" Nathanael looked around and saw the same thing everywhere. All the disciples were thronged with people, and everyone who reached into the basket pulled both hands out filled with food. Only when the last people had taken all they wanted were the baskets finally empty. Everyone ate, and they ate their fill.

"Go around now and pick up all the leftover food," Jesus said to his disciples. "People took more than they could eat." They worked their way from group to group, and the leftover food was dropped into the baskets. When they came back to Jesus, every one of the twelve disciples had a basket full of food. "Now each of you has plenty to eat too," Jesus said. "When you share what I give you with others, there will always be enough left for you, and more to spare."

By now the word was spreading through the crowd. "It's a miracle," they said to each other. "Just like the wine at the wedding, did you hear about that one? He must be the prophet God promised. He must be the new king!"

Jesus Walks on Water

AFTER FEEDING THE five thousand people, Jesus went away into the wilderness to pray. The disciples got into their boat to sail back across the lake, even though it was a bad time for sailing. Peter, Andrew, James, and John had sailed on Lake Galilee all their lives. They knew that in the evening the wind blew out of the west, and that was the direction they had to go. But Jesus had told them to sail, and so they sailed.

The sun was nearly down as they set out from shore, leaving the disappointed crowd behind them. They were not more than half a mile out onto the water when the wind shifted and began to blow directly against them. They could make no headway against the wind, and so they had to furl the sail and break out the oars. It was getting dark quickly now as they pulled and heaved on the oars; the wind was blowing stronger all the time and the waves were getting higher.

For half the night the disciples battled the waves, rowing against the wind. Then suddenly John pointed back toward the other shore. "Look there!" he shouted. The others peered through the darkness. Then they saw it too. But it couldn't be! It was a man walking toward the boat! But there was no land out there. How could he—he must be walking on top of the water!

"There's nothing there!" Andrew shouted. "Our eyes are playing tricks on us. We're just too tired!"

"But we all see it," Matthew answered. "Why would we all see the same thing if he isn't real?"

The figure kept coming closer and closer. "It's a ghost!" Peter shouted, and the other disciples cried out in fear. Now the figure was almost upon them.

"Don't be afraid," the man called out. "It's only me." They knew that voice. It was Jesus! Peter squinted against the wind. "Is it really you, Master?" he asked, his voice trembling. How could he be sure? Then he had a wonderful and terrifying idea. "If it's really you, Lord, tell me to come to you on the water."

"Come to me," Jesus said.

The other disciples watched in amazement as Peter stepped over the side of the boat into the water. No, not *into* the water—*onto* the water! Peter was walking on top of the water, straight toward Jesus! One step, then another. The water felt like solid ground under his feet, not even cold or wet. Another step . . . and then Peter had a terrible thought. "What am I doing here?" he asked himself. He looked away from Jesus and saw the

99

waves surrounding him, and he was scared to death. "I'm going to sink!" he thought. Suddenly the solid feeling under his feet gave way and his feet were wet and cold. "Help!" he shouted. "Help! I'm sinking! Lord, save me!"

In an instant Jesus was at his side. He reached out and grabbed Peter's hand to hold him up. "Oh, Peter," Jesus said sadly. "Your faith is so halfhearted. Why did you doubt me?"

Peter had no answer. Jesus helped Peter into the boat, and as soon as they were both inside, the wind and the waves died down. The men in the boat knelt down in front of Jesus, thanked him, and said, "You really are the Son of God, the Lord of Creation."

A light breeze sprang up from the east, and the disciples raised the sail. By sunrise they were back on the western shore near the town of Gennesaret. But there was no rest for them. Fishermen along the shore recognized them at once and spread the word to the nearby towns. Within an hour they were again surrounded by hundreds of people who brought their sick friends to be healed by Jesus. He healed them all and taught the people about the kingdom of God.

The Bread of Life

THE PEOPLE JESUS had fed the day before were still on the other side of the lake. They knew the disciples had sailed off by themselves in the direction of Capernaum, but they couldn't figure out where Jesus was. When Jesus could not be found, many of the people sailed across the lake with fishermen who were nearby. When they found Jesus already in Capernaum, they were amazed. "How did you get here, Rabbi?" they asked curiously.

"What difference does it make?" Jesus answered. "You only came because you wanted to see some more miracles. I fed you bread and fish yesterday. But that isn't the kind of bread you should be looking for. Work for the food that lasts, the food that gives life forever. That's the kind of food I really came to give you—food from your Father in heaven."

"How can we do the work of God, Rabbi?" they asked. Then they waited to hear which one of the commands of the law he would talk about.

"This is the work of God," Jesus answered, "to believe in the one he has sent."

"But what sign will you give us so we can believe in you? Was the bread you gave us yesterday a sign? When our ancestors were in the desert, Moses gave them manna to eat."

"Moses gave them nothing to eat! It was God who gave them the manna. It was bread from heaven. That is where the real bread comes from. The bread I gave you yesterday only filled your stomachs. The real bread from heaven will give life to the whole world."

"Give us some of that bread, Rabbi," they begged him.

"I am the bread of life," Jesus answered. "Anyone who comes to me will eat and be filled and will never be hungry or thirsty again. You have seen me, but you have not believed. If you believe and come to me, I won't turn you away. I came from heaven to do what my Father wants. He wants everyone who believes in me to have life that lasts forever. If anyone believes in me, I will raise that person to life on the last day."

There were some in the crowd who came from Jesus' home town of Nazareth. "Who do you think you are, talking like that?" they demanded. "You're just a carpenter's son. We know your mother and father, Mary and Joseph. What's this about coming from heaven? You were born just like the rest of us!" And there were many who went away shaking their heads. They never came back to hear the Lord again.

When he saw them leaving, Jesus turned to the twelve disciples and asked, "What about you? Do you want to leave too?"

"Where could we go, Lord?" Peter answered. "No one else has eternal life to offer. We believe you! We know you are God's chosen one." Then some of the disciples remembered that Jesus once had said to them, "Don't think that I have come to bring peace. I have brought a sword that will divide people from their friends, even from their own families." They were beginning to see that Jesus himself was that sword. More and more, things were narrowing down to the one question: who is this man Jesus?

Jesus at the Pool of Bethesda

BY THIS TIME there were many who believed Jesus was the Messiah, but there were many more who did not. Sometimes the question nearly caused a riot. One such time came when Jesus was visiting Jerusalem, and it started when he healed a crippled man. It happened this way.

There were many gates in the great wall around the city of Jerusalem, and the one where sheep and goats were brought in to the market was called the Sheep Gate. Not far from the Sheep Gate was a pool of water called Bethesda, meaning the House of Mercy, because it was said that a person could be healed of his sickness at that pool. Sometimes the water in the pool was stirred up by some mysterious force, and it was said that the first person to step into the pool after it was stirred up would be healed. Some said it was an angel who stirred the water. Others said there was a spring far underground that sometimes spurted out healing water.

Whatever it was that caused the water to move, people did believe that healings took place there. So many sick people came to the pool to wait for the stirring of the water that a platform had been built around the pool. It was a kind of open porch with pillars holding up a roof to keep out the rain and steps leading down into the water of the pool. The floor of the porch was always covered with the beds of men and women who were sick with all kinds of diseases. All of them were people the doctors had given up on, or they were too poor to afford doctors at all. Their last hope was to be first into the pool when the water of Bethesda was stirred.

One day Jesus came to the Bethesda pool. He was in Jerusalem for the Passover celebration, just as he had been every year since he was twelve years old. This day happened to be the Sabbath, when the Jews were not allowed to do any work. Jesus was not alone with the sick people at the pool. Some of his disciples were with him, and there were also some spies sent by the ruling council of the Jews, the Sanhedrin. They were watching everything Jesus did now and reporting it back to their bosses.

As Jesus walked among the crippled and sick who lay at Bethesda, he came upon a man who looked more miserable than the rest. He was all alone, whereas most of the others had someone else with them.

"What brings you here to Bethesda?" Jesus asked him.

"I am lame in both legs, sir," the man replied. "I cannot walk."

"And how long have you been lame?"

"Thirty-eight years, sir."

Jesus looked at him steadily. "Do you really want to get well?" he asked.

The man was puzzled, What could this man mean? Of course he wanted to get well! At that moment the years of waiting and hoping crushed him down, and he began to cry. "Sir, I have no one to help me," he said. "When the water of the pool is stirred, someone else always gets into the pool ahead of me. I don't think I will ever be well again."

"Then this is what I'll tell you," Jesus said. "Stand up now and pick up your bed. You can walk again."

At once the man felt strength flowing into his legs again. He stood up and tested his legs. The left knee would bend—and the right knee too. He could stand on one foot. He could even jump up in the air! He turned in his happiness toward the man who had healed him, but Jesus had disappeared into the crowd. The man quickly rolled up his mat and put it on his shoulder. He walked out of the Bethesda porch, enjoying each new step. But suddenly he was stopped by a group of angry-looking Pharisees. "What are you doing carrying your mat on the Sabbath day? It is against our law to work on the Sabbath."

The man could only grin at them. If only they knew how long it had been since he had been able to work on *any* day! "There was a man here who made my legs work again," he said to the Pharisees. "He told me to pick up my bed and walk home!" He waited for them to share his joy, but they only seemed to become more angry.

"Who told you such a thing?" they demanded. "Point him out to us!"

But the man could only look around helplessly. He shrugged his shoulders and said, "I never saw the man before, and he isn't here any longer."

"Just leave your mat here and don't carry it on the Sabbath," they replied. "You should go to the temple now and give glory to God. It is God who has healed you, not this man you're talking about!"

And the man did just that. He went to the temple to thank God that he could walk again. Still, he could not help wondering. Who was the man God had used to make him well?

An Argument in the Temple

WALKING ON LEGS he had not used in many years, the man from the pool of Bethesda moved cheerfully toward the temple. As he entered the courtyard, who should he see but the very man who had made him well, surrounded by some of his friends. He hurried up to one of them and asked, "Please, sir, will you tell me your master's name?"

The disciple turned to look at the man. "He is Jesus, of Nazareth," he answered.

"Jesus of Nazareth!" the man called out. At the sound of his name, Jesus turned to face the man. "Now that I know your name," the man said, "I can thank you for making me whole again!"

"Yes, you have been made well," Jesus answered him. "But it is not only your legs that must be healed. Your sins have been forgiven. Go on with your life, but don't fall back into the ways of sin, or you will end up worse off than before."

Happier than ever, the man went to find the Pharisees who had confronted him earlier. Surely they would also want to find this man of God! But when he found them and told them that it was Jesus who had healed him, they were not happy at all. Their faces grew dark with anger, and they strode off to the temple to find Jesus.

"You have broken the law of God," they scolded Jesus when they found him in the temple courtyard. "You broke the Sabbath when you helped that man, and you told him to break it too. You are twice guilty!"

"You have missed the whole point of the Sabbath," Jesus answered. "My Father has never stopped working, not even on the Sabbath, and now I am doing his work."

At this the Pharisees became so angry they could hardly speak. "It wasn't enough for you to break the Sabbath," they shouted. "Now you make yourself equal with God! Blasphemy! That is the sin of Satan! Death is what you deserve!"

"Do you really think I could heal this man on my own? It is only the power of God that can heal. The things I have done speak for themselves. God is telling you that everything I have said is true. You don't believe me because you do not have God's word in yourselves. You study the Scriptures because you think you will find the secret of eternal life there.

And you will, if you read them right. Scripture is talking about me. But you don't have the love of God in you. I have come from the Father, but you don't believe me. Still, I won't be the one to accuse you. Moses accuses you. If you really believed Moses, you would believe me, because Moses wrote about me. If you won't believe him, how can I expect you to believe me?"

And Jesus turned on his heels and walked away, leaving the Pharisees shouting after him, "Death! Death to the blasphemer!"

So the more clearly Jesus spoke about himself, the more people were divided into two camps: those who believed in him and those who rejected him. Only those who truly understood Scripture recognized him as God's chosen one.

Jesus and Nicodemus

A MAN IN Jerusalem named Nicodemus was both a Pharisee and a member of the ruling council of the Jews, the Sanhedrin. Nicodemus wanted to serve God, and he tried to obey the law of Moses in every way. But he had heard things, disturbing things, about this man named Jesus who went around teaching that the leaders of Israel had missed the most important point of the law. Not only that, but this man showed signs and performed miracles as well, and the people said he came from God. Was it true? Could Jesus of Nazareth really be a prophet of God? Nicodemus had to find out for himself.

On the other hand, he wasn't sure he wanted to be seen talking to Jesus. After all, there were so many questions about the man, and Nicodemus had his position in the community to think about. So it was night when he stepped out of his house and slipped through the silent streets of Jerusalem out to the hill where he had heard that Jesus was staying with his disciples. He saw the glow of their fire from a distance and hesitated a moment, then strode on until he entered the circle of firelight.

The disciples could see by their visitor's clothing that they were in the presence of a rich and powerful man. But Nicodemus paid no attention to them. His eyes scanned the circle of men until they came to rest on the one who was certainly their leader. "My name is Nicodemus, Rabbi, and I am a member of the Sanhedrin." The disciples were surprised, but Jesus' face showed no change. "We know you are a teacher who has come from God," Nicodemus went on. "No one could do the things you have done unless the power of God was with him."

This was more than most Pharisees were willing to admit. But Jesus knew the real question on Nicodemus' mind, and he decided to challenge him. "Listen to me, Nicodemus," he said. "No one can even begin to see what the kingdom I have taught about is like unless he is completely reborn!"

The statement took Nicodemus completely by surprise. "But Rabbi, that's impossible!" he protested. "How can a grown man be born again? He certainly can't become a fetus inside his mother again and be born a second time!"

"Nevertheless, what I have said is true, Nicodemus," Jesus answered. "Entering the kingdom of God is not a matter of obeying the law. It's a brand new life, which only God can give you. When the Spirit of God makes you live, only then are you truly alive."

"How can this happen?" Nicodemus asked.

"Do you mean, how do you know when the Spirit of God has made you alive? The Spirit of God is not mysterious, Nicodemus. The Spirit is like the wind, which blows where it wants to; you can't tell where it comes from or where it is going. But you certainly know it's there, because you hear the sound of it blowing through the trees. You know because you see it working."

Nicodemus had never heard anything like this before. "I still don't understand," he said.

"Do you mean to tell me, Nicodemus," Jesus said, "that you instruct others, yet you don't understand these things? I am not telling you anything new. Don't you remember the story of the brass snake? When the people of Israel were bitten by poisonous snakes in the desert, God told Moses to make a brass snake and set it on a pole. If people wanted to be healed, they only had to look up at that snake. Those who truly believed God looked up, and God really healed them; those who did not believe God died there in the wilderness.

"The Son of man is going to be lifted up on a cross, just as that snake was lifted up, and people will only have to look to him to be saved. Everyone who believes in him will have eternal life. Nicodemus, God loved the world so much that he sent his only Son, so that everyone who believes in him may not die but have eternal life. God didn't send his Son into the world to judge it. He sent him to be the Savior of the world. So those who have been made alive by God's Spirit will believe in me. Those who do not belong to God will also reject me."

Through the stillness of the night Nicodemus walked back to his own house, his head swimming with the things he had heard. What a surprising evening this had turned out to be! Jesus had turned everything upside down for him. All his life he had studied the Scriptures. Now he wondered if he had ever really understood them. Jesus had spoken with such power, and his words had rung so true; but he had talked about himself, not about the law. It was more than Nicodemus could take in all at once. He would have to think it over, study the Scriptures some more, and see if what Jesus had said was true. And he would watch, wait, and wonder.

"You Are the Christ!"

THINGS WERE DIFFERENT now, ever since that day in Capernaum when the thousands of people Jesus had fed came to him again. He told them openly that he was the bread of life come down from heaven, and that without him no one could have true life. Most of them left then. His words were too much for them to take. Now the crowds were gone, and Jesus began to press his disciples toward that same point of decision, toward the choice Mary had made.

"Who do people say I am?" he asked them suddenly one day.

The disciples thought for a moment. "Well, some say that you are John the Baptist come back to life. Some think you are Elijah the prophet come to earth again. Others say you are a prophet."

"I know what others say," Jesus replied. "But who do *you* say I am?"

This was the test. What would the disciples say now that so many others had deserted Jesus? Finally it was Peter, the rough fisherman, who looked at him steadily and said, "You are the Christ, the Son of the living God."

"Blessed are you, Simon," Jesus said. "You didn't learn that on your own; my Father in heaven showed it to you. From now on, Simon, your name will be Peter, 'the Rock.' This faith is the bedrock for my church. That kind of faith will stand up to anything, even to hell itself. You, my disciples, will have the keys of the kingdom of God, and you will open it for all those my Father has called to come in."

The disciples stood silently, watching Jesus. They knew they had reached some kind of a turning point. Peter at last had said it openly: "You are the Christ, the Son of the living God." And Jesus had accepted Peter's words. There could be no doubt about the meaning of Jesus' words. But now that it was out in the open, what would he say next? What would the Messiah do? What new surprises lay in store for them now?

IV.
The Surprise
of the Kingdom

The longer Jesus worked and taught among the people of Israel, the sharper his message became. More and more, the people were forced to make a choice, to give an answer to the question, Who is this man? Peter had spoken for all the disciples when he said, "You are the Christ, the Son of the living God." But they still had much to learn about who Jesus really was. Jesus had to teach them that the powerful Son of man promised by the prophet Daniel was also the suffering servant spoken of by the prophet Isaiah.

THE MESSIAH MUST SUFFER

The King Must Die

THE WORDS OF Peter's confession still hung in the air when Jesus turned suddenly to his disciples and said, "The time has not yet come for you to tell this to the world. First, I must go to Jerusalem, where I must suffer many things from the rulers of Israel. They will reject me, and they will put me to death. But I will rise from death on the third day."

This was too much for Peter. His head was still filled with the vision of Jesus as the new King David who would sit on the throne in Jerusalem. How could he think about death? "Don't say that, Lord!" Peter protested. "You can't die!"

"Get away from me, you Satan!" Jesus snapped. The words stung Peter like a hard slap in the face. "You're only thinking about what you want," said Jesus, "not about what God wants! Don't try to turn me away from what I must do." Then Jesus turned abruptly and went off by himself.

The disciples followed him in silence, each lost in his own thoughts. Their minds were reeling. First Jesus had openly admitted that he was the Messiah. Then he had talked about dying. But how could he be king of Israel if he died? Would his life have meant anything at all?

It was Jesus who at last broke the long silence. "If the people really want to follow me," he said, "they must be willing to give themselves up completely. Those who try to save their own lives will lose them in the end. But those who are willing to give up their own lives because of me, because of the good news, will keep their lives forever. What good will it do you if you hold onto your life, and everything it has to offer, only to lose it in the end? How much would you be willing to give to keep your life forever? I will set the example by giving up my own life for you.

"And there is more. The Son of man will come with his angels, in the glory of his Father, and will reward every person for his deeds. And I tell you this: some of you will not see death before you have seen the Son of man coming in his kingdom."

Then there was silence again as Jesus and his disciples walked along the dusty road. The disciples had much to think about, more than they could take in all at once. Jesus talked about death—and at the same time of coming in the glory of his kingdom. How could these things go together? Only after Jesus had died and risen again would the disciples fully understand that the king had come to die for the sin of the world.

The Transfiguration

JESUS AND THE disciples were exhausted after another week of preaching the good news of the kingdom in town after town. "Stay here and rest," he said to them. "I will take only Peter, James, and John with me. Come, you three. We'll go up into the hills to pray." So they set out, wearily making their way to the top of the hill. By the time they got there, the three disciples were completely exhausted. They lay down on the ground to rest, and soon they were fast asleep. But Jesus went on ahead a little ways and knelt down to pray.

Jesus knew that from now on life would be harder than ever for all of them. He had to teach his disciples quickly, because there was so little time left. Soon—all too soon—he would be arrested and brought to trial. And he was already so tired. He asked his Father for strength to go on doing his work. He prayed for his disciples, asking that God would open their ears and their hearts to hear what he was saying. And more than anything else, he asked for courage to face the trials of his last few months on earth.

As Jesus talked with his Father, something wonderful began to happen. His robe became glistening white, whiter than an angel's robe, and his face began to glow with the presence of God, the way Moses' face had shone when he came down from meeting with God on Mount Sinai. Suddenly there were two men with Jesus, also with robes shining white and with faces aglow. They were Moses and Elijah, men whom God had chosen to lead Israel in earlier times. Jesus talked with them about the mission that lay ahead for him, about his death, and how he would bring salvation to the world. For a long time they talked, while Moses and Elijah reminded Jesus of the sufferings they had gone through, and of all the believers who had died before his coming who depended on his faithfulness. Their words gave him comfort and encouragement.

Peter, James, and John slept on through all of this, then woke up with a start as if someone had shaken them. They looked around for Jesus, and they saw the brilliant glow where he stood with Moses and Elijah. Now they saw their Lord as one day the whole world would see him, coming in his glory. They trembled with fear and excitement as they watched.

Just then they saw Jesus begin to say good-bye to Moses and Elijah. But the disciples wanted the wonderful moment to last. Peter, who was always the first to take action, jumped up and rushed over to where the three men in shining robes were standing. "Lord, it is wonderful for us to be here! If you like, I'll put up three shelters, one each for you and Moses and Elijah."

At that very instant a bright cloud came down over the disciples, shutting Jesus away from their sight. If they had been frightened before, now they were terrified. They threw themselves down on the ground and waited for God to do something to them. But instead, they heard a voice speaking to them from the cloud saying, "This is my Son, the one I love, the one I have chosen. Listen to him!"

When the disciples finally dared to look up again, the cloud was gone. Jesus was standing alone, and his robe and his face were no longer shining. Peter felt like a fool for trying to tell Jesus what to do. And three of the disciples saw Jesus in a new way from that moment on, because they had seen him as the Lord of heaven.

On the way down the mountain, Jesus instructed Peter, James, and John not to tell anyone what they had seen there. "It isn't time yet," he said. "The time will come after I have been raised from the dead."

The disciples still could not understand what Jesus meant by this. Things were going too fast for them. Their minds were spinning as they tried to understand how all the old Scriptures fit into this. Finally one of them asked, "Is it true that Elijah must come before Messiah is shown to Israel?"

"Yes, it is true," Jesus answered. "And I tell you that Elijah has already come, but the people did not know him. Instead, they treated him as they pleased. In the same way, I must suffer many things. They will reject me, just as they rejected him." Then the disciples realized that Jesus was talking about John the Baptist. And they finally began to understand that Jesus' way would also lead through suffering and death.

Faith Like a Mustard Seed

WHEN PETER, JAMES, and John came down from the mountain with Jesus, they found the other nine disciples surrounded by a crowd of spectators and arguing hotly with some of the teachers of the law. Even from a distance they could see the waving arms and hear the loud voices. Then someone in the crowd spotted Jesus and cried out, "Look! Here comes the Master himself!" The crowd gathered around him quickly, and the disciples came toward him with worried looks on their faces.

"What are you arguing about?" Jesus asked.

"Rabbi," came a voice from the crowd, "I brought my son to your disciples. He is controlled by an evil spirit that makes him fall down and grind his teeth and foam at the mouth. Sometimes he has fallen into the fire or into the water. If we didn't watch him all the time, he would be dead by now. But even when he isn't violent, he can't hear or speak a word. I asked your disciples to free him from the evil spirit, but they couldn't do it."

"I see," Jesus said and turned to the law teachers. "And you decided that they never really had any power against evil spirits at all, and that was what the argument was about." They all nodded in silence. "This whole generation has no faith!" Jesus cried out. "How long will I have to put up with you? Bring the boy to me!"

His father led the boy to Jesus. But the moment the boy saw the Lord, the evil spirit took hold of him again. He screamed and trembled, then fell on the ground and foamed at the mouth, all his muscles twitching violently.

"How long has he been like this?" Jesus asked.

"Ever since he was a baby," said the tearful father. "Please, if you can do anything, please take pity on us and help him!"

"If? What do you mean, if? Everything is possible for one who believes!"

The poor man was so confused that he hardly knew what to say. He had heard so many things about Jesus; but everyone who had met Jesus said something different about him. Now his disciples had been unable to do anything, and he just didn't know what to think anymore. But he wanted to believe in Jesus, and finally it all burst out of him. "I do believe! Please put an end to my unbelief!"

Jesus knew his Father would never let anyone down who came to him really wanting to know him. So he turned to the boy and said to the evil spirit, "I command you to come out of the boy, and never to go into him again!" One last time the spirit attacked the boy, and then with one final, terrible scream, the boy lay still.

"He's dead!" one of the bystanders cried.

But Jesus reached down, took the boy by the hand and lifted him to his feet, and turned him toward his astonished father. "Father!" cried the boy, holding out his arms. His father hugged him so hard the boy thought his ribs would crack. "You can talk again!" the father said over and over. "You're free!" And all the way home he shouted praises to God.

"Why wouldn't the evil spirit obey us and come out of him?" the disciples asked Jesus later, when they were alone.

"Because your faith is not great enough," Jesus answered. "Have you ever seen how a tiny seed can put down its roots and crack a great boulder in two? If you had faith like that, you could say to a whole mountain, 'Move over there!' and it would move. Nothing is impossible for one who has that kind of faith."

THE TRUE CITIZENS OF THE KINGDOM

THE DISCIPLES WERE still thinking about the Messiah as the son of David. They hoped he would drive out the Romans and make Israel a great nation again. Then, they thought, those who served Jesus well before he was crowned king—themselves—would have high places in that kingdom. The Pharisees and the scribes, on the other hand, hoped to get into the kingdom by obeying every command of the law of Moses—down to the last detail. For both the disciples and the Pharisees, Jesus had a surprise in store. The rich and the powerful, those who were proud of keeping the law, even the twelve disciples, did not become citizens of the kingdom by their own efforts. Jesus had to teach them what it means to be true citizens of the kingdom.

Who Is the Greatest?

ONE DAY AS they were walking back toward their home base in Capernaum, the disciples got into an argument. It started innocently enough. "It won't be long now," Peter said. "Soon Jesus will be king in Jerusalem, and we will all rule with him."

"I wonder what kind of positions he'll give us," Nathanael said.

"Well, Judas can be treasurer," said Philip, and the others laughed because Judas kept the money bag for them now, and some of them suspected that sometimes he took money out for himself.

"Well, I think I deserve some reward," Judas said, his face flushing hotly. "Look at what I have given up to follow him."

"You?" said James indignantly. "John and I should share the highest place in the kingdom. We gave up our fishing boats, our family, everything we had to be his disciples."

"But I was the first one to follow him," growled Peter. "At least, Andrew and I were together. Besides, didn't he say I was like a rock?"

"You have a head like a rock, for sure," James teased him. And so it went, all the way to Capernaum, the disciples arguing over who would become prime minister and other cabinet officers when Jesus became king.

When they finally came to the house in Capernaum and had a chance to rest, Jesus turned to them and asked, "What were you arguing about on the way here?"

The disciples looked at one another in embarrassment. "Oh, nothing," John answered.

"What were you arguing about?" Jesus insisted

And then it all came bursting out, all the disciples talking at once, every one of them wanting an answer to the same question: Who will have the number one position in the kingdom? When at last they all fell silent, Jesus answered their question. "The one who tries to be first will end up at the bottom," he said. Now the disciples were really embarrassed, because every one of them had wanted to be number one. "You still think my kingdom is going to be like the empires of the Gentiles, don't you?" Jesus went on. "Those rulers lord it over the people and use their power in any way that will benefit themselves. That isn't the way it should be with you! The kingdom of God doesn't mean power to make others obey you; the kingdom means serving other people and helping them. If one of you wants to be great in the kingdom, let him first become the servant of all the rest. Follow my example. I didn't come into the world to have other people serve me. I came to serve others and to give my life to save others."

There were some children in the house playing their games as Jesus talked. He called one of the children over to sit on his knee. Then he said to the disciples, "The person who stops trying to be great, and instead becomes like this little child, will have the first place in my kingdom. Unless you become like children, you will never get into the kingdom at all. And anyone who accepts a little child in my name is accepting me. The one who is least important among you will be the greatest."

But John was not satisfied with Jesus' answer. If anyone who acted in the name of Jesus could be great in the kingdom, did that mean that some people who weren't even disciples might get high positions? "Rabbi," he said to Jesus, "we saw some men who were driving out evil spirits in your name. We told them to stop, because they weren't following along with us."

"Why did you stop them?" Jesus asked. "Did you really think that a person has to go everywhere with me the way you do in order to be my disciple? I'll tell you who my disciples are. A disciple is anyone who listens to me and obeys me. If someone isn't against us, then that person is on our side. The person who gives you a cup of cold water in my name will have a proper reward.

"No, don't look down on people just because you don't think they are important. That's the way people of this world live. If a man has a hundred sheep, and one of them gets lost, don't you think he will leave the other ninety-nine and go looking for the one? And if he finds it, he'll be happier about that one than he is about the others who never got lost. The world is full of lost sheep. Don't think they aren't important. Your Father in heaven doesn't want a single one of them to die. So stop arguing with each other over who will be greatest. Serve one another instead."

The disciples looked at each other in surprise, almost bewildered by what they had just heard. The kingdom Jesus was talking about was not what they had expected at all!

Jesus Receives the Children

THE DISCIPLES WERE not the only ones who were confused about the meaning of the kingdom. The leaders of Israel still expected a king like David also, and they thought that those who obeyed the law best would have the highest places in his kingdom. Some of the Pharisees in a crowd around Jesus one day wanted to find out whether he was going to make himself king. So they asked him, "When will the kingdom of God come?"

"It won't come by your looking for it," Jesus answered. "No one will be able to say, 'Look! There it is!' The kingdom of God is already among you. But only those who truly obey God will ever see it."

Just then there was a commotion at the edge of the crowd. Some people had brought their children to see Jesus, but the disciples were turning them away. "The Master is too busy to see you now," they said. "He has more important things to do than to be bothered by a bunch of kids."

"But we want our children to see the Master for themselves," the parents protested. "All we ask is that he put his hands on them and bless them."

"That's impossible," the disciples answered. "Come back some other time."

As soon as Jesus realized what they were doing, he turned to the disciples and said, "Don't stop them! Let the children come to me. The kingdom of heaven belongs to them."

The disciples stood aside then, and the children came running to him. They were shy with strangers, but one look at Jesus' face told them they could trust him. Jesus knelt down, opened his arms wide, and hugged every one of them. Then he took one of the children onto his

lap. He looked up over the heads of the other children and said to his disciples, "Listen to me. Anyone who wants to enter the kingdom must come like a little child, humble and trusting. Don't ever stop them again."

Then Jesus laid his hands on the children and blessed them. But the Pharisees walked away shaking their heads in anger and amazement. How dare he say that little children would get into the kingdom before they would! They still wanted to believe that they could earn their own way into God's kingdom.

The Woman of Samaria

"THAT'S THE WRONG road, Master," one of the disciples said.

"No, it's the right road," Jesus answered.

"But it goes through Samaria," the disciples protested. "No Jew goes into Samaria if he can avoid it."

"I cannot avoid it," Jesus said. "We must go through Samaria."

His disciples shook their heads in wonder, but they followed him. They were hot and dusty by the time they reached the town of Sychar. There was a well there, which people said had been dug by Jacob. Tired from the journey, Jesus dropped down on the ground beside the well. "Go on into town and buy us some food," Jesus told his followers. "I'll stay here by the well."

Once the disciples were gone, there was silence around the well. The only sound was the sound of flies buzzing lazily in the air. Jesus was thirsty, but he had no jug for drawing water from the well. He would just have to wait until his disciples returned. Certainly no one came to the well in the noon heat. Yet when he looked up, there was a woman walking toward him with an empty water jug on her shoulder. She had her own reasons for coming to the well at this time of the day. The people of the town considered her a great sinner, and the other women of the town would not have anything to do with her. So she avoided their taunts and their name-calling by staying away from the well during the cool morning and evening, when the others drew water.

Cautiously, the woman approached the well. Avoiding Jesus, she went to the other side of the well, tied the rope hanging there to her jug, and lowered it into the well. Suddenly Jesus turned to her and said, "May I have a drink of water, please?"

The woman nearly dropped her jug. "You are a Jew," she said, "and I am a Samaritan. You Jews won't even use the same cups we use. How can you ask me for a drink?"

"If you only knew what God can give," Jesus answered, "and if you only knew who it is asking you for a drink, you would do the asking, and he

would give you life-giving water."

What a thing to say! the woman thought. She knew that the water from deep in the well was much fresher than the water at the top. Perhaps that was what he meant by life-giving water. But the man couldn't even get a drink for himself. How could he get water for her? And why should he?

"Mister, you don't even have a bucket," she said, hauling her jug out of the well. "Don't you know how deep this well is? How would you ever get that life-giving water? This well was dug by our ancestor Jacob. He and his sons and his cattle drank from it, and even they couldn't do it without a bucket. You don't claim to be greater than Jacob, do you?"

"You can drink all the water you want from this well," Jesus said, "but you will still get thirsty again. Every day you will have to come back for another jug. But whoever drinks the water I can give will never be thirsty again. The water I give will become a spring inside that person bubbling over with eternal life."

Think of it! Never to be thirsty again, never to carry another heavy water jug, never to be forced to face the ugly looks of the people of the town as she walked to and from the well! If this man could make that happen, she would do anything for him. "Give me some of that water," she said eagerly. "Then I won't ever have to come to this well again."

How could Jesus get her to see that she needed more than water from a well? He knew her real need, but he would have to shock her into seeing it. "Go call your husband," he said, "and then come back."

119

The woman hesitated. This was something she did not want to talk about. "I don't have a husband," she said.

"That's right, you don't," Jesus answered her. "But you have had five husbands already, and right now you are living with a man you are not married to. So your answer was correct, wasn't it?"

The woman was stunned. How did this man know about her? Had someone told him? No, that was impossible. He was a stranger, and no one else came to the well in the heat of the day. There was only one answer. He had to be God's prophet. But if that was true, he would tell her how evil she was, and she didn't want to hear that again. How could she get him off the track, get him onto another subject? She had an idea.

"I can see that you are a prophet, sir," she said. "So will you please answer a question for me? We Samaritans worship God here at Mount Gerizim. But you Jews say that the only place to worship God is in Jerusalem. Who is right?"

But Jesus was not going to let her get away with that trick. He answered her question, but not in the way she expected. "Believe me," he said, "the time has come to stop arguing about the right place to worship God. It's true that God has made himself known to us Jews, and that the Savior will come from among us. But do you think God can only be in one place at a time? He is not a person who has to go here and go there. God is Spirit and is present everywhere. People can worship God anywhere—but only by the power of the Holy Spirit. True worship has nothing to do with the place. It has to do with the Spirit of God."

Somehow she knew his words were true. She went through the ceremonies at Mount Gerizim, but she could never really worship God. Her heart was too full of guilt. But how could she change her life? That was too hard for her. She had only one hope. "I know that the Messiah is coming, just as you said," she replied. "And when he comes, he will make everything clear."

"I am he," Jesus said. "The Messiah is talking with you right now."

The woman's eyes opened wide with wonder. Could it really be true? He did know all about her, even though he had never met her. How could that be if he were just an ordinary man? She had to tell someone—ask someone. Without a word, she turned and ran back toward the town, leaving her water jug at the well. She stopped everyone she met and said excitedly, "I met a stranger at the well who knew all about me. He told me everything I ever did. Could he be the Messiah?" And she kept on telling about Jesus until she had a crowd of people ready to follow her back to the well.

At the well Jesus was talking with his disciples. They had come back from the village and found him talking with the woman. They were amazed that he would take time to talk to a woman. As far as they were

120

concerned, women were good for nothing but having babies, keeping house, and serving food. Like all Jewish men, they had learned to pray, "I thank you, O Lord, that you did not make me a woman." Now here was their master talking with a woman, and in broad daylight in a public place. What was worse, she was a Samaritan woman; Jews never spoke to Samaritans. But none of them had the nerve to say, "What are you doing?" So they stood at a distance, watching.

When the woman ran into town, the disciples approached Jesus and unwrapped the food they had bought. "Eat something, Master," they said. It was well past noon, and they knew Jesus was hungry. But Jesus merely sat by the well, looking toward the town as if he were waiting for something. "Rabbi, won't you eat something?" they asked again.

Jesus turned to his disciples and said, "I have food to eat that you know nothing about."

Puzzled, the disciples began to whisper among themselves. "Do you suppose that woman brought him something to eat?" one of them asked.

"Why are you whispering?" Jesus asked. "You don't understand, do you? Doing the will of God is food and drink to me. Doing his work is my greatest joy. I want to finish the work he gave me to do, and there isn't much time. You look out at the fields and say, 'Another four months, and it will be harvest time.' But in my field the harvest is ready now. Others planted the seed, but you will work in the harvest. Look there!" He pointed toward the crowd of people coming toward them from Sychar. "There they come. That is God's harvest."

The people of the town stopped some distance away from the well. Then one of the elders approached Jesus and said, "This woman has told us about you. 'He told me everything I ever did,' she said. We would like to hear more from you. Will you stay with us a while and teach us?"

So for two days Jesus and his disciples stayed in the Samaritan town of Sychar. Many of the people of the town believed in him. And they said to the woman, "Now we have more than just your word. We have seen him with our own eyes and heard him with our own ears, and we know that he really is the promised Savior of the world."

121

The Man Born Blind

BACK IN JERUSALEM, Jesus and his disciples were walking through the streets one day when they saw a beggar, a man who had been blind since he was born. He had never seen a flower or a tree, never known the beauty of a sunset. Since he could not work, he had to sit on the street corner and hope that someone would drop a few pennies in a bowl for him. God had made a law that did not allow beggars in Israel, but his law was not being obeyed. So there the blind man sat, day after day, all alone in a darkness other people could not know.

Why did these things happen to people? the disciples wondered. It had to be because of someone's sin, but they had never been able to figure it out exactly. But now they had a chance to ask someone who ought to know.

"Rabbi," they said to Jesus, "what sin caused this man to be born blind? Was it his own sin or the sin of his parents?"

"Neither one," Jesus answered. "Don't you understand? Sin has brought disease and death into the world. We all have to suffer the consequences. Any parents could have a blind child, not just people who have been very wicked. Did you hear about the tower that collapsed last week and twelve men working on it were killed? Did you think they were more sinful than the ones who lived? A man is not a good man just because no disaster has ever happened to him.

"But there was a special reason for this man to be born blind, because now God's power over sin will be shown in what happens to him. We have to do God's work while it is still daylight, because there is a night coming when no one will be able to work. But as long as I am here, I am the light of the world."

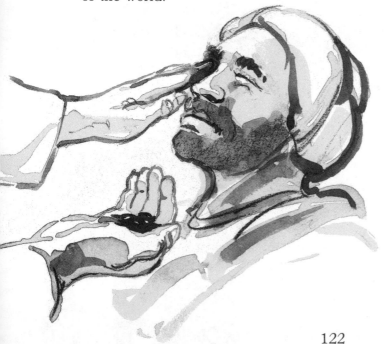

Then Jesus did a very strange thing. He spit on the ground and made a little bit of mud. If it had not been for his kind voice, the blind man would have stopped this man when he felt the mud being stroked onto his closed eyelids. But there was something about Jesus that made the man feel he ought to let him do this strange thing.

"Now go and wash yourself in the pool of

Siloam," Jesus told him. Now Siloam was a good distance away, about half an hour's walk. Still, although the man did not know quite why, he trusted Jesus. So with the help of some passers-by, he made his way to the pool and washed the mud from his eyes. Even before he could dry them, he knew that something was different. There was a glow in this darkness, a glow that looked the way Jesus' voice had made him feel. He knew even before his eyes were open that he could see—for the first time in his life.

All the way back to Jerusalem he laughed to himself and sang praises to God. Strange things kept happening to him, things that made him laugh even more. He found that his eyes didn't help him to find his way. Those who could always see recognized streets and shops, but he had never seen them before, although he had been this way many times. He found he had to close his eyes in order to find his way back to his begging corner! Somehow that seemed very funny to him, and he began to laugh again.

People who often came by his corner saw him and said, "Aren't you the blind man who used to beg here?"

"No, it can't be," another said. "This man isn't blind. He must be someone who looks like the beggar."

"No, it's really me," said the beggar, grinning from ear to ear.

"What happened to you? How is it that you can see again?"

"A man named Jesus came by. I heard him spit on the ground, and then he put some mud he made from that on my eyes and told me to go wash at the pool of Siloam. So I did, and here I am—seeing everything! Isn't it marvelous?"

"Where is Jesus now?" they asked.

"I don't know. But I can see! I can see!"

"You come along with us. Now we can show the Pharisees that Jesus really can heal people." So they took him with them to the leaders of the Pharisees at the temple, and he had to tell his story all over again.

"Have you always been blind?" they asked when he was finished.

"Ever since I was a baby," the man answered.

"So Jesus made mud and put it on your eyes. But today is the Sabbath! No one is supposed to work, not even a little bit of work like that, and Jesus knows it. He can't be from God if he breaks the Sabbath!"

"Just a minute now, don't be so hasty," one of the other Pharisees objected. "If he is such a sinner, how can he do these miracles?" And they began to argue among themselves. Finally one of them said, "Let's ask the man himself. Let's see what he thinks."

"I think he is a prophet," the man said.

"And I think you were never even blind!" one of them shouted back. "You're just one of those lazy bums who pretends to be sick so you can beg and never have to work. You're a fake!"

"Well, there's only one way to settle that," one of them suggested.

"Send for the man's parents." So they asked him where he lived and sent a messenger to fetch his parents. They came, trembling with fear. These were dangerous times, and the leaders of the Pharisees were powerful men. What did they want with the parents of a poor blind man? It had to be this business about Jesus of Nazareth. That could get them into trouble. They would have to be careful.

"Is this your son?" they demanded.

"Yes, he is our son."

"And was he really born blind?"

"Yes, he has been blind since birth."

"Then how do you explain the fact that he can see now?"

Now it was getting tricky. Better not to take sides. "How should we know?" they answered. "He's old enough to speak for himself." After all, a person could be banished from the synagogue for saying anything good about Jesus.

So the Pharisees turned on the young man again. "You should give glory to God for what has happened. As for this Jesus, he could not have healed you. We know he is a sinner."

"That may be," the man answered. "I only know one thing. This morning I was blind. Now I can see."

"What did he do to you? How did he open your eyes?"

"I already told you that once," he said impatiently. "You didn't listen the first time, so why should I bother to tell you again? Unless—" and here a mocking smile crossed his lips "—unless you want to become his disciples, in which case I'll tell you again."

That was more than the pompous Pharisees could take. "*You* are the one who follows him," they shouted. "But we follow Moses. We know God spoke to him. As for this Jesus, who knows where he came from?"

"Well, I don't know very much about these things, of course," the beggar replied, "but I was always taught that God only listens to people who worship him and obey him. He doesn't listen to sinners. Now from the beginning of the world, nobody ever heard of a man who could open the eyes of a man who had been born blind. How could Jesus do it if the power didn't come from God?"

"Who do you think you are, trying to teach us?" they demanded. "Get out! Out of the synagogue! Out of Israel! You aren't worth being called a child of Abraham!" And they shut him out and told him never to return.

What would he do now? Had he left the world of the blind only to be thrown out of the world of the seeing? Jesus did not leave him to wonder for long. When he heard that the man had been shut out of the synagogue, he searched for him until he found him. The man had never seen Jesus before, but he recognized his voice.

"Do you believe in the Son of God?" Jesus asked.

"Lord, tell me who he is, so that I can believe in him."

"You have seen him already. He is talking to you right now."

The young man knelt down on the ground, took Jesus' hand and looked up into his face. "Lord," he said, "I believe." Now he knew that it made no difference whether he would be allowed in the synagogue or not. He had found a center and a purpose for his life. From now on he would follow Jesus.

The Good Shepherd

JESUS LOOKED DOWN at the man kneeling at his feet. A few hours before he had been blind. Now he could see, but the Jewish leaders had put him out of the fellowship of the synagogue.

"It is a strange judgment that I bring into the world," Jesus said. "The blind can see, but those who see have gone blind."

There were some Pharisees there, some of those sent to watch his every move, who thought they knew what he meant. "Are you calling us blind?" they asked.

"If you were truly blind, you wouldn't know any better," Jesus answered. "But you claim to see. You even think you can teach others. So you don't have any excuse for your sin.

"Listen to me," Jesus went on. "If a man has to climb over the fence to get into the sheep pen, he's a thief. The real shepherd comes in through the door. He calls each sheep by name, and they know his voice, so they follow him. They won't follow a stranger."

The Pharisees stared at him with puzzled looks on their faces. "Shall I explain my story to you?" Jesus asked. "The sheep are God's own people, and I am the door to the sheep pen. Many have come and claimed to be the Messiah. But the sheep did not follow them, because they could tell there was something wrong. They were thieves, and they spoke with strange voices.

"But I am the door. If someone comes into the pen through me, he will find safety. He will be able to go in and out and find good pasture. And I am the good shepherd. A thief only comes to steal and to kill. But I will give my life for the sheep.

"There are other sheep too, sheep that are not from the sheep pen of Israel. I must bring them in also, and then there will be only one flock and one shepherd.

"The Father loves me because I will give my life for the sheep. No one can take my life from me. I will give it up myself. I have that power from the Father."

The people who were listening began again to argue among themselves. Some said, "He has an evil spirit. Why are you listening to him?" But others replied, "That's not the voice of a man with an evil spirit. Who ever heard of a demon making a blind man see again?" They just could not agree on what to make of him.

Mary and Martha

NOT FAR FROM Jerusalem, in the town of Bethany, lived three people who were special friends of Jesus: two sisters, Mary and Martha, and their brother Lazarus. Jesus visited their home often. On one such occasion Mary sat quietly with the other disciples, listening eagerly to what Jesus said. She didn't want to miss a single word because she knew that he spoke the word of God. Meanwhile, her sister Martha was bustling around in the kitchen trying to put on a good meal and get the whole house tidied up at the same time.

The longer Martha worked, and the longer Mary sat and listened, the more upset Martha became. "Who does Mary think she is, one of the disciples?" she thought to herself. "She ought to be in here with me, instead of sitting there with the men. Why does she leave all the work to me?" The more she thought about it, the more frustrated she became, until

she simply could not stand it any longer. It was time for Jesus to put Mary in her place.

Martha came bustling in from the kitchen, her face flushed with work and impatience. "Lord," she blurted out, "don't you care that Mary has left me to do all the work by myself? She belongs in the kitchen with me. Tell her to come out and help me."

"Martha, you have a great many things on your mind," Jesus answered. "There will always be plenty of things to worry about. But hearing my teaching is the one thing that is really important. Mary has chosen to be my disciple, and she has made the right choice. That can never be taken from her."

Stunned and speechless, Martha turned and went back to work. Her world was being turned upside down, and she scarcely knew what to do next. Did Jesus really mean that he would accept a woman as his disciple, just like a man? Shaking her head in wonder, she returned to her cooking.

The Great Banquet

ONE SABBATH, JESUS was invited to have a meal at the home of one of the leaders of the Pharisees. As the guests lay on their couches at the table, enjoying the feast their host had provided, one of them remarked, "It is a real privilege to enjoy a meal like this. But how much more wonderful it is for the one who sits down to eat in the kingdom of God!"

"Let me tell you a story about that," Jesus said to him. Everyone fell silent as Jesus began to speak, and this is the story he told:

Once upon a time, there was a man who gave a great wedding banquet for his son, and he invited all his friends. When the great day came, he sent his servants out to tell the guests that everything was ready. But when the servants came to the guests, they all started to make excuses.

"I can't come," one of them said. "I just bought some land and have to go out and look it over." Another one said, "I just bought some new teams of oxen, and I have to make sure they can really do the farm work. I can't come." Still another said, "I just got married, and I want to spend time with my wife. I can't come to the feast."

When the servants returned and reported what had happened, the master was very angry. "Go out into the city and bring in the outcasts," he commanded. "Find the blind and crippled people, the beggars, and bring them to my feast." But when the servant had brought in all those who would come, there were still empty places at the banquet table. "Go back out into the streets and *make* them come," the master said. "I want my house full for this feast. But not one of those who were invited in the first place will eat one bite of my banquet!" So the servants went out and rounded up everyone they could find, good and bad alike, and the banquet hall was filled.

Everyone who came into the hall was given a robe to wear for the banquet. But when the master came in to meet the guests, he saw that there was one man still wearing his own clothes. He couldn't be bothered to dress up for the banquet. "Why aren't you properly dressed?" the master asked. But the man had no answer for him. So the master said to his servants, "Tie him up hand and foot and throw him out into the darkness to weep and grind his teeth."

"For you see," Jesus said in conclusion, "many are invited, but few are chosen." So he made it clear in the story that the true citizens of the kingdom are not those who rely on their own goodness; the true citizens are those who know they need God's mercy. The message did not please the Pharisees, who tried so hard to show everyone how good they were.

"Do you mean to say that we Pharisees won't feast in the kingdom of God, but the sinners and the outcasts will?" one of the guests demanded. "How dare you say such a thing!" And they were very angry with Jesus

128

because they did not want to hear the message of God. After that, some of them began to plot to get rid of Jesus.

The Love of the Father

IN THE CHANGING face of the crowds who followed Jesus the story of the great banquet was being acted out. More and more, it was the tax collectors and other outcasts who came to hear him. Clearly, it was they, not the proud and mighty ones, who were eager to hear about the kingdom. The Pharisees and the teachers of the law did not like that at all. "He keeps company with the worst kinds of people," they snorted. "It just shows you what kind of a man he really is. Birds of a feather flock together, you know."

But Jesus knew what they were saying as they stood whispering together on the fringes of the crowd, far enough away so that people would not think *they* were disciples. Jesus looked at them over the heads of the crowd and spoke directly to them. And this is the story he told:

Once upon a time, there was a man who had two sons. One day the younger son came to his father and said, "Dad, I just can't stand it around here any longer. I know I won't get the farm after you die anyway; that always belongs to the oldest son. So why don't you give me now whatever you planned to give me in your will and let me go. I want to find my own place in the world."

So his father reluctantly gave him his part of the estate. The son sold everything he could, took the cash, and went out into the world to seek his fortune. He traveled to a distant country where he could be as far away as possible from his family and live his own kind of life.

It didn't take people there long to find out that the young man had plenty of money—and not much sense about how to spend it. He made friends fast, friends who showed him lots of places where he could spend his money. They all had a high old time together while the money lasted, drinking and partying until all hours of the night, and sleeping it off the next day. The young man thought he had never had so much fun in his life.

Of course, all that sleeping in the daytime meant that he couldn't work and earn a living. His father wasn't around to remind him that the money wouldn't last forever, or to challenge him about whether the things he was doing were right. The young man kept on living it up, never thinking about tomorrow, until he reached the bottom of his money bags. Then he suddenly found that he didn't have any more friends. Once they saw that he was broke, they started looking around for someone else to pay their way.

At last, the young man woke up to reality. After sleeping off his last hangover and finding that he didn't have a cent left to buy food with, much less another drink, there was only one answer. He would have to find a job. But times were hard. There was a drought in the land, and the farmers of the countryside watched their crops dry up through long months without rain. When the harvest came, there was little to be taken in, and no one could afford to hire any workers. The young man walked from farm to farm trying to quiet his growling stomach as he asked for work. Time and again he was refused.

At last he found one man who said, "I'll feed you one meal a day if you will tend my pigs."

The young man swallowed hard. Pigs! The very thought was disgusting. But he had no choices left. "I'll do it," he said.

He went out to the pig pen and began his chores. He was so hungry that he could almost have eaten the slop he was giving the pigs. "Here I am, an Israelite," he thought, "a man who would never touch a pig if he could help it, and now I am practically sleeping with them. Why, my father would never even have a pig on the place!"

His father! He hadn't thought about his father in months. Now he remembered what it had been like at home. There he had a warm bed and plenty to eat, and a father who loved him. Here he was starving—and nobody cared. Even the servants in his father's house were better off than he was! They sat down every night to a meal of bread and cheese and . . . at the thought of food, the young man's stomach began to growl louder than ever.

"What a fool I've been!" he said aloud. "I'm starving to death while my father's servants eat all they want. I'll have to go back." Quickly he stood up to leave, and just as quickly he sat down again, discouraged. "How can I go back?" he wondered. "I just deserted my father, and I've wasted every penny I had coming to me. There's no sense pretending to be his son any longer. Maybe he would take me on as a hired hand. He always needs a few men to work in the fields."

"That's it!" he decided. "I'll go back to my father and I'll say, 'I know I have done wrong before God and before you. I can't be called your son any longer. Will you take me on as a hired man?' " So he set out on his way, leaving the pigs to fend for themselves.

Meanwhile, the young man's father waited every day for some word of his son. "What can be happening to him," he wondered. "He never was very good with money. But he had to learn his lesson some day. Better he should learn it now, while I'm still around to get him started again. I hope he hasn't gotten sick. What if outlaws killed him on the road and stole his money?"

Days stretched into weeks, and weeks into months, and still there was no word. Late every afternoon he went up onto the roof of the house and scanned the horizon, looking for some sign of his son. "Some day he will come home," he told himself. "Some day."

And then one afternoon he looked and saw a weary figure trudging down the road, far out in the distance. Perhaps it was just another stranger. No, wait! That walk! He could never forget how his son walked. It was his boy coming home at last! Then he found himself running, down the stairs and out into the road, racing to meet his son. When he reached him, he threw his arms around him and kissed him, and there were tears running down his cheeks.

Softly, the son began the speech he had practiced. "Father," he said, "I have sinned against God and against you . . ."

"It's just so good to have you back, Son," his father interrupted.

"I know I can't be called your son any longer," the young man continued.

"What kind of nonsense is that?" the father exclaimed. "Welcome home, Son!" Then he shouted to one of his servants, "My son has come back! Hurry up, bring him some decent clothes. Bring the best robe, and put my ring back on his hand, and butcher that fat calf we've been saving up for a feast, because we're going to feast tonight! My son was dead, and now he's alive! He was lost, but now he's been found! Praise the Lord!"

With tears in their eyes, father and son hugged each other. Never in his wildest dreams had the son imagined such a homecoming. Almost before he knew it, he found himself bathed and dressed in fine clothes and sitting down to eat a feast such as he had never seen—even on his journeys. There was music and dancing, and the whole household celebrated together.

But there was one member of the family who wasn't at the party. The older son was out in the fields working when his brother came home. As he came close to the house, he heard the music and the laughter coming from inside. He called to one of the servants and asked, "What's going on in there?"

"Haven't you heard?" the servant grinned. "Your younger brother has come home, and your father is giving a party to celebrate! We butchered that fat calf, and there's plenty to eat. Come on in!" But the older brother turned on his heels and stalked away. "So the rascal is back," he muttered. "I thought we were rid of him! What a disgusting display, giving a party because a stupid, ungrateful kid comes whining back to his daddy!"

The servant meanwhile went to the father and told him what had happened. Immediately, the father went outside to see his son. "Come in. Join the party," he said. "It's a happy day for all of us. Your brother has come back. Please, come back to the house with me."

The older son turned to his father, and there were tears of anger and frustration in his eyes. "I've worked for you all my life, and I never once disobeyed you," he said. "You never gave a party for me, and you never gave so much as a cent so I could celebrate with my friends. But now this—this son of yours comes back after wasting all your money on wine and women, and you make all this fuss over him. No, thank you, I'd rather stay out here."

The father put his arm around his older son's shoulders. "Son, you have been right here with me all along, and I appreciate that. All this time, everything I own has been yours as well. All you had to do was to ask for whatever you wanted, and I would have given it to you. I love you just as much as I love your brother. That's why we should celebrate together and show our joy. Your brother was dead, but he's alive again! He was lost, but now he's found! Won't you come in and enjoy the evening with us?"

The Pharisees and the rest of the people looked at Jesus expectantly. What about the rest of the story? they wondered. What did the older son do next? Then Jesus looked at them as if to say, "The rest of the story is up to you. You are the older sons, angry that the sinful ones will feast at their Father's table. I tell you, these sinners and outcasts are coming back to their Father. Do you think he will turn them away?"

THE TRULY CLEAN

THE LONGER JESUS lived and taught, the more surprising his message became. First he announced to his disciples that the king had come, not to take over but to die for the sin of the world. Then he began to turn upside-down the people's ideas of who was fit for the kingdom of God. It was the repenting poor and outcasts who had nothing to offer that would get into the kingdom, he said, not the Pharisees and those who tried to get in by their own effort. He even opened the doors to Samaritans and foreigners, something unheard of in his day.

There were many people in Israel who were proud of keeping the law of Moses. They spent so much time thinking about what was clean and what was not clean that they forgot the most important parts of the law—justice, mercy, and love. The time had come for Jesus to surprise his hearers again, this time by teaching that God did not judge by the same standards that people judge by. These stories tell how Jesus made this clear.

All Things Are Clean

AS USUAL THERE were some Pharisees standing by while Jesus was teaching, men who believed that the only way to please God was to obey every rule in the law of Moses, no matter how small. Among other things, the law said that the people of Israel were not supposed to eat certain meats—pork, for example. "But how can you be absolutely sure you are keeping the command?" the Pharisees wanted to know. "What if a fly landed on a pig, then flew on and landed on your hand? Then when you eat, you might accidentally make God angry because you touched the fly who touched the pig. So before you eat, you have to wash your hands and your plates and everything, no matter how clean they were before."

Jesus and his disciples didn't eat their food with dirty hands, but they didn't bother pouring water over perfectly clean hands either. One day some of the Pharisees came to Jesus and said, "Our people have always said it was wrong to eat without washing your hands first. Why don't you obey the teachings of our ancestors? You and your disciples just go ahead and eat."

"The prophet Isaiah was certainly right!" Jesus answered. "He said, 'These people say all the right things, but they don't really obey me. They teach their own words as if they came from me.' Look at you! You take what some of the old rabbis said about the law and make it sound as if it

133

came from God's own mouth. How many of God's laws do you get around that way?

"Do you remember that God said, 'Take care of your mother and your father'? But there were many people who wanted to keep everything for themselves. So the old rabbis said, 'If a man dedicates his property to God, then he is not required to support his parents.' So they cancelled the word of God by their own teachings.

"Now let me tell you what God really meant when he spoke to his people about keeping their hands and their dishes clean. He wanted to teach people to keep themselves away from sin. He wanted them to know that there is a difference between good and evil. But where do you think evil really comes from? It doesn't come from the outside. There isn't anything a person can eat that will make him evil. What dirties a person are the things that come from deep inside him."

When the Pharisees heard this, they turned and left in disgust. The disciples came to Jesus and said, "Don't you know that you made the Pharisees angry when you said that?"

"Then let them be angry," Jesus answered. "They aren't teaching the word of God. They are like blind men trying to lead other blind people around. They'll all fall into the ditch unless they let God open their eyes. Didn't you understand what I was saying? Food can't make you disobey God. It all goes into your stomach, and anything your body doesn't need, it gets rid of. The things that make a person dirty are the things that come from inside, things like killing, stealing, lying, and cursing. These things make a person dirty, not eating without washing your hands."

The Syrophoenician Woman

WHEN JESUS TAUGHT the Pharisees about what makes a person clean, he had more in mind than just food. As far as the Pharisees were concerned, there were many people who were unfit for the kingdom because they were unclean. Now Jesus had something new to teach his disciples. The very next day, he led them out of Israel into the country around the cities of Tyre and Sidon, where Gentiles lived. Even there, among people whose houses most Jews wouldn't even enter, the name of Jesus had been spread far and wide, and there were some who had believed.

As they came into a town in Syrophoenicia, a woman who had heard they were coming rushed out to meet them. She fell down on her knees and said, "My lord! Son of David! Please help me! My daughter is controlled by an evil spirit, and it is destroying her. Please, come and help!"

The woman was a Gentile, and the most devout Jews would have had

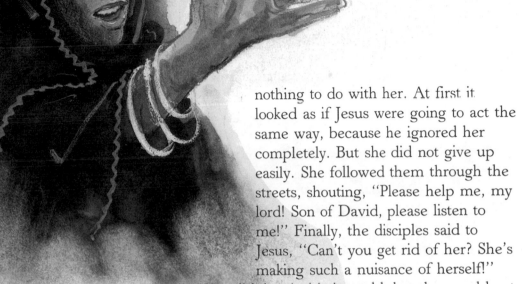

nothing to do with her. At first it looked as if Jesus were going to act the same way, because he ignored her completely. But she did not give up easily. She followed them through the streets, shouting, "Please help me, my lord! Son of David, please listen to me!" Finally, the disciples said to Jesus, "Can't you get rid of her? She's making such a nuisance of herself!"

So there it was. The disciples didn't mind being told that they could eat all kinds of food without going through the hand-washing ceremony first. But they couldn't see that this also had something to do with this Gentile woman. As far as they were concerned, she was unclean—like the pigs they were forbidden to eat.

"I only came to help the lost sheep of Israel," Jesus said. That was just as the disciples had thought. He wouldn't have anything to do with her. But she called out one more time, "Son of David, please help me!"

Jesus stopped and turned around. "Would you take bread from your children and give it to the dogs?" Jesus asked her.

The woman knew what Jesus meant. The Jews thought she was no better than a dog under the table. She knew that was not true, but she also knew that God had chosen the children of Israel to be his special people, and that other nations should be blessed through them. So she said, "I know, Lord, but certainly the dogs eat the scraps that fall from the children's table."

"Your faith is very great, my daughter," Jesus answered her. "Go back to your house. The evil spirit has left your daughter." And when she returned home, it was true.

This was new to Jesus' disciples. They swallowed hard. Jesus was teaching them that even in gentile territory, when people showed faith, the old rules no longer held. Much later, they would see what Jesus really meant: that God's salvation is not for Israel alone but for all mankind.

135

Jesus Heals Ten Lepers

GENTILES WERE NOT the only ones whom the Jews regarded as unclean. There were the lepers also, people who were afflicted with a terrible skin disease. They were not allowed to live with healthy people, and they certainly were not allowed to go into the temple to worship God. Many people believed that the disease was God's punishment for some great sin. Jesus knew better than that, and he wanted to show his disciples that even lepers were fit for God's kingdom.

As he and his disciples were walking into a small town one day, they heard voices calling out, "Jesus, have pity on us!" They stopped and listened. "Master," the voices came again, "be kind to us!"

There in the distance stood ten men, their skin white with scales, their bodies disfigured by leprosy. They did not dare to come closer, because no one was permitted to touch them. They had heard about Jesus and how he had healed many sick people. He was their last hope. Since they could not come any closer to him, they shouted loudly enough for him to hear, "Jesus, have pity on us!"

When the Lord saw the men shouting there, his heart was touched by their suffering. "Go and show yourselves to the priest," he shouted back at them.

The ten lepers looked at each other hopefully. That could mean only one thing. Jesus was going to heal them! The law of Moses said that if a person was cured of leprosy, he was to go to the priest to be pronounced clean again. Quickly they turned to go into the town to find a priest. But while they were still on their way, they suddenly noticed that something had happened to them. They pointed at each other, almost speechless with surprise.

"You've been cured!"
"And you too!"
"And you!"

They pulled frantically at their clothing, looking at their arms, their legs, their hands, touching their faces. It was true! Their sores were gone. They were healthy again! Shouting for joy, they ran to find the priest. Now they could go home, back to their families and back to their friends! So great was their joy that they forgot all about Jesus, the one who had made them well again.

But there was one man who did not run to the town. As soon as he saw that he was well, he turned around and ran back to where Jesus was. He fell down at Jesus' feet and said, "Thank you, Lord! Thank you for making me well!"

"Weren't there ten of you who were made well?" Jesus asked. "Where are the other nine?"

The man just shook his head and said nothing. He didn't know why the others had not come back with him.

"Look at this man," Jesus said to the people around him. "He is not even an Israelite, but a Samaritan. And he is the only one who came back to give God praise for being made well. Then he spoke to the man, who still clung to his feet. "Stand up and go on your way," he said. "Your faith has made you well." The man went back to his home and family, the only one of the ten who had been made truly clean.

Who Is Without Sin?

THE TIME HAD come for the celebration of the feast of booths. At this feast the Jews remembered the forty years their ancestors had spent in the wilderness living in tents. To help them remember what it was like, they put up booths, or tents, made of branches and leaves. For six days the people lived in these booths rather than in their own homes. They praised God for bringing their fathers out of the desert into the land of plenty. During the feast thousands of pilgrims came to Jerusalem to bring their offerings to God.

Jesus also came to Jerusalem with his disciples for the feast. Many people wanted to hear him teach, and there were some who believed he was the Messiah. But there were also some Pharisees, who wanted to try to trap him, to make him say things they could use against him. So the day after Jesus arrived, they dragged a woman into the temple court and brought her in front of Jesus. She stood there trembling with fear, surrounded by a mob of angry men, all carrying rocks.

"Now what do you say about this, Rabbi?" one of the Pharisees demanded. "This woman was caught in bed with a man who is not her husband. Our law says that she should be executed. These men are ready to kill her with rocks. Now, what do you say? Should they go ahead?"

But Jesus didn't seem to be paying any attention. He sat on the ground, looking down and drawing idly with his finger in the dust.

"What's the matter, are you afraid to answer?" the Pharisees shouted. One of two things would happen now, they hoped. He might say that the law was wrong, and that would be enough to get him arrested. Or he might say that it was all right to kill her, and then he'd be in trouble too, because only the Romans claimed the right to kill anyone.

Finally Jesus looked up at the Pharisees. He stood and turned toward the angry crowd of men who were ready to stone the woman. "If there is any man here who has never sinned," he called out, "let him be the first one to throw a stone."

The men looked at one another uncomfortably. One by one, they looked down at the ground, and their faces began to turn red. They shifted the rocks in their hands. One of them turned and left—then another, and another. At last, Jesus was alone with the woman.

"Where did they go?" Jesus asked. "Didn't one of them condemn you?"

"Not one, Lord."

"Then neither do I. Go back to your house, and don't sin anymore."

The Pharisees had walked away in confusion because they could not argue with Jesus. They could not grasp that the kingdom of God is for sinners, and that all of us are sinners whom only God can make truly clean.

The Pharisee and the Tax Collector

THERE WERE MANY in the crowd around Jesus who thought they were better than other people. They thought their own good deeds would be enough to get them into the kingdom of God. Some who came to Jerusalem for the feast thought they could impress God with their obedience and observance of rituals. So Jesus told them this story.

"Once there were two men who went to the temple to pray. One of them was a Pharisee, and the other was a tax collector. The Pharisee stood up and congratulated himself on the holy life he was living. He looked up toward the heavens and said, 'Lord, I thank you that I am not like other people. I have never robbed or killed or taken another man's wife, or stolen other people's property the way that tax collector over there has. I deny myself food twice a week, and I pay my 10 percent on everything I get to the synagogue.'

"But the tax collector didn't even dare look up toward

heaven. He kept his eyes fixed on the ground and beat himself on the chest with his fist and said, 'O God, have mercy on me, sinner that I am!'

"Now I tell you," Jesus said, "the tax collector went back to his house with his sins forgiven. But the other one went back still in his sins, because he thought that he had none, and that he could please God by his own acts of holiness."

But the hearts of the self-righteous were not touched by Jesus' words. Some of them began to complain about him, saying, "Why does he have so much to do with these tax collectors and sinners?"

Then Jesus said, "People who are well don't need a doctor; sick people do. I didn't come to call people who think they are holy. I came to call sinners back to God."

How Much Will It Cost?

THE PHARISEES AND other leaders of Israel were surprised when Jesus brought his message to the poor and the oppressed, to women and children, to tax collectors and prostitutes, to gentiles and lepers—in other words, to all those they themselves despised. He taught that people could never please God by their own efforts but could be saved only by believing in the Son of God. But there was another surprise in what Jesus said. He began to talk about what it would cost to follow him: from the rich and poor alike, God asks the surrender of their hearts.

Who Is My Disciple?

DURING JESUS' YEARS on earth, many people followed him. Some came to hear him once; others followed after him, listening to his teaching for days or even weeks. And then there were the twelve disciples, whom Jesus chose to be near him constantly. But time and again, when crowds of people gathered around him, Jesus said something that was more than they could take, and most of them left. He was making it more and more clear that to be a disciple meant more than following him from place to place. It meant following the way of obedience to God.

One day, one of the teachers of the law came to him and said, "Teacher, I will follow you wherever you go."

But Jesus said to him, "The foxes have holes to live in, and the birds have their nests. But the Son of man has no place to call home." The law teacher walked away sadly; he was not willing to give up the comforts of home to follow Jesus.

To another man Jesus said, "Follow me." But the man replied, "Lord, let me wait until my father dies. When I am head of the household, I will be able to follow you. Right now I am needed at home."

Jesus said, "You follow me. Let those who stay at home take care of things there."

Then Jesus turned to the people who were following him and said, "The person who wants to be my disciple must love me more than his own family, more than his very self. He must be willing to give up everything for me. If a man sets out to build a tower, he sits down first and adds up how much it will cost him. If he doesn't do that first, he may get the foundation laid and then have to quit building because he's out of money. Then his neighbors will make fun of him and say, 'Look at him! He started something he couldn't finish.'

"If a king goes into battle, he had better first decide whether his army of ten thousand men can defeat his enemy's army of twenty thousand. If not, he should make peace before the battle even starts. So it should be with you. Before you say you will follow me, think first about what it will cost. Are you ready to commit your life to me?"

Who Is My Neighbor?

IN ORDER TO be Jesus' disciples, some people had to give up their ideas of how to please God. One such person was a lawyer who stood up in front of Jesus and asked, "Master, what must I do to earn eternal life?"

Jesus knew immediately what this man's problem was. He was trying to work himself into God's graces. He wanted to get everything down to a few rules so that he could be sure to keep them all. So Jesus answered him, "What do you think? What is the most important commandment of them all?"

"Love God above everything else," the lawyer replied, "and love your neighbor as you love yourself."

"You are exactly right," Jesus answered. "If you do as you have said, you will have eternal life."

But that command was so big! It would be impossible to keep, the lawyer thought. There had to be some limits—some details. Thinking quickly, he said, "That's all well and good, but who is this neighbor I am supposed to love?" He said this because he wanted to think that he pleased God even though there were many people he did not love at all.

Jesus thought for a moment and then said, "Let me tell you a story." And this is the story he told.

Once upon a time, there was a man who had to travel from Jerusalem down to Jericho. It was a lonely and dangerous road. As he came around a bend, he saw a bunch of outlaws waiting for him. Before he could turn around they were on top of him, punching and kicking. They beat him so badly that they thought they had killed him. Then they stole his money and his clothes and left him lying by the side of the road.

He lay there unconscious for a long time. When he finally came to, he was too weak to stand. He tasted blood in his mouth where his teeth had cut his lips. He tried to move his legs, but they hurt so badly that he groaned and gave up. It was all he could do to turn his head far enough to see down the road. In the distance he could see a man walking quickly, as if he knew the dangers of being on this road alone. As the stranger drew nearer, the wounded man could see by his robe that he was a priest, probably on his way to the temple in Jerusalem.

The moment the priest saw him a look of fear came into his eyes, and he began to walk even faster. "No time to stop now," the priest thought. "The outlaws could be back any minute. Besides, he's probably dead. And if I touch a dead body, according to the law it will be a week before I can serve in the temple." He crossed to the other side of the road and kept on walking.

Once again the man was alone, moaning in pain. Then he heard footsteps behind him, but they didn't even slow as they came closer. A Levite, on his way home from helping in the temple in Jerusalem, was striding quickly down the road. "Poor fellow," thought the Levite when he saw the man in the ditch. "I really can't do anything for him. Who knows, if I stop to help him, the outlaws may be on *me* in a minute." And he broke into a little run until he was safely past the spot.

Time passed slowly for the wounded man, so he couldn't be sure how

141

long it had been before he heard another sound on the road. This time it sounded like donkey's hooves clopping slowly along. He looked up hopefully, then slumped back down in despair. The man on the donkey was a Samaritan, a person despised and hated by all Jews. Such a man would never stop to help him.

But the Samaritan had something else in mind. As soon as he saw the wounded man by the road, he kicked his donkey into a trot so he could hurry to the man's side. He stopped his donkey, slid off his back, and knelt beside the man to see if he was still alive. Then he reached into his saddlebags and took out a

small wineskin and a bottle of oil. He tore pieces of cloth from a clean robe he had with him, and used the wine to wash the wounds. Then he gently rubbed the healing oil onto the cuts and bruises, and used more strips of cloth as bandages. All the while, he spoke comforting words to the wounded man.

"Well, you aren't as bad off as you look," he said. "Here, have a sip of wine. Your mouth must be as dry as dust now. There now, we have to get you to an inn. You ride on the donkey, and I'll lead him. I'll try to take it slow so he won't bump you around too much. Here we go."

So they traveled that way to the first inn, several miles down the road. The Samaritan rented a room and put the wounded man to bed. The rest of that whole day he took care of him. By the next morning the wounded man was feeling much better, although he still had to stay in bed. The Samaritan had to continue on his journey, so he went to the innkeeper and paid the bill. "Here, I'll give you a few dollars extra," he said. "Take care of that fellow until he's ready to travel, will you? And if it costs you more than that, I'll pay you next week when I come through again."

When Jesus had finished telling his story, he paused and looked closely at the lawyer who had asked him the question. "Now, which of those three men proved to be a neighbor to the wounded man?" he asked.

The lawyer shifted his feet uncomfortably. "I suppose the one who was good to him," he said.

"Exactly," Jesus answered. "Now you go and do the same."

The lawyer opened his mouth to reply, closed it again, then turned and walked away. He had plenty to think about on his way back home. His head was spinning with questions. Could he obey God as Jesus told him to? Would he be able to love even a Samaritan? Would he be willing to pay the price of following Jesus?

The Rich Young Ruler

THE LAWYER WAS not the only one who came to Jesus wanting to know what it would cost to obey God. One day a young man who was one of the leaders of the local synagogue came to Jesus. One look at his clothing made it clear that he came from a rich family. "Good Master," he said, "what do I need to do to obtain eternal life?"

"Why are you calling me good?" Jesus answered. "Don't you know that God is the only one who is truly good? But if you want to find life, keep the commandments."

"Which ones?" the man asked.

"You know what the law says," Jesus answered. "Don't murder, or take another man's wife, or steal any of his property, or tell lies about him; take care of your father and your mother; and love your neighbor as yourself."

The young man was still not satisfied. "But Master," he said, "I have done all those things ever since I was a child. What else do I need?"

There was the problem. This man thought he could please God by keeping the commandments; but even when he kept them, he still felt that something was missing. Jesus could see that what really stood between this man and God was his money. He held on to it more than anything else, and he loved it more than he loved God. To truly please God, he was going to have to give himself completely to God, and that meant giving up his idol—money.

"You only lack one thing," Jesus said to him. "Go and sell everything you have and give it to the poor. Then come and follow me. If you do these things, you will have treasure in heaven."

The young man went away very sad, because he could not bear to part with his riches. Jesus stood and watched him go. He was even sadder than the young man was, because he saw how this man's possessions kept him from the kingdom. Jesus turned to his disciples and said, "It is hard for a rich man to enter the kingdom of God!"

"But Lord," Judas protested, "things are so much easier for the rich. They have enough money to do so many good things. They can build synagogues and give help to poor people and beggars."

"Nevertheless, I tell you that it is easier for a camel to go through a needle's eye than it is for a rich man to enter the kingdom of God."

"If it's so hard even for them," Peter said, "who *can* be saved?"

Jesus answered, "Even the things that are impossible for men are possible for God."

Can You Follow Me?

THE DISCIPLES SAT near the Lord and watched the rich ruler disappear in the distance after Jesus told him to sell everything he had and give it to the poor. Well, what about them—the fishermen who had left their nets and their boats to follow Jesus? And Matthew, who had left his well-paying job as a tax collector? All the disciples were thinking the same thing, but it was Peter who leaned forward and said, "Master, we have left everything and followed you, just as you told that rich young man to do. Does that mean we will have eternal life?"

"If anyone gives up his house and his possessions, or leaves his family and friends because of the kingdom of God," Jesus answered, "he will receive back much more from my Father in heaven. He will have a whole new family—brothers and sisters of the kingdom. And more than that, he will have eternal life. But don't think that this is going to earn you high places in the kingdom. There are many who will come to me in later years, and they will have just as great a place in the kingdom as those of you who have been with me from the beginning."

James and John, the two sons of Zebedee, looked at Jesus anxiously. "But in your kingdom, we will still have the places we have now, won't we?" It was James who was speaking for them. "I mean, we have always sat right beside you, at your right hand and at your left."

"You don't know what you are asking," Jesus said with a frown. "Can you be baptized as I will be? Can you drink the cup that I must drink?"

"Of course we can," they answered, but the answer was too quick and too easy. They did not understand what Jesus meant. He was talking about the suffering he would have to go through in Jerusalem.

But Jesus did know what lay in store for his disciples, so he said to them kindly, "It will be just as you have said. You shall be baptized as I will be, and you shall drink the same cup that I must drink. But the seats of honor by my side are not prizes to be handed out by me."

The Rich Fool

WHAT WOULD IT cost to follow Jesus and become children of the kingdom? For each person who asked him, Jesus had a different answer, because each person had something different that stood in the way of his surrender to God. There were some people whose whole world centered on things they could get their hands on right now, right here on earth. One such man shouted out to Jesus from the crowd one day, "Master! My father died a few months ago, and my brother took everything he owned.

145

Make him give me some."

"What makes you think I came to be a judge over you?" Jesus asked. "Be careful, the things you want are far too important to you. Do you really think human life is made up of the things you own? Listen, and I'll tell you a story.

"Once upon a time, there was a very rich man. One year the weather was very good, and his crops grew better than ever before. At harvest time there was so much grain that his barns and silos weren't big enough to store it all. So what did the rich man do? He said, 'I'll just have to tear those barns down and build bigger ones. There's enough there to last me for the rest of my life.' So that's exactly what he did. He gave orders to have the old silos torn down and new ones built. But that night God came to him and said, 'You fool! You made many preparations for your future. But tonight you are going to die. Who will get all those things now?' "

The man who had cried out so boldly to Jesus a few minutes before, demanding a share of his father's estate, now looked down and scuffed the ground with his toe. Jesus said to him, "That's what it's like for those who have their hearts set on the things they can get for themselves. So don't spend your life worrying about food and clothing. Look at the way God feeds the birds who never plant or harvest. Look at the way he clothes the earth with grass and flowers. Don't you think you are more important than birds and plants? If God can take care of them, he certainly will take care of you. So don't be like the people of this world, who work and sweat as if there were no God to take care of them. Seek God's kingdom, and follow his ways. And trust that he will take care of your needs."

The Unforgiving Debtor

JESUS CAREFULLY TRIED to teach his disciples that in order to share in the kingdom they needed to trust God and love him with their whole heart. And he wanted them to understand that, for him, such love for God would lead him to suffering and death—to pay the price for the sin of the world. "When we go to Jerusalem," he said to his disciples, "I will be handed over to my enemies, and I will be put to death. But on the third day after dying, I will rise again."

The disciples were not at all sure what Jesus meant, but they thought they understood the kingdom, and the old question of their place in it came up again. "Lord," they asked him, "when you do come into your kingdom, who will be the greatest in it?"

Just as he had done once before, Jesus called a little child to stand beside him. "Unless you change and become like little children," he said to his disciples, "you will never set foot in the kingdom of God. The one who becomes as humble as this little kid will be the greatest one in the kingdom. So stop arguing for once about who's going to be the greatest! Serve each other instead. If your brother is angry with you, go and talk to him about it. You take the first step: put yourself second and your brother first."

"But Lord," Peter protested, "you can't just keep on forgiving forever! How many times should I forgive my brother when he wrongs me? Seven times?"

"No, not seven times," Jesus answered. "Seven multiplied forever! Don't ever stop forgiving! Listen, and I'll tell you a story about forgiveness."

Once upon a time, there was a man who owed ten thousand dollars to a great landlord. First he put a mortgage on his land, then on his house, then on his servants, and finally on himself and his family. And he still couldn't make the payments. So the landlord said to him, "I'm going to sell everything, including you and your family, to get my money back."

But the man fell down at his landlord's feet and cried, "Please, give me more time! I'll pay the whole sum, I promise. Please!"

The landlord felt so sorry for him that he said, "All right, I forgive you your debt." And the man went out, shocked but happy and carefree.

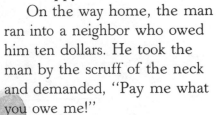

On the way home, the man ran into a neighbor who owed him ten dollars. He took the man by the scruff of the neck and demanded, "Pay me what you owe me!"

"Oh, please," said the neighbor, "I don't have the money right now. Just give me a little more time. I'll pay you everything, I promise!"

"Not a chance," the man said and took him to court. The judge sent the poor neighbor to jail until he could pay the debt.

When the others who lived on the great landlord's estates heard about what the man had done, they told the landlord about it. Then the lord called the man before him again. "You cruel little miser!" he said. "I forgave you your whole debt because you asked me to.

But you couldn't even give your neighbor a few more months to pay his debt to you. Why did you need to collect from him at all, since you don't owe me anything any more? I was merciful to you. Couldn't you have treated him the same way? Now I am going to pass sentence on you. You will stay in jail until you pay every cent.''

"That is what it is like to live in the kingdom," Jesus concluded. "The Father has forgiven you every debt you owed him. You must forgive one another in the same way."

The Rich Man and Lazarus

FOR MANY PEOPLE the message of Jesus was really beginning to pinch. He saw through their questions to the idols they were serving—idols such as money and power. More and more, the rich and the powerful tried to find ways to get rid of him. There were only a few—like Nicodemus—who struggled to fit what Jesus was saying into their lives. There were many more, Pharisees and teachers of the law among them, who were disturbed by what Jesus taught about money. "A man cannot serve two masters," Jesus said to them one day. "You cannot be loyal to God and money at the same time." They laughed at him, but he answered them with this story.

Once upon a time, there was a rich man who lived in a beautiful house, surrounded by the finest things in life. He wore the best clothing money could buy, and every meal he had was a feast. Outside the gate of his house lay a poor beggar whose name was Lazarus. Lazarus was old and sick, too sick even to beg any longer, and he had no one to look after him. His body was covered with sores, and dogs would come along and lick at them. All he could hope was that the rich man's servants would at least bring him the scraps from the table. But the rich man gave him nothing, and Lazarus slowly starved to death. But no matter how much he suffered, he never gave up his faith in God. When he died, God's angels took him into heaven.

Some time later, the rich man also died, and they buried him. He went to hell, where he was in agony. Far away, through the darkness, he saw a glow of light. There sat Lazarus, the poor beggar he had seen so many times lying at his gate. But Lazarus was no longer old or begging or covered with sores; and his head was resting on father Abraham's shoulder. "Oh, Father Abraham," the rich man called out, "please send Lazarus here with a drop of water to cool my tongue. I am in agony in these flames."

Abraham said to him, "Remember, my son, that you were very comfortable in life, while Lazarus had nothing. You never gave him anything. Now things are turned around. But Lazarus cannot come to you. There is a great chasm between us and you, and nobody can cross it."

"But what about my brothers?" the rich man pleaded. "I have five of them, all as bad as I was. Please, send Lazarus to warn them, or they may also end up in this terrible place."

"They have the Scriptures," Abraham replied. "They have everything that Moses and the prophets have said. They should listen to them."

"But surely, Father Abraham, if someone came back from the dead, they would believe him!"

"No, they wouldn't," Abraham answered. "If they won't listen to Moses and the prophets, they won't be convinced even if someone were to rise from the dead."

The rich leaders of the Jews knew exactly who Jesus was talking about—them. Speechless with anger, they turned away from Jesus, more determined than ever to get rid of him. As Jesus watched them go, his heart was touched by a deep sadness. God asked them to give up everything for the sake of the kingdom, but they had so much that they could not bear to part with it—not even for the sake of God, who had given it to them in the first place. For them, the cost of the kingdom was higher than they were willing to pay.

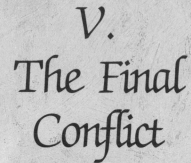

V.
The Final Conflict

Jesus knew that the time had come for him to go to Jerusalem. "I must go," he said to his disciples. "Everything the prophets have written about me will take place there. I will be turned over to the authorities, who will make fun of me and spit on me. They will beat me, and finally they will put me to death, but on the third day I will rise again." The disciples could not understand how this fit into the picture of Jesus as the Messiah. But they had followed him this far; they would follow him still.

THE ROAD
TO JERUSALEM

The Stage Is Set

SOON IT WOULD be Passover time. Many lambs would be killed on
Passover night—in memory of the night long ago in Egypt when the angel
of death passed over the houses where lamb's blood was painted on the
door posts. But all the blood of all those lambs could not take away the sin
of the people. Jesus knew that he was the Lamb of God, the one who
would die at this Passover to pay for the sin of the world. Soon all the
people who were to play a role in his death would be gathered in
Jerusalem.

There was Pontius Pilate, the calculating Roman governor who was
trying to keep the Roman peace in a land where the Romans were hated
bitterly. He was an ambitious man, anxious to be promoted to a higher
post. If he could not keep the peace in Judea, he could never hope for
promotion. Pilate knew that Passover would be a dangerous time. The
Zealots were everywhere, plotting to overthrow his government. He
mounted special security guards, but still he was nervous. He had already
arrested a rabble-rouser named Barabbas, who had killed someone while
trying to lead a revolt. But there might be more. Pilate wanted to be ready
for them.

There was Herod Antipas, the son of Herod the Great, who had tried to
kill Jesus, the newborn king, by murdering the children of Bethlehem.
Herod Antipas was as cruel as his father, but he was also weak and
cowardly. He had already killed John the Baptist. Now he lived in fear that
Jesus the prophet might be John coming back from the dead to haunt him.
He also feared that the Romans might take away the title he loved so
much, "King of the Jews." If only he could find a way to please Pontius
Pilate, without making the Jews angry at him.

There were the Pharisees, the reformers who tried to lead the people of
Israel back to God by teaching them to obey the law of Moses in every
tiniest detail. They saw Jesus as a threat, but more than that, as a man who
worked against God. He broke the Sabbath, he kept company with tax
collectors and people of the worst sort, he called the Pharisees hypocrites
and snakes, and, worst of all, he claimed to be the Messiah. They had to
get rid of him.

The Sanhedrin was also in Jerusalem: they were the ruling council of
the Jewish people. They were trying to keep the people of Judea in line so

that the Romans would not come and destroy them all. To them, Jesus was a threat to the peace. There were a few members of the council, men like Nicodemus, who really listened to what Jesus said. The rest hoped to trap Jesus into violating either the law of the Jews or the law of the Romans. Then they could have him executed and be rid of him forever.

There were the Zealots, the Jewish underground plotting to overthrow Roman rule in Judea. The people were restless under the oppressive rule of the Romans, and the smell of rebellion was in the air. The Zealots were guerrillas looking for a strong man to lead them, someone the people would look up to, someone who would lead them to victory over Rome. For a while they had hoped that John the Baptist would be the one; now he was dead. But there was a new prophet on the scene, one who claimed to be the promised Messiah. Would he be the one? If he would join them, they would make him king; if he would not, they would have to get him out of the way.

And soon Judas Iscariot would also be in Jerusalem—Judas, the one disciple who never truly believed in Jesus. Like the other disciples, he had hoped that Jesus would be the new King David, the one who would rid them of the Romans and make Israel great again. But Jesus began to talk about his death and about a kingdom that was not like the kingdoms of the gentiles. That was when Judas began to turn against him. Judas was one of those Jesus had spoken of when he said, "You will listen and listen, but you will not understand, because you have closed your ears."

As Passover approached, all these forces began to move toward Jerusalem, and events moved quickly toward their climax. Satan's plans to destroy Jesus were coming together. He had enlisted the men who wanted power for themselves; the people who thought the kingdom of God was a kind of Jewish Roman Empire; the men who wanted to rule the world for Rome; and the people who thought they were defending the law of God. All of them, whether they knew it or not, were serving Satan's dreams of power. Not one of them had any way of knowing that when they finally had "conquered" Jesus, it would mean their own defeat. The death of Jesus would complete God's plan to bring salvation to his people.

With all the powers of darkness gathered against him, knowing what suffering lay ahead of him, Jesus still was determined to go to Jerusalem. He had come into the world for this. The time when he would complete his work was coming quickly. Very quickly.

Bartimaeus the Blind Man

IN ORDER TO reach Jerusalem, Jesus and the disciples had to cross the Jordan River. They crossed near the city of Jericho, the first city the

Israelites had taken when they entered the land of Canaan in the days of Joshua. God had wanted the city to remain in ruins as a reminder that he had fought on the side of Israel. But in spite of God's curse, the city had been rebuilt, although the man who rebuilt it lost both his sons in the process.

Jesus could have taken another route, but he decided to go through Jericho because he had work to do there before his death. Even in this city that had been built on pride, he came to bring blessings to the poor and the afflicted. A large crowd gathered around him as news of his visit spread through the city. Eagerly they flocked around him, hoping he would become their king and free them from the Romans.

Outside the gates of the old city sat a blind man named Bartimaeus. It was a good place to beg, right on the road between old Jericho and the new city raised by Herod the Great, with its impressive buildings of Greek designs, including a palace built for Herod himself. Many travelers went by on this road, and for Bartimaeus that meant coins clinking into the cup he held in his hand. But there was more noise than usual today. It sounded like a whole crowd of people was coming from old Jericho.

"What's all the fuss?" he asked of anyone who might be listening. "Can you see what's going on?"

"It's Jesus, the prophet from Nazareth," someone answered. "They say he may be the Messiah."

Jesus! Bartimaeus had heard stories about Jesus, how he cured sick people and made blind people see again. Perhaps he would even help a poor blind beggar! Bartimaeus decided that there was only one way to make sure Jesus paid attention to him. He began to shout: "Jesus, Son of David, have pity on me! Son of David, have pity on me!"

"Shut up!" someone in the crowd snapped. "Jesus doesn't have time for the likes of you."

But instead of keeping quiet, Bartimaeus began to yell even louder, "Jesus, Son of David, have pity on me!"

Jesus stopped in the middle of the road. It took faith for someone to call him "Son of David," to recognize him as the Messiah whom God had promised to Israel. "Who is that calling me?" Jesus asked.

"It's nobody," one of the followers said. "Just a blind beggar by the roadside."

"Bring him to me," Jesus

commanded. Instantly, several people hurried to help the man they had just been scolding. Bartimaeus jumped to his feet and threw his coat aside so he could walk faster.

"What do you want me to do for you?" Jesus asked when Bartimaeus was led to him.

"Rabbi, I want to see again."

Jesus touched Bartimaeus' face and said, "See!" And immediately Bartimaeus was dazzled by the brightest light he had ever seen. His whole head seemed to be filled with a light that was almost painful. Then shapes formed out of the light, and he could see people standing around him. He could see again! Then his eyes blurred again, this time because of the tears, tears of joy that streamed down his cheeks, while his face glowed with a radiant smile.

"Your faith has made you whole," Jesus said. Shouting praises to God, Bartimaeus set off down the road following after Jesus and the disciples. Jesus had truly come to save the lost!

Zacchaeus Climbs a Tree

"HEY, SHORTY! WHAT'S the matter, can't you see?"

"Yeah, come on, Shorty! You want to sit on my shoulders?"

The crowd roared with glee. There, at the back of the crowd that lined the road, they could just see a bald head bobbing up and down. This was the tax collector, Zacchaeus, trying to jump high enough to see over their heads. He hopped up and down like a rabbit, hoping to get a glimpse of Jesus. The tax collector had become so rich from the money he had cheated people out of that the crowd really enjoyed making fun of him. They crowded together so he could not see between them, then they laughed some more. "Better luck next time, Shorty!" they shouted. "Why don't you get a Roman soldier to hold you up? After all, you support the Romans the rest of the time!" And they laughed even louder than before.

Zacchaeus, hopping up and down at the back of the crowd, was getting more and more upset. He could understand why the people in the crowd didn't like him. But he had waited for a long time to get a look at Jesus, ever since he first heard about a prophet from Nazareth who went around healing people and talking about the kingdom of God. People who had heard him said he talked like a man who really knew God, not like the Pharisees, who could only tell people to be as good as they were themselves. Zacchaeus hated their sermons. He didn't really like the Romans much either, but he knew who had the real power in Judea.

Just then, Zacchaeus noticed the sycamore trees that lined the road. "Why not?" he thought. "If they won't let me see over their heads, I'll jolly well climb a tree." And that is exactly what he did. From his new perch in the branches of the sycamore tree, Zacchaeus could see the crowd of people coming from the old town of Jericho. And who was that tagging along behind? Wasn't that the blind beggar—Bartimaeus? Only he wasn't blind anymore!

A new kind of excitement filled Zacchaeus as he tried to get a glimpse of Jesus. Then he saw him. "Why, he doesn't look like a king," Zacchaeus thought. "He looks too—well, he looks too gentle, too kind to be a king, at least the sort of king I know about. But what a man he must be! How I wish I could hear him speak. They say he has the words of God."

Suddenly the crowd came to a halt. Jesus was standing right below Zacchaeus. He seemed to be looking for something—or someone. Then he lifted his head and looked right up at Zacchaeus. "Hurry and come down, Zacchaeus," he said. "I'm staying at your house today."

Zacchaeus was so surprised he almost fell out of the tree. How did Jesus know his name? And why did he want to come to his house? What in the world was going on? In a second, he had scrambled down from the tree to meet Jesus. He had never been so happy before in his life. Beaming with joy, he led Jesus through the streets of New Jericho to his own home. The people standing by, grumbling as usual, said, "Look at that! With all the decent people there are in Jericho, he picks a real sinner to stay with!"

On the way to Zacchaeus' house, Jesus talked with him about the kingdom of God. Zacchaeus listened eagerly. When Jesus said that a man who had his heart set on treasures on earth could never enter the kingdom, he felt as if Jesus were seeing right through him. Before they went into the house, he turned to Jesus and said, "Lord, I am going to take half of everything I own and give it to the poor."

"That's easy enough for him to say," one of the bystanders muttered. "He's only giving back what he stole from us in the first place."

155

But Zacchaeus was not finished. "If I have cheated anyone," he went on, "I will pay him back four times as much as I stole."

Jesus knew that these were not mere words; the change in Zacchaeus was real. "Today," he said, "salvation has come to this house. Zacchaeus is a true son of Abraham, because he has believed God and has obeyed him from the heart. I came to find those who were lost, and to save them."

So Jesus went in and spent the afternoon with Zacchaeus and his family. He talked about the kingdom of God, while Zacchaeus and the curious crowd that had followed him listened. As in every other place Jesus visited, some heard his every word. But some turned away in anger or mockery, and there were always some of the Pharisees around to question everything he said. But for those who really listened, his words were words of life.

Then, after spending this time with Zacchaeus, Jesus and his disciples set out again for Jerusalem and the Passover feast.

The Death of Lazarus

THE HOUSE AT Bethany was very quiet—too quiet. Lazarus lay on his bed, pale and still. Mary sat beside him, holding a cool cloth to his forehead. She was worried about her brother. He had been sick for several days and was not getting better. Each day the fever seemed worse, and Lazarus had not eaten anything in three days. Quietly she got up and went into the main part of the house. Her sister Martha was just returning from the well with a fresh jar of cold water.

"I'm afraid Lazarus isn't getting any better," Mary said.

"I know," Martha answered. "Mary, I haven't dared to say this before, but I don't know how much longer he can live."

Mary bit her lip, and tears came into her eyes. "If only Jesus were here," she said. "I know he would help him. Oh Martha, he has done so much for so many people, why do they hate him so? He had to cross over to the other side of the Jordan to get away from the mobs."

"Well, he isn't at the other end of the earth, Mary. We could send for him."

And that is how it happened that

a messenger came to Jesus on the other side of the Jordan River with the news that his friend Lazarus was very sick.

"Take this message back to Mary and Martha," Jesus replied. "Tell them this sickness is not meant to end in death. It has come to bring glory to God."

Joyfully, the messenger hurried back with the good news. But when he reached Bethany, he found the house of Mary and Martha in mourning. Lazarus was already dead! He had died the very day the messenger left and had already been buried by the time he returned. What good was his message now? But he dutifully reported to the two sisters what Jesus had said.

"But Lazarus is already dead!" Martha cried out. "How could he say that?"

"Do you think he means to bring Lazarus back to life again, the way he did that widow's young son we heard about from Nain?"

"Then he might be on his way here right now! Oh, let's hope he comes soon!"

The sisters waited and watched, but Jesus did not come that day or the next. By the end of the second day, they had given up all hope. After all, their brother's body had been in the tomb almost two days. There was no chance that life could come back into his body now.

For a full two days after he heard the news, Jesus stayed with his disciples on the other side of the Jordan. The disciples thought about Lazarus occasionally, but they were comforted by Jesus' words that his sickness would not end in death. Then, on the morning of the third day, Jesus surprised them all by saying, "We must leave today and return across the Jordan to Bethany."

"But Master!" they protested. "Only a few days ago the Jewish leaders there were ready to have you killed. It's too dangerous to go back now."

"I know, but we are still going. This is my Father's will. I am not going in the dark, but in his light. It would be right even if I should lose my life. Our friend Lazarus has fallen asleep, and I must go wake him."

The disciples looked at him curiously. "But Lord, if he's sleeping, he must be getting better. You won't have to go."

Then Jesus said to them plain and simple, "Lazarus is dead."

The disciples didn't dare to say what they thought next. If Lazarus was dead, what was the point of going back to Bethany? And why had they stayed so long if Lazarus had been that sick? Why hadn't they gone back sooner, when it would have done some good?

"I'm glad I wasn't there," Jesus went on. "Glad for your sakes, so you may learn to believe. Come, let us go to Lazarus."

Thomas, the twin, could only think of one meaning in that. Lazarus was dead, the Jewish leaders were trying to kill Jesus, and Jesus was going to join Lazarus in death. "Let's go," he said to the rest. "If he dies, we may as well all die with him."

Jesus Raises Lazarus from the Dead

MARY AND MARTHA'S house was filled with people. Friends, relatives, neighbors, and other people from Jerusalem had come to comfort them on the loss of their brother. A friend beckoned Martha away from the crowd and said, "I have just heard that the Master has been seen walking toward Bethany. I didn't want to upset Mary by telling her."

"Quite right," Martha said. "I must speak to him before he comes. He has to know how much grief he has caused here." And she quietly left the house and went to find Jesus. But when she saw him, the speech she had been practicing died on her lips. She fell down on the ground in front of him and cried out in her grief, "Lord, if you had only been here, my brother would still be alive!" She sobbed for a moment, and then she looked up at Jesus. "Still, Lord, I know that even now, God will give you whatever you ask from him."

But did she really believe that? Did she believe that God could even raise Lazarus from the tomb? Jesus wanted to help her to believe it. He looked down at Martha and said, "Your brother will rise from the grave."

"Yes, Lord, I know," she said. "He will rise from the grave at the resurrection of the dead."

"Martha," Jesus said gently, "*I* am the resurrection. I am life. Any one who believes in me will live, even though he dies. The one who believes in me will never die. Do you believe that, Martha?"

"Yes, Lord, I believe," Martha answered. "I believe that you are the Christ, the Son of God, the one God promised long ago that he would send into the world."

Martha quickly got up and hurried back to the house to tell her sister the news. Quietly she said to her, "The Master is here and wants to talk to you."

Mary sprang to her feet so suddenly that people in the room were startled. She rushed out the door and into the street, with the friends and other mourners following behind her. "She must be going to the tomb to weep," they said to each other. "Let's follow her. She shouldn't be alone at a time like this."

But Mary led them not to the tomb but to Jesus. As soon as she saw him, she knelt down at his feet, weeping, and said, "Lord, if you had only been here, my brother would still be alive!" And her friends were so touched by her grief that they began to weep again too.

The Lord Jesus himself could scarcely hold back the tears. How he

hated death, the terrible enemy. Then he wept, not only for Lazarus but for all who were in the grip of sin, disease, and death.

"Look, he's crying," some of the bystanders said. "He must have loved Lazarus very much."

But others asked, "If he loved him so much, why didn't he come sooner? He cured the man at the pool, and he raised the daughter of Jairus. Couldn't he have cured Lazarus?"

"Where have you put Lazarus?" Jesus asked at last.

"Come this way, Lord," Mary answered, and she slowly led the way to the tomb where the body of Lazarus lay. It was a cave carved into the soft rock of the hillside. A heavy stone had been rolled in front of the grave to seal it.

"Take away the stone," Jesus said.

The people standing around were dumbfounded. Was he so stricken with grief that he actually wanted to see the body of Lazarus? "Don't do it, Lord," Martha begged him. "His body has already been in the tomb for four days. It will be decaying already."

Jesus turned to her and said, "Didn't I tell you that if you believed you would see the great things God can do? Take away the stone!"

Several men leaned their shoulders against the stone and pushed. Slowly, slowly it gave way, until the mouth of the tomb was exposed. Then Jesus looked up toward heaven and said, "Father, I thank you that you have heard me. I know that you always hear me, but I have said this for the benefit of this crowd of people, so they may believe that you sent me."

Then he turned toward the cave and called out, like a father calling his son home, "Lazarus! Come out!"

Has he taken leave of his senses? the people wondered. Perhaps his grief has made him crazy! But then there was a hint of movement in the cave, and a hush fell over the crowd. Then someone cried out, "He's coming out! Lazarus is coming out!" Some of the people in the crowd screamed with fear, and some were too frightened even to scream. And then there in the doorway of the tomb stood Lazarus, his body still wrapped with the linen cloths, his legs so tightly wound that he could scarcely move. If it had not been the middle of the day, they would have thought he was a ghost.

"He's alive!" someone shouted, and the whole crowd began to shout praises to God and to hug one another and shout some more.

"Set him free," Jesus told them. "Let him go home." And the men who had pushed away the stone ran and cut the linen strips, allowing Lazarus to move his arms and legs. One of them took his own robe and covered Lazarus so that the body wrap could fall free.

Overwhelmed with joy, Mary, Martha, and Lazarus walked back to the house. They had always loved Jesus, but now they would love him more than ever. And even though they knew that Lazarus would someday die again, now they knew for sure that he would rise again to eternal life.

Many in the crowd that day believed in Jesus. But some of them went to the leaders of the Pharisees and told them what had happened. And at once the Pharisees called together the Sanhedrin, the ruling council of Israel.

"What are we going to do about this fellow?" they demanded. "He is doing so many signs and wonders that all the people are starting to follow him. If they turn him into a king, the Romans will come and destroy our whole nation."

Then the high priest, Caiaphas, beckoned for silence. "It is better for one man to die than for the whole nation to be put to death. If he is killed, the people will be saved." Caiaphas had no way of knowing how true his words were in a much deeper sense. The Holy Spirit put the words in his mouth, words that said, although Caiaphas did not know it, that through Jesus' death salvation would come to all those who believed in him.

From that day on, the leaders in Jerusalem plotted ways in which they could get Jesus killed.

The King Enters Jerusalem

THE ROADS WERE crowded as Jesus and his disciples made their way to Jerusalem that Sabbath morning. The word flashed on ahead through the throngs of people, faster than Jesus could walk: "Jesus is coming to the feast!" "Jesus of Nazareth is on his way to Jerusalem!" "Don't you want to see the one who raised Lazarus from the dead?" "The Messiah is coming! They'll make him king for sure now!"

When they came close to Bethphage, a village on the slopes of the Mount of Olives, the Lord called two of his disciples. "Go into that village up ahead," he told them. "You will find a donkey colt there that has never been ridden before. Untie it and bring it here. If anyone asks you, say, 'The Master needs it.' "

The two disciples had long since learned to do whatever Jesus told them. They went into the village and found the colt tied outside a house. "Why are you untying it?" asked the owner of the colt, stepping out of the shadow of the house. The disciples turned, startled. "The Master needs it," they stammered. The owner only nodded and disappeared back into the shadow. They led the donkey away, and as they walked they began to think about what was happening. Only a king required a mount that had never been ridden before! Was Jesus at last going to declare himself the king of Israel? They had waited so long! Perhaps the day had finally come!

Eagerly now, they led the donkey back to Jesus. The other disciples were feeling the same excitement. As they led the donkey toward Jesus, the crowd began to whisper, and the word spread quickly: "Jesus is the new king of Israel! Jesus is coming to assume the throne in Jerusalem!"

The disciples put their own cloaks on the donkey and helped Jesus mount. They could hardly believe this moment had finally come. Quickly, the rest of the disciples also took off their cloaks and laid them on the road in front of the donkey, just as they had seen King Herod's servants do many times.

There were Zealots in the crowd, who hoped that Jesus would lead them to victory against the Romans. "Hail to the king!" they began to shout. "Hail to God's chosen one!" And others in the crowd took up the cry, people who had been in Bethany when he raised Lazarus from the dead, people who had been in the desert when Jesus fed five thousand people with five little bread rolls and two dried fish. There were even some there who were walking, talking, and seeing now only because Jesus had

healed them. Gladly they took up the shout, "Hosanna! Welcome to the King!"

The crowd became a cheering throng. Hundreds of people began to lay their cloaks on the ground in front of Jesus. Those who had no cloaks cut branches off some nearby palm trees and spread them in his path. And all the while the crowds cheered and waved and cried out, "Long live the new King David! Hail to the king! He comes in the name of the Lord!" Even those who didn't know what they were shouting about were caught up in the noise and the joy and found themselves shouting, "Hail to the King! Hail to God's chosen Messiah!"

But there were some who refused to join in. A group of Pharisees standing nearby pushed their way through the crowd to Jesus, their faces dark with anger. "Stop them! Stop them!" they demanded. "Make them stop saying those things!"

"No," Jesus answered. "This time they have to cheer. I tell you, if I stopped them, God would make the stones shout in their place!"

The Pharisees drew back and let the crowds go by. "It's no use," they said. "There's no stopping him now. He has everyone on his side."

On and on the procession went, and new crowds took up the shouts of "Hosanna! Welcome, Son of David!" But as they came close to Jerusalem, those who looked closely could see that there were tears flowing down Jesus' cheeks. Only the disciples who were holding the donkey heard him when he said, "O Jerusalem! If only you knew what you need in order to remain in peace! But you refuse to see it. Days are coming when your enemies will surround you and tear down your walls and destroy you. They will kill your women and children, and they will not leave a single stone in its place. And all because you did not recognize the day when God himself was visiting you."

Inside the city itself, everybody was buzzing. "Who is this?" some said. "This is the prophet Jesus from Nazareth," the crowds replied; and they followed him all the way to the temple. As Jesus walked into the temple court, the beggars who sat outside, plus the blind, the deaf, and the crippled—all crowded around him, and he healed them all. Some of the children who had been in the streets were still carrying little palm branches. They ran around the courtyard shouting, "Hosanna! Hosanna to the Son of David!" just as they had heard their parents shout.

When the rulers of the temple, the law teachers, and the chief priests heard what was going on, they rushed angrily out to face Jesus. "Don't you hear what those children are saying?" they demanded. "They are calling you the Messiah!"

"Yes, I know," Jesus answered. "Haven't you ever read what it says in the Scriptures: 'You have made perfect praise come from the mouths of children'?" The astonished priests did not know what to say. But some of them became more determined than ever to get rid of Jesus—once and for all.

163

JESUS IN JERUSALEM

Jesus Cleans Out the Temple

FOR THE MERCHANTS and shopkeepers of Jerusalem, Passover meant sales. Most people came from long distances and could not bring their own animals to sacrifice on the temple altar. Instead, they had to buy a young sheep or goat, or if they were poor, two young pigeons. So the merchants crowded around the temple, selling animals for sacrifices. The priests got in on the action too, allowing the merchants inside the temple court where the priests could inspect the animals—for a fee. As a result, those who came to worship there were surrounded on every side by the peddlers, who shouted and grabbed at people's arms, all the while talking about bargains, bargains, bargains!

And then there were the moneychangers. Judea was ruled by the Romans, and the money of Judea was Roman coins. But Roman coins had a picture of Caesar stamped on them. The rabbis of the temple said, "Our law says that we must not carve any images. Since this Roman money has an image of Caesar, it must not be used in the temple, which is a holy place." So when the pilgrims brought their tithes, the tenth that God required from all that he had given them that year, they could not pay the tithe in their own money. They could not even use it to buy animals for sacrifices. Instead, they had to exchange their Roman coins for special temple money. Seated at tables in the temple courtyard, the moneychangers did their business, always keeping an exchange fee for themselves. So God's temple had become the best place in Jerusalem for a businessman to make a profit.

As Jesus looked around at the crowds and heard the shouts of those selling animals and the clink of the moneychangers' coins, his face grew stern and angry. He quietly turned to his disciples and asked them to take off the cords they used as belts around their waists. He held the cords together and tied them all in a knot at one end. Then he raised this whip over his head and walked swiftly toward a corner of the temple court, where some cattle were waiting to be sold. Suddenly Jesus swung his whip and cracked it in the air over the heads of the cattle. Again and again he snapped the whip, and the frightened cattle began to run; people in the temple had to scramble to get out of the way of their horns.

The merchants looked up in astonishment to see Jesus driving their cattle and sheep and goats toward the temple gates. People were running in every direction, confused and frightened; and the panicked animals were running wildly through the temple, knocking over tables and pigeon cages.

As the pigeons fluttered away to the tops of the pillars, Jesus grabbed the edge of one of the moneychangers' tables and jerked it upwards. The table—and the man behind it—crashed heavily to the ground as coins of all shapes and sizes scattered across the floor. Greedy people rushed to pick up the coins, while angry merchants crowded around Jesus, shaking their fists and shouting in anger. But Jesus raised his whip and cracked it over their heads, and they turned and ran for the gate just as their scared sheep had.

"You thieves!" Jesus shouted after them. "My Father's house is supposed to be a house of prayer. You have turned it into a crooked business! How dare you dirty God's holy place with your animals and your money!"

"What is the meaning of this?" came some voices from behind Jesus. He turned to face the rabbis and priests of the temple. "What right do you have to act this way in God's temple?"

"You are more to blame than the rest of them," Jesus said, his eyes blazing. "You are supposed to know what the Scriptures say. 'My house shall be called a house of prayer for all the nations,' God said. But you have turned it into a den of thieves. Those merchants only bought and sold. But you are the ones who let them into the temple court, yes, and even make a profit yourselves on what they sell! How are people supposed to see God's grace and love with all the commotion going on in this place?"

"So you think you can tell us what to do!" they shouted back. "Why should we listen to you? Who do you think you are, a prophet? What sign do you have from God that you have a right to do this?"

"This will be the sign for you," Jesus answered them. "Destroy this temple, and in three days I will build it again."

"You must be crazy!" they said. "It took forty-six years to build this temple. What makes you think anyone could build it in three days?"

Jesus did not answer. He motioned to his disciples to follow him, and together they left the temple and returned to Bethany for the night. On the way, the disciples were scratching their heads, wondering what Jesus had meant when he said, "I will build this temple again in three days." Only later, after Jesus had risen from the dead, did they realize that he was talking about his own body that he would raise up again in three days.

At the temple the merchants and the moneychangers rounded up their animals, recovered their coins, set up their tables, and went back to business. The angry priests met together to decide what to do. "He has to go!" one of them said. "He undermines our authority. We are all that stands between these people and the anger of the Roman armies. He is putting all Israel in danger. The last thing we need right now is another Messiah!"

"But what can we do?" asked another. "The people are all on his side."

"Hah! Ignorant peasants!" shouted the third. "They have no idea of what is really happening. They don't understand politics, and they don't know the Scriptures well enough to know what a fraud he really is."

"Still, we can't do anything to him with those crowds around. They think he *is* the Messiah. If we act against him now, they will turn on us."

"Then we'll just have to wait. If he comes to the temple tomorrow, we can question him. Sooner or later, he will say something that will turn the people against him. And don't worry, our time will come."

Jesus in the Temple

AFTER SPENDING THE night in Bethany, Jesus came to the temple again. This was the opportunity the Jewish rulers had been waiting for. They confronted him in the halls of the temple, where he was already teaching a small group of people. "Who gave you the right to teach here?" one of them asked. "By whose authority do you do all these things?"

"I will answer that if you will answer another question first. When John came baptizing, where did he get his authority? Was it from God? Or was

he a fraud?"

The rulers put their heads together. "He asks some tough questions, I'll grant him that," one said.

"If we say John's authority came from God, then he'll say, 'Why didn't you listen to him?'"

"Yes, but if we say it was just from a normal human source, the people will be angry, because they think John was a great prophet."

Finally they stopped their buzz of conversation and looked back at Jesus. He faced the man who asked the first question. "Well, what is your answer?"

"We, uh, we don't know," the man answered lamely.

"Then I won't answer your question either," Jesus said. "But when you do know about John, then you will know about me also.

"Listen to me. Once upon a time, there was a man who had two sons. He said to the first one, 'Go out and work among the grape vines today.' And the son said, 'No, I don't want to.' But later he thought it over and decided to go out to work.

"Then the father came to his second son and said, 'Son, go out and work among the grape vines today.' And the son said, 'I'm on my way, Father.' But he didn't go.

"Now, tell me this: which one of them did what his father wanted?"

"The first one, of course," they answered.

"And I tell you this. The tax collectors and the prostitutes will get into the kingdom of God ahead of you. John the Baptist came to tell you the way to please God; but you wouldn't believe him. The tax collectors and the prostitutes believed him, though, and they gave up their sinful ways and obeyed God. You claim to be so holy, but you won't turn away from your sins."

The Jewish leaders began to grumble among themselves. But Jesus was not finished with them yet. "Listen to me again," he said. "Once upon a time, there was a man who owned a field of grape vines. He built a hedge all around it to keep out thieves, and he built a press to squeeze out the grape juice and make wine. Then he built a lookout tower so the field could be guarded. When the preparation work was all finished, he rented out the vineyard to some farmers and went on a trip.

"When harvest time came, the owner sent a servant to collect some of the fruit as a rent payment. But the renters decided they didn't want to pay; so they beat up the servant and sent him back empty-handed. The owner sent a second servant, and they did the same thing to him. When he sent a third servant, they killed him.

"But the owner decided to give them one last chance. 'I won't send a servant this time,' he said to himself. 'I'll send my son. Surely they will respect my son.'

"But when the renters saw him coming, they put their heads together. 'Here comes the owner's son,' one said. 'What shall we do, give him what he wants?'

" 'No. Let's get rid of him too,' said another.

" 'If we kill him, and the old man dies, then we'll get the property.'

"So when the son came to the vineyard, the renters attacked him and killed him, and threw his body out into the road."

It was a shocking story, and it got Jesus' listeners to thinking. Then he put his question. "What do you suppose the owner of the vineyard will do to those renters when he comes back?"

"That's easy," one of the Jewish leaders answered. "He'll kill those miserable wretches and find new renters for his vineyard who will give him the fruit when the harvest comes."

"You are exactly right," Jesus said. "Now, have you ever read this in Scripture?

> The stone the builders would not use
>> Has become the cornerstone of the building.
> This was from the Lord,
>> And it is wonderful to see.

You have rejected the one God has sent. Therefore, I tell you that the kingdom of God will be taken away from you and will be given to others who do what the kingdom requires."

After that, the Jewish leaders were determined to get rid of Jesus. But they didn't dare do anything to him then, because so many of the people were on his side.

Setting a Trap

THE JEWISH LEADERS had only one hope left. If they could trap Jesus into breaking either the Jewish law or the Roman law, then they could have him executed. So now the questions came thick and fast. They made sure that there were always some Pharisees around, those who defended the Jewish law, and also some of those who admired King Herod and thought the Jews ought to obey the Romans. That way, they thought, no matter which way Jesus answered some questions, one group or the other would be offended by him.

But they didn't want Jesus to think they were trying to trap him. So they put on their most polite faces and tried to flatter him instead. "Master," they said—and that was the first time they had ever called him that —"we know that you always say what you really believe. You don't care what people think, but you always teach God's ways. So tell us, please, is it right for us Jews to pay taxes to Caesar or not?"

But Jesus knew what they were up to. "Are you trying to trap me, you hypocrites?" he said. "Give me the coin that they collect for the tax and I'll show you something."

One of the Herod party dug into his purse and pulled out a Roman coin. He handed it to Jesus. "Whose image is stamped on this coin?" Jesus asked.

"That's Caesar," the man replied.

"Then give Caesar what belongs to him," Jesus told him. "And give God what belongs to him."

There was not a word from any of them. They had been caught in their own trap. They knew that as humans they themselves were stamped with the image of God, and Jesus' words said a lot about their money too!

Next in line were a group of Sadducees, religious teachers who believed that there was so such thing as the resurrection of the dead. So they came to Jesus and said, "Master, we want you to explain something to us about this idea of the resurrection. As you well know, Moses commanded that if a man died and his wife had no children, his brother was to marry her. Now there was a man who had six brothers. The first man died, so the second one married her; and then he died, and still she had no children, so she married the third brother. And so it went until all seven of them had died. And then the wife finally died.

"Now, Master, please tell us this: When the resurrection comes, which one of the seven brothers will be the husband? They all married her."

"Do you think that in the resurrection they will be just like they are now?" Jesus asked. "No, I tell you, in the new age it will be quite different. People won't get married then, not any more than the angels do."

"Good for you, Rabbi," one of the Pharisees called out.

"But now about the resurrection, my Sadducee friend," Jesus went on. "Have you ever read in Scripture how God appeared to Moses in a burning bush?"

"Of course, we all know that story."

169

"Moses asked God who he was. Do you remember what God said?"

"He said, 'I am the God of Abraham, and the God of Isaac, and the God of Jacob.'"

"Now then," Jesus said, "why do you suppose he didn't say 'I was the God of Abraham?' He said 'I am' because Abraham and Isaac and Jacob rose from the dead and are with him. God isn't the God of the dead. He is the God of the living."

And while the Sadducees walked away in confusion, the laughter of the Pharisees, who often argued with them over religious issues, rang in their ears. Now it was the Pharisees' turn to put Jesus to the test. They spent so much time talking about the law that they often argued among themselves which commandment was most important. So they sent one of the law teachers to him with a question. "Master," he asked, "which commandment of the law is the greatest?"

Jesus said, "You must love God with your whole heart and mind and soul. That is the most important commandment. And there is another one just as important: you must love your neighbor as you love yourself."

The teacher was amazed, for Jesus had gone back to the heart of all the commandments. "That is a good answer, Rabbi," he finally said. "Loving God and your neighbor is more important than all the sacrifices and offerings we can bring to the temple."

"If you know that," Jesus answered him, "then you are not far from the kingdom of God."

The common people who sat around listening to Jesus enjoyed seeing the pompous Pharisees and Sadducees put in their places for a change. Then Jesus turned to them and said, "The Pharisees and the law teachers have taken the place of Moses as your leaders. When they read to you from the Scriptures, you should obey them. But don't follow their example. They talk a great deal, but they don't do much. The way they burden you with the law is like tying rocks to a drowning man. But they won't help carry the load they put on you.

"Don't be like them. Don't look for other people to praise you. Praise from God is all that really counts." Then he turned to the Pharisees, his voice full of fire. "You Pharisees are like blind men trying to lead other blind people around," he said. "You find ways to get out of obeying the really important things in the law. You pay your tithes down to the tiniest seeds from your garden. But important things like justice and mercy and love, those things you ignore! You wash every cup before you use it, but you don't care what's inside! You make a big show of your piety, but you don't look after the helpless widows. You're just like painted tombs. They look pretty on the outside, but inside they smell of decay and are full of the bones of dead men! You are just like that: you appear holy on the outside, but on the inside you are full of hypocrisy and evil."

When he was finished speaking, Jesus sat down opposite the box where people brought their offerings of money. The crowd watched with him as several rich men made a great show of dropping in stacks of coins. But one woman came there dressed like a widow from a small town, obviously very poor. Without looking to see whether anyone was watching, she dropped two pennies into the box and then went on into the temple. Jesus turned to the people and said, "Look at that poor widow. She gave more than all the rich people who came ahead of her."

They looked at him in surprise. She had only put in two pennies! But Jesus said, "The rich men gave much, but it was only a small amount of what they had. The widow had very little, and she gave it all to God. Those were her last two pennies." Then, leaving the people to wonder about all that had happened that day, Jesus left the temple with his disciples and went to be alone with them on the Mount of Olives.

WAITING FOR THE KINGDOM

THREE DAYS HAD passed since Jesus rode into Jerusalem on a donkey, with the crowds shouting "Hail to the king!" Still he had done nothing to make himself king. In spite of everything he had said, the disciples were still expecting him to take the throne of David and rule like an emperor. Jesus wanted to prepare his disciples to see that the kingdom would come through his suffering and death, and that they themselves would face a long time of turmoil and distress that would test their patience, their endurance, and their faith. Once again he taught them in stories that only those who had been made alive by the Spirit of God could ever truly understand.

Jesus' Story of the Ten Girls

ONCE UPON A time, there were ten girls who were invited to a wedding. They were all happy to go, so they put on their best dresses and took lamps with them to light the way, because the wedding was at night. They went to the bride's house, but they did not go inside. They had to wait outside for the bridegroom so that they could escort him into the house, their lamps shining brightly and their faces aglow with happiness.

Now it happened that five of the girls were wise, but the other five were foolish. It never occurred to the foolish ones that they might have to wait some time for the groom to come. They only had enough oil in their lamps to light their way to the bride's house and back home again.

The five wise girls realized that it might take a while for the groom to arrive from his distant home. No matter how long they had to wait, they wanted their lamps to be shining brightly to welcome him. So they took along some extra oil, just in case they had to wait a while. And they did have quite a long time to wait. Either the road was too crowded, or the groom got a late start, but his trip took longer than anyone expected. Far into the night they waited, until it looked as if the groom might not come at all. The girls grew tired of waiting and sat down on the ground. One by one, they drifted off to sleep.

At midnight a shout rang out. "The bridegroom is here! Come out to meet him!" It was the call for all the guests to bring their lamps and escort the bridegroom into the house. The ten girls woke up at once. The five wise ones trimmed off the burnt ends of the wicks so their lamps would shine brighter. But when the five foolish girls did the same, their lamps flickered and went out!

"Our lamps are out of oil!" they wailed to the other five girls. "Please give us some of yours!"

"But we don't have enough left," the others answered. "You'll have to run to the store and buy some."

The five foolish girls ran as fast as their legs would carry them, but while they were gone the bridegroom arrived. The guests, including the five wise girls, came out to meet him with their lamps shining brightly, and they went in with him to the wedding feast. When all the guests were inside, the bride's father shut the door and locked it, and the party began.

Soon there came a knocking at the door. "Open up, my lord. Open up!" cried the girls outside.

"Who's there?" the bridegroom asked.

"Five girls. We're here to join the party. We were here before. We were invited!"

"I'm sorry," the bridegroom answered, "but I don't know who you are. All my friends waited for me. It's too late now, I can't let you in."

When he had finished the story, Jesus said to his disciples, "So be on the watch. You don't know when the bridegroom may come."

Would it take that much patience and trust before they could celebrate the coming of God's kingdom? the disciples wondered. How long might they have to wait?

Jesus' Story of the Three Servants

JESUS WAS SITTING with his disciples on the Mount of Olives, trying to tell them what the coming of the kingdom was really like. This would be his last opportunity to teach them before he died. He wanted to remind them of the image he had used before, about the wheat and the weeds growing together until the final harvest. But he also wanted to tell them what they were to do during the long time between his death and when he would return in judgment. He wanted them to keep on expecting him but in the meantime to be stewards of everything he had given them. So he told them this story.

The kingdom is like a man who took a trip to a far-off country. Before he went, he divided his estate among his servants so they could take care of it for him. He gave one of them five thousand dollars, and another two thousand, and to the third he gave one thousand dollars. Then he said, "Manage the money for me while I am gone. I have given each of you as much as I think you can handle. When I come back, each of you will report to me." Then the servants went their own ways.

After a long time the master came back. He called his three servants together and asked, "How did you make out with my money while I was gone?"

The first servant came to him and said, "Sir, I used your money to buy wheat and corn when they were plentiful, and then I sold the grain again when it was scarce. Your five thousand dollars has earned five thousand more. Here is the whole ten thousand dollars."

"You have done a good job," the master said to him. "You were careful with this small amount of money. I will put you in charge of greater things. Enter into your master's joy." And he set him up to rule over five cities.

Then the second servant came to the master and said, "Sir, I used your money to buy silks and spices from the East. I traveled far to find the very finest, and sold them here again. Your two thousand dollars have earned you two thousand more. Here is the whole four thousand dollars."

The master said to him, "You have done a good job. You were careful with this small amount of money. I will give you more responsibility. Enter into your master's joy." And he set him up to rule over two cities.

Then came the third servant, the one who had started with only one thousand dollars. "Sir," he said, "I knew that you were a hard man to

please. I was afraid I would lose the thousand dollars, so I buried it in the ground. When you came back, I dug the money up. Here is your thousand dollars, safe and sound." And he stood back, wondering what his reward would be.

Instead the master roared at him, "You lazy, ignorant bum! You knew I was hard to please. The least you could have done was put the money in the bank where it could have earned some interest while I was away. But you did nothing with it! Nothing at all!" The master turned to his men and said, "Take the thousand away from him and give it to the man who has ten thousand. And take this worthless servant and throw him into the darkness outside. Let him weep and wail out there!"

When Jesus had finished the story, the disciples looked curiously at one another, wondering just what Jesus meant. He was the master in the story, no question about that. But what was this part about a long journey? Did he mean he was going away? Yes, it must be that, and he wanted them to take care of things while he was gone. And then when he did come back, he would judge them by what kind of stewards they had been. But how long would he be gone from them? One of them was just about to ask, when he remembered the story of the ten girls coming to the wedding. They didn't know how long it would be before the bridegroom came, but five of them were ready when he did come, with their lamps lit. Just then, Jesus began to speak again.

"When I come in my glory with all the angels," Jesus said, "I will sit on my throne and judge all the nations of the earth, just the way a shepherd separates the sheep from the goats. I will put the sheep on my right side and the goats on my left. Then I will turn to the sheep on my right and say, 'You have my Father's blessing! Come and enter the kingdom that was prepared for you before the world was even created. For you fed me when I was hungry; you gave me a drink when I was thirsty; you gave me clothing when I was naked; and you visited me when I was in prison.'

"And they will say to me, 'When did we ever see you hungry, or thirsty, or naked, or in prison?'

"And I will answer, 'When you did those things for one of the least important of my people, you did it for me.'

"Then I will turn to the goats on my left hand and say, 'Go away from me and get lost! You are cursed to the eternal fire that was made for the devil and his angels. When I was hungry, you did not feed me; when I was thirsty, you gave me nothing to drink; when I was naked, you gave me no clothing; when I was in prison, you did not visit me.'

"Then they will say to me, 'Lord, when did we see you hungry, or thirsty, or naked, or in prison?'

"And I will answer them, 'When you refused to do it for one of the least important of my people, you refused to do it for me.' And those wicked ones will be punished forever; but those who helped others for my sake will enter into eternal life."

With these stories Jesus prepared his disciples for the surprising events soon to come. He showed them how they would have to wait and work, patiently and energetically and without giving up hope, until his return as king of all creation.

JESUS PREPARES FOR HIS DEATH

THE TIME WAS very close now. Jesus' work on earth was nearly finished. For three years he had gone through Galilee and Judea announcing the good news of the kingdom. He had chosen twelve disciples to follow him, to watch him closely, and to learn from him. He had already sent them out to preach the good news and to bring healing to the sick and the lame and the blind. How joyful they had been when they returned!

Things had not been so joyful since that time. Jesus had begun to tell them what would happen in Jerusalem, and they were confused, disappointed, and discouraged. Then he taught them that the kingdom would not come as they expected it, even though he knew they would not understand him fully until after his death. Now there was so little time left. The time for teaching was nearly over. Jesus had to prepare himself and his followers for the struggle that lay ahead. He would begin in Bethany with a final visit among his friends there.

Mary Anoints Jesus

SHORTLY BEFORE THE Passover, Jesus was invited to have dinner at the home of a man named Simon, who lived in Bethany, where Jesus was staying with Mary, Martha, and Lazarus. The disciples were there as well, including Judas Iscariot. None of them knew that this was the last time Jesus would visit Bethany, and none of them knew what Jesus was about to go through.

For at that very moment members of the Sanhedrin were meeting to discuss what they could do about Jesus. "He must be arrested," they agreed. "The man is a danger to our whole people, although they don't know it. We'll have to be careful, though; if we have him arrested right in the middle of the feast, the people will turn against us. We must find a time when he will be alone." So they plotted and schemed far into the night.

In her own house in Bethany, Mary was preparing to do something quite different. Her heart was filled with love for Jesus, and she wanted to show him how much she loved him. On a little shelf in her room lay a beautiful white bottle made of stone cut so thin that the light could shine through. Inside was a very expensive perfumed oil that could not be used until the bottle was broken. She had made up her mind. She was going to use the oil to anoint Jesus. Quickly she tucked the bottle into her robe and set out for the house of Simon.

The meal was long and leisurely, and the guests lay on their couches and talked for hours. They scarcely noticed Mary as she quietly entered the room and knelt by the feet of Jesus. Then suddenly the room was filled with a sweet scent that made them look around to find what it was that smelled so good. There was Mary, the ointment jar still in her hand. She had broken off the top and was pouring the fragrant oil onto Jesus' head. Then she poured the rest of the oil on his feet and wiped them dry with her own hair.

Judas could not see that what Mary was really pouring out was her love for Jesus. He could only think about what the bottle of perfume must have been worth. "What a waste!" he said. "She could have sold that bottle for a huge amount of money and given the money to the poor."

"Leave Mary alone," Jesus said to him. "What she has done is right. There will never be a shortage of poor people to give money to. But I will not always be with you. She did this to prepare my body for burial. And I tell you that in days to

176

come, when the good news is preached all over the world, they will tell about Mary and what she has done tonight."

This was the last straw for Judas. He did not want a Messiah who talked about dying. That very night, he stole away to Jerusalem and made his way to the council chamber of the Sanhedrin. The babble of voices in the chamber stopped suddenly when Judas entered the room. Caiaphas, the high priest, looked at him coldly and said, "What is a follower of Jesus doing here in the middle of the night?"

"You are looking for a chance to arrest Jesus when he is away from the crowds, isn't that right?" Judas asked. There was no answer. "Well, I can help you. For a while, I thought he was the new king, and so I followed him. But now I see that nothing will come of it." He could see the frowns turning to looks of interest. "I know where he stays when he wants to be alone. How much would you pay me to turn him over to you?"

"So you've finally seen the light, have you, Judas?" Caiaphas looked around at the other members of the Sanhedrin and smiled. "I knew it would only be a matter of time before his disciples began to desert him. It happens to all of them, these Messiahs. Gentlemen, how much is it worth to us to have Jesus handed over to us secretly, away from the crowds?"

They haggled for a while, but at last they agreed to pay Judas thirty pieces of silver. "Just wait for the word from me," Judas told them. "I'll let you know when you can find him alone." Then he went out into the night and crept back to the house in Bethany. He had done his work. And he was so good at fooling himself that he did not even know he was working for Satan's cause. That night, for the last time, he slept with the other eleven disciples, close to the Lord he was about to betray.

Passover Night

THE SUN HUNG like a great red ball, low in the western sky. People scurried through the streets of Jerusalem in the lengthening shadows. At sunset the new day would begin, the holy day of Passover. All work had to stop then; so people hurried now to finish their errands and chores.

In a borrowed room on the top floor of a house, the disciples of Jesus made the last preparations for their Passover meal. In every Jewish household in the world that night, the same preparations were being made. A young lamb, one that had been carefully watched for a week to make sure it was without any flaw, was slaughtered for the Passover meal. Bitter herbs and flat bread were placed on the table. And on that night, when the family sat down to eat, everyone was dressed for a journey. The father in each household then told his children the story of Passover.

"Long ago, the children of Israel were slaves in Egypt. But God raised up a man named Moses to save his people. He brought terrible plagues on Egypt, but still the Pharaoh refused to let God's people go. Then Moses told us each to kill a lamb and paint its blood on the top and sides of our doors. Our ancestors sat down to this meal of roasted lamb, the very lamb that was killed to provide the blood for the doorway. They were dressed for a journey because that night God was going to lead them out of Egypt. They ate flat bread to show that they were in such a hurry to leave that there was no time for the bread to rise. And they ate bitter herbs because of the sorrow of that night.

"For outside in the night an angel of death went through Egypt, and in every household the oldest son died. Only in the houses with the blood around the door did no one die, because the blood was a sign for the angel to pass over those houses. That is why we call this feast Passover, because that night the angel of death passed over our houses. God saved us from the terrible plague of death and delivered us from slavery in Egypt."

Not even the disciples knew that before the long night was over, Jesus himself would become the Passover lamb, the Lamb of God who would be killed, and whose blood would take away the world's plague of sin and death.

Earlier that day, Jesus had called Peter and John and talked with them privately. "Go into town," he had said. "There you will meet a man carrying a jar of water. Follow him to the house he enters and go in. When you meet the owner, say to him: 'The Teacher says, "The time has come. Where is the guest room where I may eat the Passover with my disciples?"' And he will show you a large upstairs room provided with everything you need. There you must prepare for the Passover meal."

Now Peter and John were welcoming Jesus and the others as they arrived just before dark. But since it was a borrowed room, neither of them was really the host. So the disciples talked and waited, wondering who would wash the others' feet, as was the custom in those days. Each of them wanted to be the honored guest, and no one wanted to act like a servant. Soon they began talking about it, and before long they were arguing again about who was the most important, and who was going to have the highest place in the kingdom of God. The babble grew louder and louder. It was John who first caught sight of what Jesus was doing, and he fell silent. Then others saw John and turned to see what he was looking at. There was Jesus, with his robe laid aside and a towel wrapped around his waist, filling a basin with water.

The disciples watched with astonishment as Jesus knelt down to wash the feet of Judas Iscariot. He did the same for Thomas, and then for Matthew, and for the other Judas, before he came to Simon Peter. "I won't let you wash my feet," Peter cried out. "I won't let you humiliate yourself like that."

"Peter," the Lord said kindly, "I don't expect you to understand this now. Later you will understand what I am doing."

"No, Lord! I will never let you wash my feet!"

"If you won't let me wash you," Jesus said, "you can't have anything to do with me."

"In that case," Peter said, changing his mind completely, "don't stop with my feet. Wash me all over!"

"No, Peter," Jesus answered him. "You bathed before you came here. You are clean. Only your feet need washing, because of the dusty road. A man who has had a bath only needs to have his feet washed. But not all of you are clean." He said that because he knew that Judas was going to betray him.

Slowly Jesus went on around the circle, washing the feet of Andrew, then Philip, and Bartholomew, then Simon the Zealot, and James, the son of Alphaeus, and finally James and John, the sons of Zebedee. When he was finished, he put down the basin and the towel, put on his robe and lay down on his couch at the table.

"Do you understand what I have done tonight?" he asked.

"I—I think so, Master," John answered.

"You call me Master," Jesus said. "Peter, you called me Lord. You are both right, because I am your Master and Lord. Yet I have washed your feet. If I, your Master and Lord, wash your feet, then you should follow my example. Wash each other's feet. Serve each other, just as I have served you. Do you think that a servant can be greater than his master?"

"No," the disciples answered.

"If you know that," Jesus answered, "then you should practice it. Do as I have done. Then you will have my Father's blessing. But I cannot say that to all of you. One of you who is eating at this table tonight will betray me."

There was a startled gasp from everyone at the table. It was John, the disciple who was closest to Jesus in every way, who asked the question that was on everyone's mind. "Do you mean me, Lord?"

"Do you mean me?" the others echoed. "Am I the one?" Peter leaned across the table to John and whispered, "Ask him who it is."

So John leaned over again so his head was next to Jesus'. "Lord," he asked softly, "which one of us is it?"

Just as quietly, Jesus answered, "It is the one who will dip his bread into the dish along with mine." Almost idly, Jesus reached out his hand to dip his bread into the bowl of sauce made with bitter herbs. From the crowd of hands around the table another hand reached out. The two pieces of bread touched the bowl at the same time, and the hand of Judas brushed against Jesus' hand. Judas looked up, straight into Jesus' eyes.

"Do you mean me, Lord?" he asked.

"It is just as you have said," Jesus answered. "Hurry out and do what you must."

Only Peter and John heard the quiet conversation. The other disciples could only wonder why Judas got up so quickly and went out into the night. "But then," they thought, "he probably has to buy something more for the feast. After all, he is the treasurer." And they turned back to their meal.

Outside, Judas shivered slightly in the cool night air. "He knows," Judas thought, as he slipped through the streets to find his cohorts on the Sanhedrin. Now he was completely in the grip of Satan.

The Last Supper

ONCE JUDAS HAD gone out into the night, Jesus continued the celebration of the Passover meal. He picked up one of the loaves of flat bread and asked God to bless it. Then he broke it in half and passed the bread to his disciples, who each broke off a piece and ate it in silence. This was the bread of remembrance, which they ate to remember what God had done when he brought their people out of slavery in Egypt. Suddenly Jesus broke the silence. What he said startled the disciples, set their minds reeling, and gave a whole new meaning to that night.

"This bread is my body, which is given for you," he said. "From now on, when you eat it, remember me."

Peter nearly choked on his bread. He had been thinking about Moses in Egypt and about the lamb that was killed and eaten at Passover; but suddenly Jesus said to remember him instead. What could he possibly mean? The other disciples were wondering the same thing, but it was John who remembered something Jesus had once said: "Unless a man eats my body and drinks my blood, he has nothing to do with me."

Then Jesus picked up the cup of wine, the third cup that was drunk during the feast, called "the cup of blessing." The red wine always reminded the Jewish people of the blood their ancestors had painted on the doors of their homes in Egypt so that they would be saved from the angel of death. That night in Egypt, God had shown that he was keeping his covenant with his people. Now Jesus took the cup of wine and said, "This wine is my blood, poured out for your sins, to establish God's new covenant. When you drink it, remember me."

Not really understanding what Jesus was saying, the disciples drank the wine. Then Jesus said, "Whenever you eat this bread and drink this wine, you will be announcing my death, and this you will continue to do until I come again." And to this day, followers of Jesus Christ still eat the Lord's Supper, remembering together how he gave his body and blood for our salvation.

But the disciples were still trying desperately to understand what was happening. "Master, why are you talking about death?" Peter asked.

"My children," Jesus answered, "I will only be with you a little while longer. You will look for me, but you will not find me, because you cannot go where I am going. But I am leaving this one commandment with you: love one another just as I have loved you. If you do, everyone will know you are my disciples."

"But you can't leave us, Lord!" Peter protested. "Where are you going? Why can't we go with you?"

"You cannot follow me now," Jesus said, "but later you will follow me."

"Why can't I come with you now?" Peter insisted. "Even if they take you to prison or kill you, I am ready to go with you."

"Are you, Peter?" Jesus asked sadly. "I must tell you something. Satan is going to sift your life the way a farmer sifts the wheat out of the hulls. But I have prayed for you and asked the Father to make your faith last. Once it is all over, you must teach your brothers. But I must also tell you this. This very night, before the rooster crows, you will deny three times that you ever knew me."

Peter could feel the eyes of the other disciples burning into him. "No, I won't!" he said hotly. "I will never deny you, not even if I have to die with you!"

"Neither will I," Andrew joined in.

"Nor I," said John, and all the others said the same thing.

"Every one of you will desert me," Jesus said. "But don't get discouraged. You believe in God. Believe in me too.

There was silence for a moment. Then it was John who said, "Let's sing the psalm." It was the custom to end the Passover meal with a psalm, so they all sang "I Cried to God," a psalm that David had written many years before:

> In my distress I cried to God;
> He answered me and set me free.
> The Lord is with me; I'll not fear,
> For what can men now do to me?
>
> The nations gathered all around,
> Surrounding me on every side;
> They thrust so hard I nearly fell,
> But God has saved me from their hand.
>
> The Lord's my strength, the Lord's my song;
> My tent resounds with shouts of joy;
> The Lord's right hand has done great things;
> He raises up the fallen one.
>
> I will not die, but live to tell
> The wondrous works which God has done.
> He did not give me up to death,
> But opened gates of victory.
>
> The stone the builders cast away
> Has now as cornerstone been laid.
> Let us rejoice and sing his praise
> In this, the day the Lord has made.

Then Jesus looked up toward the heavens and said, "Father, the time has come. I have told my disciples about you. They know that I have come from you. You gave them to me, and I have kept them all, except the one who has gone to betray me. Now, Father, I am giving them back to you. Please keep them through these dark hours. Keep them from falling in with the ways of this world. I am sending them out, just as you sent me into the world. Keep them holy through your Word. I pray also for those who will hear their message and believe in me, that we all may be one, just as you and I are one. The world does not know you, Father, but I know you, and now my disciples know you too. I have told them about you so that the love you have for me may be in them too."

Then he turned to his disciples. "Come now, it's very late," he said. "We must go." And they left the room and walked out into the night—toward the Mount of Olives.

Gethsemane

ON THE MOUNT of Olives there was a garden called Gethsemane, a place where Jesus often went with his disciples. On this night, after the

183

Passover meal, they went to Gethsemane once more. At the entrance to the garden Jesus stopped. He shivered—but not from the cold. He knew what he had to do, and he knew that once he entered this garden there would be no turning back.

Jesus faced his disciples. "Stay here, near the gate," he said. "I am going into the garden to pray. Peter, James, John, you come with me." He turned then and walked into the garden, followed by the three disciples who were closest to him. He was not alone, yet a great sense of loneliness came over him. For years now he had lived with them as a man among men. But tonight he would be more alone than any other man has ever been. He thought of what he would have to face in the next few hours, and tears came into his eyes. Never before had he known such sadness, a sorrow so deep that it felt as if it would kill him.

"This is the saddest night of my life," Jesus said to his three companions. "I feel as if my heart will break. You wait here and pray. I will go on ahead and pray alone." Then Jesus walked on into the garden, leaving Peter, James, and John behind. They tried to pray, but they were so exhausted and sad that, one by one, they fell asleep. All alone, the Lord Jesus himself knelt down to pray.

"I know you love me, Father," he said. "And I know that you can do anything. So please, Father, if there is any way for me to escape the suffering of this night, please let it be so. I don't want to go through with it. Oh Father, it is too much for me!" He bowed down on the ground, his body wracked with sobs and of grief.

Then Jesus felt someone touch his hand. Looking up through his tears, he saw a man standing in front of him. It was not one of the disciples come to comfort him. They were all sound asleep. It was one of God's angels. He knew that Jesus was suffering and had come to give him comfort. Jesus stood up then and walked back to where he had left his disciples. He found them fast asleep, so he gently woke them. "Peter," he said, "couldn't you even stay with me this one hour? Stay here and pray. Ask the Father to keep you from being led away by temptation. I know your spirits are willing; unfortunately, your bodies are weak.

This time Jesus went deeper into the garden alone to pray. He realized now how truly alone he was; neither man nor angel could stand with him. The burden of it all crushed him down, and again he began to pray.

"Father, I do not want to drink this cup of suffering being poured for me. If there is any other way, Father, please do not make me go through this. Take this cup away from me! But if there is no other way, then I will drink it. May your will be done!"

Once more Jesus went back to his disciples. All three had gone off to sleep again. This time he did not even wake them. None of them could really pray with him, because they could not understand what he was going

through. He left them to their sleep and went back into the dark garden once more to pray.

And for the third time he prayed, "Father, if it is possible, please take this cup of suffering away from me!" He groaned in the agony of his suffering. Everything in him said, "No! You were not meant to die but to live! You were made to enjoy God's creation, not to suffer!" Yet at the same time his whole being cried out, "You were made to do God's will! You were made to serve him!" And Jesus' suffering was so great that his sweat rolled down his forehead and neck like big drops of blood.

And then at last a great calm came over Jesus. Yes, mankind was created for life. But so that people could live again, he would have to die. "Father," he said, "I will do your will, not my own."

He lay still a few minutes more, recovering his strength, before he stood to go. Not far away he could see the glow of torches being carried slowly up the hill. "Now it begins," he thought. "Now let Satan have his way. But I will defeat him in what he thinks is his moment of greatest victory. Let it begin."

BEHOLD, THE LAMB OF GOD

The Arrest

"Y OU CAN SLEEP now," Jesus said. They lay on the ground asleep, all eleven of the disciples. He had spent his time of prayer to his Father all alone. "The time of my temptation is over," he said, "and you didn't even know it had begun."

The torches were closer now, and Jesus could already hear the muffled voices of the men outside the garden. "Wake up!" he called to his disciples. "The time has come! Look, here comes the one who is betraying me."

The disciples sat up, groggy and confused, rubbing their eyes in the eerie glow of the torches. One moment they had been asleep, and the next moment there were voices and lights and the clanging of swords being drawn. There were temple guards and servants of the chief priests, and in front of them all was Judas Iscariot.

"Which one is he?" whispered one of the guards to Judas.

"The one I will kiss," he answered.

Judas walked forward slowly until he stood directly in front of Jesus. "Hello, Master," he said, and he leaned forward to kiss him.

"Would you betray me with a kiss, Judas?" Jesus asked. Judas looked at him strangely, then leaned forward again and kissed him on the cheek.

Suddenly all was confusion. Guards were seizing everyone in sight—Peter, John, Andrew, Thomas—and some were moving quickly toward Jesus. Then Jesus stepped past Judas toward the guards, and in the same strong voice he had used to teach thousands of people in the open air, he called out, "Who are you after?"

The guards stopped short in surprise. "Jesus of Nazareth," the commander answered.

"I am he," Jesus said calmly. At his words, the men fell backward as if they had been struck on the face. A power they could not understand drove them to the ground. There was fear in the eyes of the guards now. What kind of man was this who could overpower them without lifting a finger?

"Who did you say you want?" Jesus asked again.

"Jesus of Nazareth," the officer replied at last, but his voice was not as certain this time.

"I told you I am the one," Jesus said to him. "Take me, and let these others go."

The guards slowly got to their feet and moved cautiously toward Jesus. But before anyone knew what was happening, Peter leaped in front of them, pulling a sword from under his robe. He yelled and swung at the man closest to him, one of the high priest's servants. The man ducked to one side, but the blade caught him on the side of the head and cut off his ear.

"Put down your sword!" Jesus said in a voice that made Peter drop it to the ground with a clatter. "People who live by the sword will die by the sword! If I had needed help, I could ask the Father and he would send twelve armies of angels to fight for me. But it must happen this way." Then he stooped down and picked up the servant's severed ear. Quickly he pressed it back in place, and the man's wound was healed.

"Am I a thief, that you have to come out for me with swords?" Jesus asked the priest's men as he held out his hands toward them. "I taught every day in the temple, and you didn't arrest me there. You work in the dark, and your power comes from the darkness. But it had to happen this way so that what Scripture said would come true."

When the guards saw that Jesus was not going to resist, they seized him and led him away. As for the disciples, they ran away as fast as they could, leaving Jesus alone with his captors.

Jesus Before the Council

THE EASTERN SKY was brightening with the glow of dawn when they brought Jesus to the courtroom of Caiaphas, the high priest. The scribes and the members of the Sanhedrin who opposed Jesus were waiting for him. So was Annas, the old high priest whom Governor Pilate had replaced with Caiaphas, Annas' son-in-law. In the shadows behind Jesus and his captors came Peter, slinking through the darkness, watching to see what would happen.

"I demand that you explain yourself!" Annas said. "What have you been teaching the people? What have your disciples been saying about you?"

Jesus looked Annas straight in the eye. "I have not been hiding in the hills, teaching in secret," he said. "I have spoken in synagogues all over Judea and Galilee, and in the temple itself. If you want to know about my teaching, ask those who heard me."

This answer made the men of the Council so angry that one of them slapped Jesus hard across the face. "How dare you talk to the high priest that way!" he shouted.

But Jesus said to Annas, "If I have said something evil, then come right out and say so. But if not, what right do you have to hit me?"

"Enough of this!" broke in Caiaphas. "Bring in the witnesses." And through the door came a couple of the sorriest looking men any of them had seen in a long time. For days, those who hated Jesus had searched for anyone who would accuse Jesus of breaking the law, but they couldn't find anyone, not even one of the Pharisees who had argued with him in the temple. Finally they found some scoundrels who could be bribed to say anything at all, and those were the men who now came into the Council chamber to testify against Jesus.

"There he is! There's the man!" one of them shouted, pointing his finger at Jesus.

"What did he do?"

"He's the one who cursed God's temple. We heard him, didn't we?" He nudged his companion with his elbow.

"Yes, yes, he's the one," the other agreed.

"What did he say?" asked one of the Council members.

The man looked confused for a moment. Then he remembered. "We heard him say, 'If you destroy this temple, I will build it again in three days.' He made himself greater than the temple. If that isn't a curse, I don't know what is!"

Caiaphas groaned to himself. Is that the best they could do for witnesses? This was getting them nowhere. "What kind of testimony is that?" he barked. "Get out of here, you worthless scum!"

One after another the bribed false witnesses came into the chamber. "He taught men to break the Sabbath," one said. "No," said the next, "he said he was greater than the Sabbath." A scribe said, "He made himself greater than the law," but when the council members asked him what he meant, he couldn't give an explanation. The members of the Council, like Caiaphas, just wanted any old accusation that would stick under Hebrew law. There were questions and shouts and arguments, but no one could get the witnesses to agree with each other or give consistent testimony.

Finally Caiaphas himself stepped forward. "Enough!" he shouted. "Jesus of Nazareth, what do you have to say to these accusations?" Jesus did not answer. "Nothing, I see," Caiaphas went on. "There is no reason why you should. There is only one question that is important. I command you in the name of God to answer me this question. Do you claim to be the Messiah, the—it burns my tongue to say it—the Son of the living God?"

There was a deathly silence in the room, and all eyes turned to Jesus. "I am," he said. "And the day will come when you will see me sitting at the

right hand of God, coming on the clouds of heaven."

With a loud cry of pain, the high priest snatched off his own robe and tore it in two. "There is no need for more witnesses!" he shouted. "You've all heard it with your own ears. The man has condemned himself out of his own mouth! He makes himself equal with God! It is blasphemy! What is your verdict?"

Again the room was filled with shouts and cries. "Blasphemy! Blasphemy! He has insulted God himself! He is guilty, and he must die!" In their anger and hatred some of them began to spit on Jesus. One man grabbed him from behind and held his hands over Jesus' eyes while another one punched him hard in the pit of his stomach. "Now, Prophet, tell us which one of us hit you!" he shouted.

"Stop it!" Caiaphas commanded. "Leave him alone for now. As soon as all the members of the Council are here, we will give our judgment." But everyone knew what the judgment would be: Jesus was about to be condemned to death.

189

Peter Denies Jesus

PETER STOOD OUTSIDE the high priest's courtyard, waiting in the shadows to see what would happen. But John had already gone into the court where Jesus was, because he was known by the high priest. Only these two, Peter and John, had followed Jesus; the others had all gone into hiding, still afraid that they would be arrested. When John saw Peter standing outside in the shadows, he spoke to the servant girl who was the doorkeeper. "Let that man in too," he said quietly.

She beckoned to Peter, who stepped quickly through the door. "Aren't you one of Jesus' disciples too?" she whispered.

"No, I'm not," Peter answered and walked into the courtyard. There was a fire crackling in the center of the open court, and the guards were warming their hands. Peter was so cold that he couldn't stay away from the fire. But as he stepped closer and the firelight lit up his face, one of the servants standing nearby said, "I saw you with Jesus of Nazareth."

"I don't know what you're talking about," Peter replied nervously and walked back into the shadows near the doorway. He stood there for more than an hour, listening to the laughter of the guards, wondering what was going on inside the house, frightened that he might be arrested, but too concerned to leave.

Suddenly the door to the high priest's house opened. There in the doorway stood Jesus, his hands bound. Peter stepped out of the shadow to get a better look, and the firelight once more lit up his face. "There's one of them!" shouted one of the high priest's men. "He was with Jesus when we arrested him in the garden! He cut off my cousin Malchus' ear!"

"No, no, I wasn't there!" Peter cried desperately. "I've never even heard of him!"

But the man grabbed Peter by the arm and pulled him closer to the fire. "Of course you were there," he said. "You even talk like you're from Galilee. You must be one of his disciples."

"So help me God, I'm telling you the truth! I don't know the man!" As the man let go of Peter's arm, a rooster crowed to greet the rising sun. Jesus turned and sadly looked at Peter. In that moment Peter remembered what Jesus had said, and the words went home like an arrow through his heart: "Before the rooster crows in the morning, you will deny me three

190

times." A cry of anguish rose in Peter's throat, and he ran out into the night, weeping bitter tears.

The Death of Judas Iscariot

THE FULL SANHEDRIN met at daybreak to reach a verdict on Jesus, although no one doubted what it would be. "Guilty!" the angry voices shouted, and it was done. "The sentence is death!" But the Sanhedrin could not carry out a death sentence, because the Romans had the power of life and death in Judea. So they led Jesus away to the Roman governor, Pontius Pilate.

Judas Iscariot was waiting outside when the door opened. The first to appear was one of the temple guards. Then Judas saw Jesus, bound like a prisoner. Slowly, the guards marched their prisoner past Judas and up the street, with Jesus' accusers following. Judas' heart began to race wildly. What had he done? He stumbled back against the building, his face a mask of horror. He looked around wildly. The door to the high priest's court was still ajar. In a frenzy he ran through the courtyard and into the room where the Sanhedrin had met. The heavy door opened with a clang as he rushed into the room. Caiaphas looked up in surprise. "Ah, friend Judas," he said.

"I'm no friend of yours!" Judas blurted out. "Jesus is innocent! I have betrayed an innocent man!"

"He condemned himself by his own words," Caiaphas answered.

"But he's innocent, I tell you!" Judas cried.

"That's your problem," Caiaphas said coldly. "Besides, you were well paid for your efforts. You got what you wanted."

"No, no! I never wanted the money!" His hands were fumbling at the leather purse hanging from his belt. With trembling fingers he pulled out the silver pieces and threw them on the floor, where they clattered and rolled across the stones. "You are the high priest! Tell me what I can do to take away this sin I have committed!"

"Sin?" Caiaphas said, raising his eyebrows. "Who said anything about sin? You did us a favor, that's all. Pick up your money, Judas." With a strangled cry, Judas turned and ran from the room, through the streets of the city, and out into the countryside. By the time he stopped running, he had already decided what to do.

They found his body a few days later; he had hanged himself. The priests, meanwhile, had to figure out what to do with the thirty pieces of silver. "We can't put it in the temple treasury," they agreed, "because it's blood money." So they used it to buy a field as a graveyard for foreigners. And because the graveyard was paid for with Judas' blood money, it became known as the "Field of Blood."

There were twelve disciples who betrayed their Lord that night. They all ran away from him, and they all denied him. But only Judas found no forgiveness, because he had never given himself to the Lord. He became the first of those about whom Jesus had said, "There will be many who will say to me, 'Lord, Lord,' but I will say to them, 'Depart from me. I never knew you.' "

Jesus Appears Before Pilate

"SIR, THE JEWISH elders are here, asking to see you."

Irritated, the Roman governor looked up from his work. He could tell this was going to be a bad day. His wife had been up half the night with nightmares about some Jewish prophet. He had finally decided that since he couldn't sleep anyway, he might as well get some early work done. Now the day was beginning with those insufferable Jewish elders. Why did Caesar have to make him governor of Judea? Did he deserve that? "Jewish elders, at this hour of the morning?" Pontius Pilate asked with a scowl. "Oh, all right, send them in."

"Sir, they asked me to beg the governor's pardon, but today is a holy day for them, and they are not allowed to enter a Roman building. They ask if you will be kind enough to come outside to them. They have a prisoner with them."

"Come outside to *them*?" Pilate roared. "Who do they think I am, their servant? Oh, never mind, I suppose I'll have to come." Annoyed, Pilate rose from his chair and strode outside to meet the priests and the Sanhedrin. "What do you want?" he snapped. "And who is this man? What is the charge against him?"

"If he weren't a criminal, we would not have brought him to you," the high priest answered. He hated Pilate as much as Pilate hated the Jews.

"Can't you take care of this yourself?" the governor asked. "You have your own laws."

"Yes, Your Excellency, but we are not allowed to put a man to death. Only you order the death penalty."

"Death?" Pilate said in some surprise. The man certainly did not look like a criminal, but then, you could never tell. "What has he done to deserve death?"

All the voices started shouting out at once, "Blasphemy! Treason! He says he's a king!"

"Silence!" Pilate's voice rang out sharply in the morning air. "You, Annas. You are the oldest one here, you tell me what the charge is."

"This man has been traveling all over, stirring up the people," Annas replied. "He has been teaching them that it is not lawful to pay taxes to Caesar. And he claims that he himself is the chosen king of the Jews."

"I see," Pilate said thoughtfully. He turned to Jesus. "And what do you have to say to these charges?"

Jesus looked straight at Pilate but said nothing.

"Come on, man, don't you hear what these people are saying? Those are serious charges. What do you have to say for yourself?" Still Jesus said nothing at all. "Well, well," Pilate said at last, "a prisoner who does not defend himself. This is a rare case. I will examine him myself. Guards, bring the prisoner in."

This is a messy business, Pilate thought as he walked back to his chamber. You can't be too careful with these Jews. Always some kind of plot going on. What if this prisoner is really from the old family of Jewish kings? Well, he thought, there is only one way to find out.

Pilate sat down and faced the prisoner. "Now we are alone. You may speak freely to me. Tell me, are you the king of the Jews?"

For the first time Jesus spoke. "Are you asking for yourself, or have others been talking to you about me?"

"Who do you think I am, a Jew?" Pilate barked. "How should I know about you? Your own leaders have handed you over to me. What have you done?"

But Jesus answered his first question instead. "My kingdom does not belong to this world," he said. "If it did, my followers would be fighting right now to keep me away from the Jewish leaders. But my kingdom is not like that."

"But you are a king, then?" Pilate asked.

"You say that I am a king," Jesus answered. "I will tell you why I was born. I came into the world to witness to the truth. Everyone who loves the truth will listen to me."

"And what is truth?" Pilate asked. But Jesus did not answer. What a strange man! Pilate thought. He talks about a kingdom, but he has no army. Then he talks about truth, but he won't get into a debate about what it means. Who is he; anyway? Certainly no threat to Rome, I would think."

Pilate rose from his seat and went back outside to meet the Sanhedrin. "This man has done nothing wrong," Pilate said to the Jewish leaders. "I am going to set him free."

Once again all the members of the Sanhedrin spoke at once. "No, he's a troublemaker," one said. "He keeps the people restless," said another. "He's been over the whole countryside, from Galilee to Judea," cried a third.

"Wait a minute!" Pilate snapped. "Did someone say this man is from Galilee?"

"Yes, Your Excellency, he is," Annas replied.

"Then why didn't you say so before? Herod Antipas is in charge of Galilee. Take him to Herod." As the soldiers led Jesus away, Pilate walked back to his work, smiling and rubbing his hands happily. "Two birds with one stone," he thought, "two birds with one stone. Herod will be happy I thought highly enough of him to send over the prisoner. And the Sanhedrin will be happy I took up the case. Not bad for one morning's work!" Then a frown crossed his face. "But what if the prisoner *had* done nothing wrong? Well, let the Jews handle their own affairs."

Jesus Appears Before Herod

JESUS WAS COMING to the court of King Herod Antipas. "At last!" thought Herod. "And as a Roman prisoner!" It was the best news Herod had received all week. It wasn't often that a man got a chance to see a genuine prophet, and under arrest too, where he couldn't do any harm. Perhaps Jesus would do some miracle for him. "And to think that Pilate had sent the prisoner to me. What consideration the man has, what respect for me!" He had misjudged the Roman governor. Now he was sure the two of them could get along.

"Ah, Jesus of Nazareth," Herod said when they led the prisoner before him. "I have heard so much about you. How fortunate that I was in Jerusalem this Passover season. I'm sure all this unpleasantness about your arrest can be straightened out—if you are as great a prophet as they say. Do something for me, will you, Jesus? Nothing very spectacular, you know, just a little something. I have a servant with a crippled arm. What about him? You could heal him. Or maybe you could give us all lunch from one loaf of bread. Just one little miracle to prove you really are a prophet."

Jesus just looked at Herod and did not answer him.

"You aren't going to disappoint me, are you, Jesus? You are? How sad. It seems that I must listen to your accusers after all. Well, what is it? What has he done?"

"He has cursed God by claiming that he is the Son of God," one said.

"He taught that it is wrong to pay taxes to Caesar," said another.

"He claims to be king of the Jews," said a third.

Suddenly the smile was gone from Herod's face. "What's that you say? King of the Jews?" Would John the Baptist never stay buried? He remembered John's words as clearly as if they had been spoken yesterday: "If you do not repent, God will reject you as king." Herod felt that little stab of fear he got whenever he thought of John.

"What do you say for yourself?" Herod demanded. "Do you say you are the king of the Jews?"

But Jesus still did not answer him. "What good is a prophet who won't even talk?" Herod said scornfully. He remembered how John had shouted out his message. No, this man was no threat to him. And he wasn't any fun either.

"Well, if you are a king, you certainly should be dressed like one," Herod said. "Bring out the robe for our royal guest!" So Herod's servants brought one of Herod's discarded robes and put it on Jesus. "Don't you look the part, though!" Herod laughed. "A peasant king, all tied up!" He roared with laughter at the thought, and his men joined him. But Jesus did not get angry or even put his head down, and the laughter soon died.

"How tiresome this is," Herod said at last. "Take the man back to Pilate. Tell him that he would not answer a single question I put to him, so I cannot give judgment in his case. No, no, just a minute. Instead, tell him that I respect the position of the Roman governor and don't want to take the authority out of his hands. That ought to make him happy."

But it did not make Pilate happy to see Jesus return. "I have already questioned this man," he said to the members of the Sanhedrin. "I found him not guilty of the charges you brought. Obviously, Herod could not find anything wrong with him either; that's why he sent the prisoner back to me. He has not done anything that deserves death under the laws of Rome. I will have him whipped so he will learn not to stir up the people, and then I'm going to let him go."

"One moment, Your Excellency." It was Caiaphas, the high priest. "It may be that this man has done nothing to deserve death under Roman law; but according to our law, he has committed a serious crime. He has claimed to be the chosen one of God, and has insulted and cursed God by doing so. The law of Moses demands death for such a man. If you want to keep the loyalty of the Jewish people, you must put him to death for us, since we are not allowed to do it."

"So you think the people will love me if I put this man to death?" Pilate asked. "Okay, we'll ask them. There is another prisoner here, one of those Zealot rebels, who started a riot here in Jerusalem and killed a man in the process. His name is Barabbas. It's your Passover custom to release one prisoner in honor of the festival. We shall see which one the people choose. Come to the Court of Judgment in one hour." "Surely," Pilate thought, "the people will choose to release an innocent man. Then all this unpleasantness will be over."

The Court of Judgment

THE RUMORS HAD spread through Jerusalem like wildfire that morning. Jesus of Nazareth was under arrest. The Sanhedrin was going to have him stoned to death. King Herod had put him in the same prison where he had kept John the Baptist. Jesus was going to call out armies of angels to fight the Romans. Jesus was already dead. No, he was still alive.

Outside Pilate's palace was an open courtyard where the people came to appear before the governor. There he gave his decisions on important matters. Now the courtyard was filling with people. Many of them were Zealots who hoped that their comrade Barabbas would be released. Others were friends of the Sanhedrin, leaders of the Pharisees, priests from the temple, supporters of King Herod—as many as the Jewish leaders could find who hated Jesus. His enemies tried to turn away anybody who might tell Pilate to release Jesus; the crowd inside was packed against him.

Inside his palace, Pontius Pilate paced worriedly. He knew he was in trouble: it was a mistake for any Roman ruler to get involved in the Jews' own religious quarrels. Why did he have to rule these stubborn people?

"Caius Pontius!"

Pilate whirled at the sound of his first name. "Claudia! What are you doing here?" His wife's eyes had dark circles under them from lack of sleep, and her face was creased with worry.

"Caius, I have seen the prisoner Herod sent to you."

"Claudia, you shouldn't worry yourself about these—"

"But Caius," she said, "this is the man I dreamed about! I don't know why it bothers me so much, but I am sure it has some terrible meaning for you. Please, don't have anything to do with him. I know it will mean disaster for you."

"Claudia, I am the governor," Pilate replied. "I will do what I must."

Frustrated and troubled, Pilate watched his wife leave the room. Did she think he could govern Judea on dreams? Still, her concern bothered him. He shook his head in determination. He had work to do. "Bring the prisoners out to the judgment porch," he called to his servants.

A hush fell over the crowd when Pilate appeared and took his seat in judgment. When the prisoners were led out, the crowd broke into wild cheering. On one side stood Jesus; on the other side stood Barabbas, the notorious rebel leader who had robbed and killed in his attempt to overthrow the Romans. Pilate raised his hand for silence, and once more quiet fell in the court of judgment. The only sound was the weeping of the few who loved Jesus. "It is the custom," Pilate began in his strong voice, "that the governor of Judea should release one prisoner in honor of your Passover feast. In my love for the Jewish people—" Here he was interrupted by boos from the crowd, and one or two shook their fists in the air. "In my love for the Jewish people," Pilate went on, "I have decided to honor this custom. You see before you two prisoners. On my right, accused of murder and revolution, is the prisoner Barabbas."

The crowd below him again broke out into such noisy cheering that once more he had to raise his hand to quiet them. "On my left stands Jesus of Nazareth, who claims to be king of the Jews Which one shall I release to you?"

"Barabbas! Give us Barabbas!" the crowd screamed. There were a few who cried out, "Jesus! Jesus!" But the Zealots in the crowd, and the priests and the Pharisees, shut them up quickly. Pilate frowned. He had not counted on this. He motioned to the guards to follow him back into the inner chamber with the prisoners.

"Take that man away," Pilate said, pointing to Barabbas, "but be ready to bring him back. And take the other one away and whip him. Perhaps that will satisfy that bloodthirsty mob."

They led Jesus away, down the cold stone steps to the prison below the palace. Torches in brackets on the walls flickered in the dark dungeon. Mounted on the wall were brass rings that were used to tie up prisoners for flogging. Raising Jesus' bound hands over his head, they tied him to one of the rings and took off his robe.

"What's this one here for?" asked the whipmaster as he grasped the handle of the whip in his hand. He swung the whip up over his head and brought it down with a sharp crack across the back of the prisoner.

"Some kind of Jewish prophet, I think," the captain of the guard answered. "Claims to be king of the Jews."

Again and again the whip came down on Jesus until his back was crisscrossed with bleeding welts. "That's enough," the captain said finally. "We don't want to kill him yet." He picked up Jesus' robe and put it back on the prisoner's shoulders.

"Wait a minute," said one of the men. "A king should have a robe. What about the one King Herod sent along?"

"Good idea," said the captain. So they brought Herod's purple robe and put it on Jesus.

"Now he needs a crown. What can we use for a crown?"

"There's a thorn bush in the courtyard," one of the soldiers suggested. "We could make one out of that."

"Good idea," said the captain. "Do you think he'll get the point?" And they laughed at their little joke.

The thorns were long and sharp, and the soldier who wove the crown pricked his fingers more than once. When it was finally done, he brought it back and jammed it onto the prisoner's head. Jesus winced in pain as the thorns punctured his skin, and little trickles of blood began to run down his forehead.

"Now for the scepter of authority," another soldier shouted. "Here, let him have this stick!" With a laugh, he struck Jesus on the side of the head with the stick, then put it in Jesus' hand.

"Well, boys, how does he look?"

"Like a king! Hail to the king!" They shouted it over and over, and bowed down in front of him, and they laughed the laughter of men who know nothing but cruelty. When they were finished having their fun, the captain led Jesus back to Pilate.

"A strange thing, Your Excellency," he said when he handed over the prisoner. "No matter what we did, he never opened his mouth. I never knew a prisoner who didn't curse the men who beat him."

"Yes, very strange indeed," Pilate said thoughtfully. More and more he was convinced that this man was no criminal. There was only one other reason he could think of why the Jewish leaders wanted him out of the way: they were envious of him. Perhaps he was more popular with the people than they were. If so, the people would soon have their chance to show it.

Pilate squared his shoulders and led Jesus back out to the court of judgment.

The Verdict of the Mob

WHEN JESUS APPEARED in the judgment court for the second time, there were some in the crowd who gasped at the sight. His face showed a welt where he had been struck with a stick, and he was bleeding from the crown of thorns on his head. The bloodstains from the whip lashes on his back had soaked through Herod's purple robe. A few in the crowd began to weep out loud.

"I have brought him out to you again," Pilate said to the mob, "so you can see that I have punished him. But he is not guilty of anything deserving death. Here is the man!"

The sound of weeping was drowned out by a roar of voices crying, "No, take him away! Crucify him! Crucify him!"

Pilate was shocked by the savage anger of the crowd. He could hardly believe his ears. These people could be more cruel than some of the Roman soldiers. Angrily he shouted, "Take him and crucify him yourself! I won't have anything more to do with him."

Then one of the priests stood up in front of Pilate

and said, "This man deserves to die by our law. He claimed to be the Son of God!"

Pilate turned pale. What if his wife's dream were true? If he offended one of the gods, it could surely mean disaster for him. Once more he called Jesus into the inner chamber.

"Who are you, really?" he demanded when they were alone. "Where do you come from?" But Jesus did not answer. "Can't you understand what is happening, man?" Pilate thundered. "I am trying my best to set you free, but you aren't helping me at all. Don't you know that I have the power to kill you or to set you free?"

At last Jesus broke his silence. "You would not have any power at all unless it were given to you from above," he said. "God has put you in authority. But the ones who handed me over to you are far more guilty than you are."

Pilate took a handkerchief and mopped his forehead. Strange how he was sweating, though the day was not yet hot. "I don't want to see you die," he said to Jesus, "but your own people are demanding it. Even a Roman governor, with power from above—as you put it—sometimes has to listen to the voices of the people below. Well, let's go back out to your people and see what they want me to do with you."

Pilate led Jesus out onto the balcony overlooking the courtyard and sat down in his seat of judgment again. He knew that he had only one more chance to set Jesus free. He would have to convince them that it was ridiculous to think of Jesus as a king. He looked at Jesus—dirty and bloody, dressed in Herod's castoff robe, and with a thorn bush on his head. "Look!" he said scornfully. "There is your king!"

"Take him away!" the crowd began to yell. "Crucify him!"

"Do you want me to crucify your king?" Pilate asked, hardly believing what he was hearing.

"Caesar is our only king," said one of the chief priests. "This man made himself a king. He spoke against Caesar. If you let him go, Caesar will hear about it."

"You filthy hypocrite!" Pilate snarled at him. "You hate Caesar more than you hate me. You would kill every Roman in Judea if you thought you could get away with it. Don't tell me how loyal you are to Caesar!"

"We are not talking about me, Your Excellency," the priest said with a cruel smile. "We are talking about your position as royal governor."

Pilate was trapped, and he knew it. He turned to a servant and snapped, "Bring me a pitcher of water and a towel." Then he stood and motioned for silence. "You have demanded this man's death," he said. "He is innocent, and I will not take the responsibility for his death. Look," he said as the servant poured water over his hands, "I am washing my hands of this whole affair. I will let you carry out your sentence, but I will not condemn him under Roman law."

Then Pilate turned and left the place of judgment. Back in his own room he sat down heavily. "Go to the dungeons and release that rebel Barabbas," he said to his men. "And send the prisoner Jesus along with the others who are supposed to be crucified today."

"And the accusation, sir?" one asked.

"Accusation? What do you mean?"

"What shall we write on the sign, Your Excellency, the one that goes on the cross to announce his crime."

"Oh yeah, of course," Pilate said. "I'll give those rotten Jewish leaders something to think about. Write this: 'Jesus of Nazareth, the King of the Jews.' And don't change a word of it."

Pilate listened to the tramp of the soldiers' feet as they led Jesus away, and he heard the cheers of the crowd as Barabbas was released. He stood and walked to the washstand in the corner, poured water over his hands and began to dry them on a towel. "I just did that," he thought. Then he drew a deep breath. He could not believe what had happened to him today. As he looked out the window at the mob surging out of the courtyard, he said to himself, "Of all the places in the world, why did Caesar send me to Judea?"

Golgotha

THE THIEF'S CROSS felt very heavy as he carried it through the streets, its rough edges cutting through the thin cloth of his robe. He never thought it would come to this. Stealing had seemed such as easy way to get by. Now he was headed for death, carrying his own cross on his back. He broke out in a cold sweat.

But that other fellow there—the one they called the king of the Jews. He knew there was something different about him. Something about the way he walked. He didn't curse the Romans or shout that he was innocent. Why were they taking him out to execute? The thief had heard about him, of course. They said he healed sick people; some even claimed he raised a dead man to life. Could he save himself from the cross? Maybe he could even rescue all three of us—himself and us two thieves with him.

He looked so tired, the thief thought. They must have beaten him too hard. He could hardly walk. Then he stumbled and fell down on one knee! But he didn't look like a weakling; he looked strong, like a working man. They said he was a carpenter before he became a prophet. How did the wood of a cross feel to a carpenter? the thief wondered.

He shook his head. Those were crazy thoughts. He'd better concentrate on his feet . . . left, right, left, right. Look there, Jesus fell again! He'll never make it all the way to Skull Hill at this rate. He's too weak. There, the

guards are grabbing someone from the crowd. African, looks like—Simon, he says his name is. Good, they're putting the cross on his shoulders. That should make things easier.

Look at the crowds! I'll tell you, they always come out to watch an execution. And there are so many people here, it being Passover and all. Look at that, some of them are crying! That must be for Jesus, not for me. For me all they have is jeers and dirty looks. At least I deserve it. But what about him? He never did anything wrong, I'm sure of it.

We're past the city walls now. He just keeps walking—just like a lamb to the slaughter. If it were me, I'd be telling everyone who would listen that I was innocent. Wait a minute. They aren't all crying. What's that they're yelling? "Save yourself, King! Where are your armies of angels now? Go back to your heaven, you phony Messiah! Or to hell, for all we care!" Why do they hate him like that? What did he ever do to anyone?

Oh man, here's the hill now. I don't want to go. Please, God, I don't want to die. "Okay, okay, I'll move. Stop whipping me!" What a place this is! All those empty crosses. How many men have the Romans killed here? Hundreds—maybe thousands. And I'm next. Skull Hill. What an awful name. What do the Romans call it. . . ? Calvary, that's it.

Almost to the top now. Left, right. Now I can stop. They're taking the cross off now. I don't have to carry it any more; soon it will carry me. What's that they have now? Ah, the drugged wine. Good, it'll dull the pain a bit.

He hit the ground with a crash when the Roman soldier kicked his feet out from under him. They turned him so he faced the sky and laid him on the wooden cross. Now the fear hit him full force and he began to scream, "No! No!" He struggled and twisted, but Roman soldiers held his hands and feet. They had done this many times before and knew how to handle prisoners. Screams of pain, mingled with the sound of the hammers, rang out as the nails were driven through the prisoner's wrists and feet and into the wood of the cross. Then the cross was lifted, lifted high into the air and, with a terrible thud, dropped into the hole that had been dug for it.

He could see everything now. In the distance lay Jerusalem. Closer to him stood the crowd, held back by the Roman soldiers. Some of the people were weeping and wailing, others were shouting angrily and shaking their fists. Below him he could see the other thief being nailed to his cross. Boy, how he screamed and cursed! But at last he too was nailed down, and his cross was raised up.

The soldiers came to Jesus next. The thief on the cross had never seen anyone face death as Jesus did. He wouldn't drink the drugged wine the Romans offered him; and they didn't have to trip him or throw him down. He fell to the earth beside the cross, and when they laid him on the wood, he stretched out his arms and laid them flat against the crosspiece. The soldiers hesitated a moment, not sure what to make of him. Only one soldier held him down now, and not even he was needed. "Like a lamb to the slaughter," thought the thief.

The soldiers stripped off Jesus' clothing. "No sense letting him wear a good robe up there on the cross," one of them said. Then they nailed Jesus to the cross and lifted it into position. Still Jesus did not cry out or say a word. Wait a moment! Jesus *was* saying something. The voice came faintly from the figure on the cross. "Father, forgive them," he said. "They don't know what they are doing." The thief was utterly amazed. He had never seen a man who could love as Jesus loved, love as he was being killed.

The second thief, the one whose cross was on the other side of Jesus, began to curse him. "Forgive! Hah!" he spat. "Only a weakling forgives! If you don't hate the Romans for what they are doing to you, you don't deserve to live!"

On the ground below the soldiers were quarreling over Jesus' robe. "Flavius, you got the last robe," one of them said. "It's my turn this time. That robe is too good to tear apart."

"I'll tell you what," said the man named Flavius. "Let's throw dice for it." So it happened just as David had written that it would in the Psalms many centuries earlier:

> They look at me and mock me;
> they divide my clothing among them,
> and cast lots for my garments.

But the thief on the cross could see only the cruelty of the Romans, who could crucify a man and then gamble over his clothes. His burning anger made him forget his pain for a moment. But Jesus said nothing.

The people in the crowd were beginning to shout now. "Come on, Christ!" they taunted. "I thought you were going to tear down the temple and build it again in three days. Can't you even tear down a cross?"

"If you are the Messiah, prove it! Come down from the cross!"

"You saved other people. Now save yourself!"

"If God loves you so much, how come he doesn't save you?"

The thief on Jesus' left joined in with them. "Big man!" he shouted. "If you're so great, you could save all three of us! Some Messiah you are! King of Israel! Hah!"

"Shut up!" the thief on Jesus' right blurted out. "What right do you have to talk to him that way? Don't you even respect God? We're both getting exactly what we deserve. But he didn't do anything wrong. Leave him alone!" Then his voice grew softer, and he said, "Jesus, if you are really the Messiah, will you think of me when you come into your kingdom?"

Jesus turned his head toward him and said, "I assure you, this very day you will be with me in Paradise."

The thief looked at Jesus in astonishment. "I think you really are the Messiah!" he said. Then, tired from the effort of speaking, and weak from his wounds, he allowed his head to drop onto his chest. Despite the pain that wracked his body, he felt a strange sense of joy. "Today!" Jesus had said. "Today you will be with me in Paradise!"

The Death of Jesus

BEHIND THE LINE of Roman soldiers, surrounded by those who were shouting insults at Jesus, stood a small group of his friends. His mother was there, along with Mary Magdalene, and several other women who had faithfully helped him during his ministry. And the disciple John was also with them. Through their tears they had watched as Jesus was nailed to the cross and raised up above the earth. They had heard the sound of the hammers striking the nails, had heard the coarse laughter of the Roman soldiers.

Now that all the crosses had been raised, the soldiers were allowing the families of the dying men to come closer. As Jesus' mother and his other friends approached the cross, the light of the sun began to fade, even though it was only noon, and darkness was beginning to cover the countryside like an approaching storm. In Jerusalem lamps were being lit. John saw this and wondered what was happening.

"Mother."

The voice from the cross was quiet, but still strong. Mary looked up at her son, wiping away her tears. "Mother," Jesus said, "take John to be your son. John, she is your mother now."

The strange darkness was deepening. The shouting of the crowd died away as the people looked fearfully at the blackened sky. The soldiers were frightened too, but they covered their fear with their joking. Their laughter, mingled with the women's weeping at the foot of Jesus' cross, and the moans of pain from the two thieves, made for a very eery atmosphere in the gathering dark.

Jesus did not cry out, although his pain was greater than the thieves'. He had to bear the pain of sin and suffering and death, the pain of the whole creation. He had become the Passover lamb, the one whose blood had to be shed so that sin might be taken away forever. In his own body he was carrying the sin of the world. Even his Father had left him now. This was the worst of his sufferings: in the darkness he was utterly alone.

"My God, my God," he cried out at last, "why have you forsaken me?" His anguished cry shattered the awful darkness and chilled the hearts of those who stood nearby. But for Jesus the worst was over. He had suffered the hatred of men and the punishment of God, and still he had cried out to his Father, "My God!" In his darkest hour he had not turned away from God.

"I'm thirsty," Jesus said to the men on the ground. One of the soldiers got a sponge, dipped it in the sour wine they kept there for the dying men to drink, and held it up to Jesus' parched lips on the end of a pole.

"It is finished!" Jesus exclaimed. The work God had given him to do, the task for which he had come into the world, was completed. Now he could give up his life, just as he had said he would. Standing at the foot of the cross, John remembered the words Jesus had spoken: "No man can take my life from me. I will give it up on my own."

Then, in a voice loud enough to be heard by all who stood around, Jesus cried out, "Father, into your hands I commit my spirit." And he bowed his head and died.

The officer in charge of the Roman guard looked up at Jesus. He had seen many prisoners die, but never one who faced death the way Jesus did. "This man was no criminal," he said aloud. "He was a son of God."

In Jerusalem men and women ran screaming from their houses as the earth began to quake and tremble. Dishes clattered to the floor and pieces of brick fell from the tops of buildings to the street below. A few of the weaker buildings collapsed completely. At the temple, the frightened priests watched as the walls began to tremble, but not a stone was shaken from its place. The earthquake passed at last, and the priests nervously went back to their duties. But moments later, a horrified priest came running from the Holy Place, where he had gone to put more incense on the altar. "The curtain is gone!" he shouted. "The curtain has torn in two! The Holy of Holies is open!"

And it was true. The curtain had torn in two from the top to the bottom, and the Holy of Holies was open to plain view, the place where the ark of God's covenant had once stood, the sign of his presence among his people. Ever since the first tent of worship had been erected in the wilderness, only the high priest had been allowed to enter the Holy of Holies. Now, because of the death of Jesus, the way into God's presence was open to everyone.

Buried

THREE HOURS LATER, sunlight had returned to the sky, and the Roman soldiers had recovered their courage. It was the middle of the afternoon now, and few of the spectators were left. The commander of the guard finished his afternoon cup of wine and stood up. "All right, men, get to work," he said to the soldiers. "Go down the line of crosses and break the prisoners' legs."

The men looked at him in surprise. Crucifixion was a punishment designed to make people suffer as long as possible. If a crucified man's legs were broken, they would no longer support his weight; his body would sag downward, cutting off his air supply, and he would die in a few minutes. "Why so soon, Captain?" the men wanted to know.

"Something about the Jews' religion," he answered. "Their leaders don't want dying men hanging here all through their high holy day, and that starts at sundown. So get to it."

The soldiers moved toward the crosses. Quickly and brutally, they broke the legs of the two thieves. But the soldier who came to the cross where Jesus was hanging turned toward the commander and shouted, "No sense in breaking this one's legs, Captain. He's already dead."

"Impossible!" the captain answered. "Are you sure?"

"We can find out soon enough," the soldier said. He took his spear and drove the sharp point into Jesus' side. Blood came from the wound, but not the heavy flow that would have come from the body of a living man. It trickled down his side, and a clear, watery fluid was already separating from it. "He's dead, all right," the soldier said.

Thus the words God had spoken to the Israelites on the first Passover came true for Jesus, the true Passover Lamb: "You shall not break any of the bones of the lamb." And the prophet Zechariah had written about the Messiah, "They will look upon the one they have pierced."

Pontius Pilate was amazed when he heard that Jesus was already dead. The man who stood before him was an honorable man, a member of the Sanhedrin, but one of the few who did not agree to the sentence passed on Jesus. "What I tell you is true, Your Excellency," Joseph of Arimathea insisted. "Now sunset is approaching, and we Jews can do no work once the Sabbath begins. So please let me take the body and lay it in a tomb before the day ends."

How very strange, Pilate thought. Here is a man who, by his own testimony, was afraid to be on Jesus' side while the man was still alive. Now that Jesus is dead, he risks his reputation to come to me. What sort of man was this Jesus?

"Send for the captain of the crucifixion detail," Pilate said. The captain confirmed what Joseph had said. "All right," Pilate said to Joseph, "you may take the body down and bury it. Captain, go with him and see to it that my order is carried out."

Outside Pilate's palace Joseph rejoined his friend Nicodemus, who had brought with him spices and oils for the burial. Joseph himself had brought a new linen cloth to wrap the body in. "Let's move quickly, before the sun sets," Joseph said. So they carried Jesus' body to the cave Joseph had ordered for his own burial. Now the grave would hold the

body of the man who, even in death, had no place to call his own. They laid his body tenderly in the tomb and began to wrap it with the linen cloth and the spices. But it was late, and there was no time to finish the task. "We will have to return Sunday morning," Joseph said. "Let's roll the stone in front of the cave to seal it now, and go home for the Sabbath."

Outside the tomb they rejoined Mary and Mary Magdalene and the other women. The sun was just setting as they solemnly left the tomb and went to their own homes. It was all over. All their hopes had come to this, to death and the grave. What would they do now that Jesus was dead? Would their lives still hold any meaning?

There were others wondering what they would do now. Among them were the Jewish leaders who had condemned Jesus to death. Early the next morning they went to see Pontius Pilate, even though it was the Sabbath.

"What is it now?" Pilate asked wearily. "Aren't you satisfied that you got rid of your king?"

The high priest ignored the remark. "Something very distressing has come to our attention," he said. "It is reported that this Jesus, while he was still alive, said that after three days he would come to life again. Of course, we don't believe a word of it. But some of his disciples might come and steal the body so they can say he rose from the dead. Therefore, we have come to ask you to set a guard at his grave."

"You have your own temple guards," Pilate answered. "Use them."

"That is true, Your Excellency," Caiaphas replied, "but some might claim that they are on our side and only say what they are told. It would be far better to set a guard of Roman soldiers, who are well known for their honesty and—"

"Oh, brother!" Pilate interrupted angrily. "All right—take your guards and do the best you can with them. Just get out of my hair!"

So the Sanhedrin set up a detail of Roman soldiers to watch the grave of Jesus. They also poured a seal of molten wax in the crack between the stone and the cave so that the stone could not be moved secretly. Then the guards sat down to watch through the Sabbath and into the night.

HE IS RISEN!

The Tomb Is Opened

IT WAS THE darkest and loneliest hour of the night, the time when it seemed that all light had gone from the sky. The moon had set, and the eastern sky showed no sign of approaching dawn. The Roman soldiers saw each other only as dark shadows against the far-off stars. They shivered in the coolness of the night. "Why do we have to pull this night shift, anyway?" one of them grumbled. "Of all the rotten luck."

For the Romans, who believed that spirits of the dead could roam the earth, standing guard over a tomb was unpleasant duty at best. The darkness did not help. "What time do you suppose it is?" another of the soldiers asked, more to hear the sound of a human voice than to know the time.

"It must be five o'clock in the morning by now," answered the first. "Only an hour at most till dawn."

The guards fell silent again and continued their lonely vigil. Suddenly one of the watching soldiers gasped. "Listen!" he hissed. "What was that?"

"Oh, Horatio, you're always hearing things."

"No, really. Listen. It sounds like thunder."

There was a distant rumbling. They could hear it clearly now, and it got louder and louder. Then they could feel it coming, not from the sky but from the ground. "It's an earthquake!" one of the soldiers shouted. "Get away from the trees!" They dove to the ground as the earth began to shake. Branches broke off trees and rocks rolled down the hillside. At the height of the quake, the guards suddenly saw a brilliant light—not the

momentary flash of lightning, but a steady glow. As the rumbling died away, the glow remained. The frightened soldiers looked up and saw a sight that struck terror in their hearts.

Seated on the stone of Jesus' tomb was a man in a white robe that glowed more brightly than any moon. He had rolled the stone aside, and the grave stood open like a yawning black mouth. At the sight of the angel and the open tomb, the soldiers fainted with fear and fell to the ground as if they were dead.

Easter Morning

MARY MAGDALENE WOKE with a start. Her bed was shaking, and the dishes in the cupboard were rattling. Then the rumbling passed, but Mary could not go back to sleep. Besides, it was nearly dawn. She woke up Mary (James's mother) and Salome, and in the early morning darkness, with the light of an oil lamp, the three women gathered their spices and ointments and the strips of linen cloth they would take to Jesus' grave. By the time they left the house, the eastern sky was already glowing red with the dawn. Near the city gate they were nearly run over by a troop of Roman soldiers who were running into the city as fast as they could. "Do you think they are after John and the others?" Mary Magdalene asked.

"I don't know," answered Salome. "But why should they be coming from outside the city?" There was no answer to her question, and the women continued on toward the garden where Jesus was buried.

At the gate to the garden, Mary Magdalene stopped short. "What about the stone?" she asked in dismay. "We forgot about the stone. We'll never be able to move it ourselves. We should have brought John with us."

"It would take more than one person to move that stone," said the other Mary. "But we could try. We'll be at the tomb in a moment anyway, and—" Her breath caught in her throat. Then she managed to gasp, "Look! The grave is open! Who could have done that?"

"Perhaps Joseph got here first—or Nicodemus," Mary Magdalene answered. "I'll run ahead and see." She hurried to the tomb and stooped to go inside. A moment later she was running toward her friends, a look of anguish on her face. "He's gone!" she wailed.

"What do you mean, he's gone?"

"He's gone, someone has stolen his body! Oh, couldn't they even leave him alone after he was dead? We have to tell Peter and John!" And before the others could stop her, Mary Magdalene was running back toward the city.

The two women had no chance to think about their companion. A strange sight caught the attention of Mary, the mother of James. "Look at those two men over there," she said. Her friend Salome looked, and then they both began to tremble. The two men approached with robes shining as bright as the sun, and the women fell to the ground in fear.

"Why are you looking for the living where the dead are kept?" one of the men asked.

"Sir, we—uh, we were looking for—" Mary stammered.

"I know who you are looking for. Jesus of Nazareth, who was crucified. He is not here."

"Where have they taken him?"

"He has risen, just as he said he would," the angel replied. "Go on in and look at the place where he was lying." But the women could only stand mute, looking at the tomb. "Go back and tell his disciples, and especially Peter, that he has risen."

Scarcely believing what they had heard, the two women turned and hurried toward Jerusalem. By this time Mary Magdalene had already reached the city and was pounding on the door of the house where Peter and John were staying. "Wake up! Peter, wake up!"

"Who's there?" came a sleepy voice from inside.

"It's Mary! Mary Magdalene. Something terrible has happened. Peter, John, open up!"

In a moment the door opened, and John peered out. When he saw her frightened look he asked anxiously, "Mary, what's the matter?"

"They have stolen the Master's body!"

John was suddenly wide awake. "Stolen his body? What are you talking about?"

"I went to the tomb this morning with Mary and Salome, and someone had opened the grave. His body is gone, and we don't know where they have taken it. Oh, John, who would do such a terrible thing?"

John's mind was racing, but he had no answer. "We'd better go and see for ourselves. Peter! Hurry up!" The two of them set out at a run for the garden, but John was faster and was already peering into the tomb from the outside when Peter arrived. "It's true, Peter," he said. "There's no one there. Only the graveclothes lying on the stone shelf."

"Let me see." Peter pushed John aside and went right into the tomb. There on the slab, just as John had said, were the linen graveclothes, still

213

wrapped in the shape of a body—but empty. The linen cloth that had covered his face lay neatly folded in a corner.

Then it began to dawn on John what Jesus had meant when he spoke of dying and rising again. Their minds still spinning in excitement, they made their way back to the city. On the way they missed Mary Magdalene, who had taken another path to the garden. When she came to the tomb, she found no one there. And she began to weep again, torn by her belief that someone had stolen the body of Jesus.

Once more Mary stooped down to look into the empty tomb; but this time it was not empty. Two men, dressed in white robes, were sitting on the rock shelf where the body of Jesus had lain. One sat near the head of the graveclothes, the other at the feet. Startled, Mary stumbled backward against the wall of the cave. "Why are you crying?" one of the angels said to her, and his voice was so gentle that she lost some of her fear.

"They have taken my Lord away," she said, and she began to weep again. "I don't know where they have taken him." She turned then and went out of the tomb. There she saw another man, who turned to her and asked the same question: "Woman, why are you crying? Who are you looking for?"

"Oh, sir," she said, "did you see anyone come to the tomb this morning? You are the gardener here, aren't you? Do you know where they have taken my Lord?"

"Mary," he said. He spoke only one word, but in that instant she knew. That voice! She knew that voice! Her heart was beating wildly as she looked up into his face. Yes, it was Jesus! "Oh, Master," she cried out, and she knelt down and grabbed him tightly around the legs.

"Don't cling to me," Jesus said. "You will never lose me again, although I must still go to my Father. Go to my brothers now, and tell them that I am going to my Father and your Father, to my God and your God." Mary kept holding on to him. He reached down and lifted her head so that she faced him again, and said, "You may not have me only for yourself, Mary. Go now, and tell my brothers." At last she got up and went back toward Jerusalem, and soon her heart was singing.

Far ahead of her, the other Mary and Salome were walking and still talking about what the angel had said to them at the tomb, trying to understand. Just then, a man met them on the road. He looked familiar—and when he spoke they knew his voice. "Oh, Master, it's really true!" they exclaimed, and they bowed down in front of him. "You really are alive again! O Lord, our faith was so small!"

"Don't be afraid," Jesus told them. "Go tell my brothers that I am going on to Galilee, and they will see me there."

So the women hurried on to Jerusalem, their hearts bursting with the good news that Jesus had risen from the grave.

Bribing the Soldiers

"YOU DON'T SUPPOSE it could be true, do you?" He was pacing back and forth, this worried member of the Sanhedrin, trying to decide what the soldiers' story meant. "After what those soldiers told us—well, what *did* happen out there?"

"They fell asleep, that's what happened," Caiaphas fumed. "Those Romans can't do anything right! Wait till their commanding officer hears about this!"

"No!" The voice of Annas was sharp. "That's the worst thing we could do. We can't have them spreading these wild stories all over Jerusalem. We have to think of something."

"You're right, of course," Caiaphas said. "I think I know what we can do. Send the soldiers back in."

They were Roman soldiers, occupation troops standing before the leaders of a conquered people, but they were nervous. "You were sent to

215

guard a tomb," Caiaphas said sternly, "but you couldn't keep those followers of Jesus from stealing his body. I could have your necks for falling asleep on duty."

"But we didn't fall—" they began, but Caiaphas cut them off.

"Be glad that we are treating this incident with such understanding," he said. "We know this has been an exhausting time for us all. We can understand how this happened. But it would be such a shame if Governor Pilate heard that you had failed in your duty. Do you get my meaning?" The men looked at each other and nodded. "Good, good. Now, if anyone asks you what happened," Caiaphas went on, "you will say that you had been on duty too long and you fell asleep. While you were sleeping, some followers of Jesus stole his body. We will, of course, be willing to pay you extra, because of the, uh, the obvious nervous strain you suffered spending the night next to a tomb."

"But sir," one of the soldiers asked, "what if Pilate does hear about this? This man was a Roman prisoner."

"Don't worry," Caiaphas assured them. "If the governor hears of it, we will explain it to him. You won't suffer for this. That is, if we can agree as to what happened in that garden, of course."

"Yes, of course," they quickly said. "We were sent out on night duty without relief after a hard day's work, and we fell asleep, and someone stole the body." So the soldiers took their extra pay. And after that, if anyone asked the Sanhedrin what had happened to the body of Jesus, they could say, "His disciples stole it. Ask the Roman soldiers. They were there."

MY LORD, AND MY GOD!

The Road to Emmaus

IT WAS A seven-mile walk from Jerusalem to the little town of Emmaus. Cleopas, one of Jesus' followers, was on his way home. He could not shake off the gloom of the events in Jerusalem during Passover week. He was glad to have a friend along, another follower of Jesus, someone he could share his feelings with. What did it all mean? What would they do next? They argued, as friends will, about the things Jesus had said and done.

In the midst of their lively conversation, a stranger fell in with them on the road. "What were you talking about so excitedly?" he asked.

"Do you mean to tell me," Cleopas said, "that you have been in Jerusalem this Passover and don't know what happened?"

"What do you mean?" the stranger said.

"We're talking about Jesus of Nazareth," the friend explained. "He was a prophet of the Lord who did great wonders for all the people to see."

"But our own leaders and chief priests handed him over to the Romans," Cleopas added. "They condemned him to death by crucifixion. We were hoping that he was the one God had sent to set Israel free."

"And that isn't all," said the friend. "This is the third day since that happened, and this morning some women from our group brought us some amazing news. They went to his tomb this morning before sunrise, but the body wasn't there. They told us a story about seeing a vision of angels who told them that Jesus is alive! Some of the men went to the tomb and found it empty, just as the women had said. But they didn't see Jesus."

"I don't think you have understood at all," the stranger said. "Don't you know that the prophets said the Messiah would have to suffer before he entered into his glory?" The two travelers were quite surprised. They had never seen this man among the followers of Jesus. How did he know so much? "Let me explain it to you," the stranger said. He began to speak to them from Scripture, quoting again and again from the prophets as he told them about the Messiah. They were so enthralled by what he was saying that they were sorry to reach a fork in the road; it appeared that the stranger was going to take the other road.

"Won't you come into the village and stay the night with us?" Cleopas asked. "Night will fall soon, and we would like to hear more from you." So the stranger went with them into Emmaus. When they came to Cleopas' house and sat down to eat, Cleopas asked the stranger courteously, "Would you say the blessing, please?"

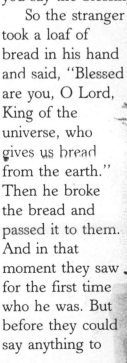

So the stranger took a loaf of bread in his hand and said, "Blessed are you, O Lord, King of the universe, who gives us bread from the earth." Then he broke the bread and passed it to them. And in that moment they saw for the first time who he was. But before they could say anything to him, he vanished from their sight, leaving them gaping in amazement.

"We should have known!" Cleopas said at last. "His words to us on the road set me afire!"

"Back to Jerusalem, right away," his friend said. "We have to tell the disciples the news!"

Fear Turns to Joy

THE SUN WAS just setting, but the windows were shuttered and the room was dark and gloomy where the disciples huddled together in fear. The door was barred, and they kept their conversation to low tones so that no one in the street could hear that there were people inside. At every unfamiliar sound the disciples fell silent and listened intently, fearing that soldiers might be coming to arrest them. As the sound passed, they would relax slowly and begin to talk again.

"You still don't really believe me, do you, James?" It was John asking his brother the question.

"I'm not convinced, John," his brother replied. At that moment there was a quiet knock at the door. It was Andrew, with his brother Simon Peter. James and John did not look up as Nathanael went to let them in.

"Don't you remember how Lazarus came out of the tomb?" John asked. "And how Jesus brought that widow's son back to life? Don't you think he can rise from the dead himself?"

"I think that if he were really alive, he would have shown himself to us," replied Matthew.

"Yes, where is he?" Jude added. "Why hasn't one of us seen him?"

"One of us has." All eyes turned in the direction of the booming voice they knew so well. It was Peter, his face flushed with excitement. He was smiling for the first time since the night he denied knowing his Lord. "I have seen him."

James was shaken. "How do you know it was Jesus? What did he say to you?"

Peter started to reply, but there was another knock at the door, a sharp and unexpected rap that startled them all. What if it was the Romans? James walked softly to the door and asked in a whisper, "Who is it?"

"It's Cleopas! Let us in!" came the shout from the other side of the door.

James quickly opened the door for Cleopas and his friend. "Where have you been?" he asked.

"We have seen the Lord!" Cleopas cried out.

"You too!" Peter exclaimed.

John leaned forward eagerly. "Are you sure? Where?"

"In Emmaus! We ran almost all the way back to tell you. Just let me catch my breath. You see, we were sitting down to eat, and—no, no, I'd better start at the beginning." The disciples gathered around him, listening intently to every word as Cleopas told them about the stranger who had joined them on the road to Emmaus. Both hope and disbelief were written on their faces as he spoke. "But when he broke the bread," Cleopas finished, "we suddenly recognized him. And then he was gone!"

"Gone?" asked Andrew. "Gone where?"

"Just gone! Vanished!"

"Vanished? Human bodies don't just vanish." This was Matthew again. "If you saw anything, it was a ghost."

"Don't be afraid," said a voice behind them. "Peace be with you." Suddenly white with fear, they turned and saw a man who a moment before had not been in the room. But the doors and windows were locked!

"I told you it was a ghost!" Matthew shouted. "There it is now!"

"God save us all!" James cried out, and as he stepped backward, he tripped and fell.

"Why are you so frightened?" Jesus asked them. "Look at my hands and my feet. See, the nail holes are still there. It really is me. Touch me, Matthew. A ghost doesn't have flesh and bones as I do."

"Oh, Lord," Matthew exclaimed, "is it really you?"

"Are you still not convinced?" Jesus asked. "Didn't Mary Magdalene and the others tell you what I said to them?"

"Yes, Lord," John answered, "but we—"

"You didn't believe them." The disciples looked down, ashamed. "Do you have something to eat?" Jesus asked.

"We have some broiled fish here," Nathanael said. Jesus took some of the fish and ate it. Now there could be no doubt. This was no ghost. It was Jesus—in the flesh! Suddenly there was pandemonium, everyone shouting and crying all at once, crowding around Jesus, touching him, hugging him, hugging each other, filled with more joy than they had ever known, more than they knew how to express. Tears streamed down their cheeks as they greeted their risen Lord.

"Peace!" Jesus said at last. Slowly the noise and excitement died down. "Once more I say, Peace be unto you. I am sending you out into the world, just as the Father sent me. You must preach this good news to all the nations of the world." Then he was gone again.

"We must go and tell Thomas," Andrew said at last. "Wait until he hears! Jesus has risen from the dead! He is alive!"

Jesus Appears to Thomas

"NO! I STILL don't believe it!" This was Thomas, the one disciple who was not present when Jesus appeared to the others. "I know, I know, I've heard all the stories. I know what you think you saw. But I just can't believe it's true." The disciples were together in the home where James and John were staying. A week had passed since the morning Mary Magdalene came running from the tomb, crying that Jesus' body had been stolen. "Mary was all worked up that morning, and so were the other women," Thomas went on.

"We've been through all that," Peter answered him. "I know you think I was having dreams too. But what about Cleopas?"

"As I say, Peter," Thomas answered, "it just doesn't convince me. For instance, did anyone recognize him at first? They thought he was a stranger. Did we have any trouble recognizing Lazarus when he came out of the grave? No, I think they saw someone who looked a little like Jesus, and they wanted so badly to believe it was he that they convinced themselves."

"But what about all the rest of us? There are fifteen of us in all now who have seen him face to face. Don't you remember what he said before he died? He said, 'I must go to Jerusalem, where I will be handed over to the gentiles and put to death, but on the third day I will rise again.' He told us! We just didn't take him at his word."

"Thomas, believe us!" Now it was John who joined in the conversation.

When Thomas turned to answer John, he was close to tears. "It's not that I don't want to believe. I do! But I can't buy your stories about Jesus rising from the dead. And I won't believe until I see him for myself, put my finger into the nail hole in his hand, and touch the wound in his side. Then I will believe, but not before!"

"Then why wait any longer, Thomas?" came a gentle voice. The disciples turned and saw their risen Lord! The faces of those who had seen him before lit up with joy, but Thomas was amazed and bewildered.

"Don't be afraid, Thomas," Jesus said. "Here is my hand. Touch the hole the nail left there. Put your hand into the wound in my side. Don't go on any longer in your unbelief, but believe."

Thomas felt his knees buckling under him, and he reached out to hold the Lord's hand for support. His doubts were gone. He no longer needed to touch the wounds. He had seen the Lord with his own eyes. "My Lord!" Thomas said. "My Lord, and my God!"

Jesus looked at him intently. "You became a believer because you saw me," he said. "Blessed are those who have never seen me, yet still have believed!"

Gone Fishing

IT WASN'T LIKE the old days—when they traveled with Jesus, ate with him, and worked with him. Now he only came to them once in a while, and when he was gone, they never knew where to find him. They were convinced that Jesus had risen from the dead, but what did it mean? What should they do now? In the old days they had followed him everywhere. Now they did not know where he was, and he had not told them what to do. With each passing day Simon Peter grew more impatient. Finally one evening he said, "I don't know about the rest of you, but I'm going fishing."

"Why not?" said James and John. "Let's all go."

They returned to Lake Galilee and found Zebedee's boat. They gathered their gear, sailed out onto the lake, and spent the whole night fishing. But by the time it was morning, they still had not caught a thing. Just before dawn, as they were giving up in discouragement, they saw a man standing on the shore. "Have you caught anything, fellows?" he called.

"No, not a thing," the disciples answered.

"Try lowering your nets on the other side of the boat. I think you'll catch something."

"What do we have to lose?" Peter asked, shrugging his shoulders. So they lowered the net over the other side of the boat. When they tried to pull it in, it was so full of fish that they couldn't lift it.

Suddenly Peter straightened up. "It's the Lord!" he shouted. He dropped the net, grabbed his robe, jumped into the water, and swam furiously toward the shore. The others followed as quickly as they could, rowing the boat and dragging the net full of fish behind them. By the time they got to land, there was already a hot bed of coals waiting for them, with some fish filleted and broiling on the fire, and bread to be eaten with the fish.

Peter was waiting on shore, ready to help the others pull in the net. In spite of the great size of the catch, the net was not broken. Then Jesus said, "Come and have breakfast with me." So they ate with him, and not one of them said, "Who are you?" because they knew it was the Lord. This was the third time he had appeared to them since his resurrection.

"Follow Me"

WHEN THEY HAD finished eating, Jesus turned suddenly to Peter and asked, "Simon, do you love me more than these others do?" Peter squirmed uncomfortably. He had always been the first to rush ahead. But ever since that terrible night of his denial, he had not been sure if he could rely on his own feelings about anything. And Jesus had used such a strong word: *love*. "Lord, you know that I am your friend," Peter finally replied.

"Then feed my lambs," Jesus said. He paused for a moment, then turned his head a little to one side and said again, "Simon, son of John, do you love me?"

Peter looked into Jesus' eyes, then looked away. "Lord, you know that I am your friend," he said again, and this time his voice showed his discomfort.

"Then care for my sheep," Jesus said. Then once more he looked at

Peter, and with a touch of sadness in his voice he said, "Simon, *are* you my friend?"

"Lord, you know everything!" Peter cried out, hurt that Jesus had stopped using the word *love*. "You know that I am your friend!"

"Then feed my sheep. Peter, when you were young, you got dressed and walked wherever you wanted to go. But when you are old, someone else will dress you and take you where you do not want to go." Peter did not understand, but Jesus was telling him that one day he would die for his faith. Then Jesus added one more thing. "Peter, follow me."

Peter looked around and saw the other disciples staring at him. Hoping to draw attention away from himself, he pointed to John and said, "Lord, what should he do?"

"Never mind about him," Jesus answered. "You follow me."

During the month that followed Jesus was with his disciples often, teaching them about himself and helping them understand Scripture. They began to see the meaning of many of the things he had said before he died, things that had been a mystery to them at the time. "I am teaching you," Jesus said to them one day, "so that you will be able to go out into the world, just as the Father sent me into the world."

With their doubts laid to rest, they were able to listen and learn, and their faith grew stronger day by day. They began to understand that their task was still the same one he had given them at the first. "Follow me," he had said to each of them when he first came teaching through Galilee. Now he was saying it again: "Follow me!" And that's what the disciples would do, spreading the word and work of Jesus all over the world.

VI.
The Book
of Acts

One of the four Gospels was written by a doctor named Luke as a letter to someone he called "Theophilus," which means "one who loves God." It may have been written to one actual person, or symbolically to all who were eager to know about the Lord Jesus. In either case, Luke said that his Gospel was about "the things which Jesus began to do and to teach." Later Luke wrote a second letter, one that told what Jesus continued to do and teach through those who believed in him. We call this letter the book of the Acts of the Apostles, or just the book of Acts.

There were many surprises for the disciples in the last months they were with Jesus, but one of the greatest surprises was yet to come. Jesus went back to his Father; but before he went, he commanded his disciples to be his witnesses in Judea, in Samaria, and to the ends of the earth. Then God gave them the power to do that by sending his Holy Spirit to live in all those who believed in Jesus.

The Holy Spirit gave them a place in a new kind of community, the fellowship of believers. They found themselves living a kind of life they could not have imagined before, and many people were attracted to it. Beginning in Jerusalem, and moving outward in ever-widening circles, the church of Jesus Christ began to grow.

But from the very beginning there was trouble. At first it was the Jewish leaders who opposed them. But as soon as the gospel reached outside the Jewish community, the leaders of other religions opposed the message too. Opposition began to come from inside the church as well, as Satan kept trying to destroy the work of Jesus. But in the power of God's Holy Spirit, the church overcame these forces and continued to spread the gospel, just as Jesus had commanded: beginning in Jerusalem, and outward to Judea, to Samaria, and to the ends of the earth.

If Jesus had only lived and died, his story would have been swallowed up in history and lost forever. But when he went to be with his Father and sent his Spirit, the effect was like dropping a pebble into a still pond. The ripples spread outward to the very edges, beginning where the pebble had been dropped—in Jerusalem.

THE PEBBLE IS DROPPED

Jesus Returns to the Father

"THE TIME HAS come," Jesus said to his disciples one day. Forty days had passed since Jesus rose from the dead, days in which doubt had turned to faith, days in which the disciples had learned more about the real meaning of what Jesus had done. Yet some had never given up the hope that he would be a king like the kings of other nations. Perhaps, they thought, now that he was risen, he will become the glorious king.

"Lord," one of them asked on the way to the mountain, "is this the time you will restore the kingdom to Israel?"

"The kingdom is coming," Jesus answered, "but it is for the Father to say when and how. First the Holy Spirit of God will come upon you, and you will receive power. You will be eyewitnesses of me and my kingdom, first in Jerusalem, then in Judea, then in Samaria, and to the far corners of the earth."

"What do you have in mind, Lord? When do we start?"

"Be patient," Jesus answered. "Stay in Jerusalem until power from heaven comes upon you."

They were nearly at the top of the mountain now. They walked on in silence, each lost in his own thoughts. At the crest of the hill, Jesus turned to speak to his disciples one last time. "The Father has given me all authority and power, both in heaven and on the earth. So when you go out into the world, preach the good news to the whole creation, and make disciples in all the nations. Baptize them in the name of the Father, the Son, and the Holy Spirit. Teach them to do all the things that I have commanded you. And don't be afraid. Remember, I will always be with you, as long as the world itself shall last."

The disciples gazed at Jesus, knowing that they were seeing him for the last time. Jesus raised his arms and touched their heads in blessing. And then, as the disciples watched in amazement, the shining cloud of God's glory surrounded him and took him out of their sight.

They were still staring after him when two angels suddenly appeared beside them, dressed in white robes. "Why are you looking up at the sky?" one of them asked. "You won't see him again this day. But one day this same Jesus will come again in the same way you saw him leave." Then the angels too were gone.

The disciples were alone now. Jesus' time with them on earth had ended as it had begun, with a visible sign of God's favor. When Jesus had begun his ministry, John the Baptist had seen the Holy Spirit descending on him in the form of a dove, and had heard a voice from heaven saying, "This is my Son, the one I love, the one with whom I am well pleased." Now the disciples had seen God raise Jesus to the highest place, the place at his own right hand. And they had heard the promise. Their Master was coming back. The day was still to come when every knee would bend before him and every tongue would confess that he is the Lord.

In the meantime they had a job to do. And so, filled with wonder and joy, they went back to Jerusalem to wait for the gift of the Holy Spirit. They spent their time praying together, along with the others who knew Jesus, including Mary, Jesus' mother, and a number of other women. They often spent their days in the temple praising God. Some of the priests and other Jewish leaders who saw them were amazed. How could these people be so happy when their Messiah was dead and gone? It troubled them deeply. "Perhaps," said one of the priests to his friends one day, "perhaps we have not yet heard the last of that Jesus of Nazareth."

God Gives His Holy Spirit

THERE WERE ONLY eleven disciples now, since Judas had killed himself. But it seemed right to them that there should be twelve again, the number Jesus had chosen, the number of the tribes of Israel. It was Peter who suggested it first when he spoke to the whole group of Jesus' followers in Jerusalem, about a hundred and twenty of them. Two names were put forward: Joseph, known as Barsabbas, and Matthias. After praying for guidance, the disciples drew lots, and the lot fell to Matthias, one who had been with them from the beginning, when Jesus was baptized by John, until the end, when they saw him risen from the dead. Now there were again twelve apostles, as Jesus had called them, eyewitnesses to his life and death and resurrection.

Ten days after Jesus went back to the Father, the Jewish feast of Pentecost, the feast of the new harvest, was held. On that day, the first loaves of bread made from the new grain were baked and taken to the temple. The first loaves were given to God as a sign that everything belonged to him, the one who made the grain grow, the one who blessed the work of his people.

The apostles and the others who knew Jesus joined the crowds of people streaming into the temple courtyard that day. They made quite a crowd, these faithful Jerusalem followers. They met in a hall close to the temple to thank the Lord for the rich harvest he had given that year, and to pray for the special harvest the Lord Jesus had promised them.

While they were praying, there came a strange sound, like the rushing

of a strong wind. It filled the room until it seemed that the walls themselves began to shake. Suddenly something that seemed like a flame of fire swept into the room; it divided up, and a small flame came to rest on each of them. It all happened so fast that they scarcely had time to be frightened.

The disciples were not the only ones who heard the noise. In the streets and in the courtyard of the temple, people looked up at the sound and then ran to see where it was coming from. There were Jews from all over the world, people who spoke many different languages, in Jerusalem for Pentecost. When they reached the place where the followers of Jesus were gathered, they found them all telling the message of Jesus, and every person heard it spoken in his own language!

"Aren't these men from Galilee?" asked a Jew from Egypt, speaking in Hebrew.

"Yes, they are," answered one from Rome.

"Then how does that one come to be speaking my own Egyptian language?"

"I don't know. But that one over there is speaking Latin!"

"That's Greek I hear," shouted a man from Athens.

No matter where in the world the person had come from, one of the disciples could speak that language, even though none of them had ever spoken a language other than Hebrew before in their lives. The Holy Spirit had come upon them like a wind from heaven, and had given them the power to speak those languages. God had kept his promise! Everyone standing there heard the good news about Jesus spoken in his own language.

But some of those standing there heard only the confusion of dozens of languages being spoken all at once. It sounded like the Tower of Babel all over again. "These men are drunk," they said. "They can't even talk straight any more!"

Peter heard what they were saying, and he held up his hands for silence. Gradually the noise died down so that everyone could hear Peter's voice. "Fellow Jews, listen to me! These men aren't drunk! It's only nine o'clock in the morning. What happened this morning is what the prophet Joel talked about when he said,

> In the last days, God says,
> I will pour out my Holy Spirit,
> And your sons and daughters will prophesy.
> I will show signs in heaven and signs on earth,
> Before the great day of the Lord comes.
> But whoever calls on the name of the Lord shall be saved.

"Listen, Israelites! Jesus of Nazareth did those signs that the prophet Joel wrote about. They proved he came from God. You all know that. God decided to put him into your hands, and you nailed him on a cross and murdered him! But God wouldn't allow death to keep him. He raised Jesus to life again on the third day. We are all eyewitnesses! Every one of us has seen him alive again! Now he has gone to be at the right hand of God. But he has sent us the Holy Spirit. That is what you are seeing and hearing this morning. Now there can't be any doubt. This Jesus, whom you crucified, God has declared to be Lord and Christ!"

Upon hearing Peter's words, many of those Jews became fearful. They knew what had happened to Jesus. They knew in their hearts that he came from God. But they had stood by while their own leaders turned him over to the Romans to be executed. Some of them had stood in the court of judgment and shouted to Pilate, "Crucify him! Set Barabbas free!" Now they could see that they had sent God's Messiah to his death.

"What can we do?" they cried.

"Repent! Turn away from your wicked ways!" Peter answered. "Be baptized in the name of Jesus Christ so that your sins may be forgiven and you may receive the gift of the Holy Spirit. God's great promise is to you and to your children, and to all those the Lord will call to himself."

They crowded around to hear Peter, and he told them how all of Scripture talked about Jesus, and how he was the Redeemer God had promised to Adam, Abraham, and Moses. That very day three thousand of them were baptized, Jews from every part of the world. Although they came from so many different backgrounds, the Holy Spirit brought them together as one body. They met every day after that in the open marketplace to hear the apostles teach them more about the kingdom of God. And every day more of them believed in Jesus and were baptized.

The love of Jesus was so real to these new believers that they took care of each other's every need. They no longer kept their own possessions to themselves: they believed that everything they had came from God and was given for the benefit of all. Their hearts were filled with warmth and generosity as they shared meals together in their homes. None of them went without food or clothing, no matter how poor they were. And all the other Jews of the city respected them, because they saw how much they loved each other.

A Crippled Man Walks Again

THE POWER OF the Holy Spirit was plain to see among these believers in Jerusalem. Many were healed of their diseases, and the power of evil spirits was broken.

Peter and John were on their way to the temple one afternoon for three o'clock prayers. When they came to one of the gates of the temple, the "Beautiful Gate" as it was called, they saw a crippled man who was carried there every day so that he could beg for money from those going into the temple.

"Help a poor cripple," the man said to them. "Please help."

Peter and John looked at him. God's law said that there should be no beggars in Israel. Yet here was one, right at the gate of the temple itself, as if to show the world how little attention the people of Israel paid to the law of God. Suddenly Peter knew what he should do. God was going to use this poor crippled man to show how much he cared. "Look at me!" Peter said. The man looked up, smiling, and held out his hand for a coin. But Peter shook his head. "I don't have any money," he said. The man frowned and started to drop his hand. "But I will give you what I do have," Peter went on. "In the name of Jesus Christ of Nazareth, get up and walk!" The man looked at him in amazement and disbelief, but Peter reached down and took him by the hand. He lifted the man to his feet, and at that very

moment his feet and ankles became strong again. He could walk!

Never had a happier man been seen in the temple. He kept running and jumping around, hugging Peter and John, and shouting thanks to God. He made such a commotion that soon a crowd of people gathered around to see what was going on. It was almost embarrassing the way he was hanging onto Peter, and then leaping and dancing around Solomon's Porch, only to run back and hug Peter and John again.

Finally Peter turned to the crowd and said, "Why are you so surprised? Why keep staring at us as if we made him walk through our own power? God did this—the God of Abraham and Jacob. He did it to honor his servant Jesus, the same Jesus you turned over to Pilate and then rejected, even when Pilate had decided to let him go. You chose a murderer instead! You turned away from God's holy one, and you killed the prince of life! But God raised him from the dead, and we have all seen him alive again. The name of Jesus cured this man. You know him. You know he was a crippled beggar. But faith in Jesus has made him well again.

"Now, friends," Peter went on, "I know you didn't know what you were doing when you killed Jesus. But God had said by his prophets that his Messiah would have to suffer, and this is how the words came true. Now you must turn away from your sins and turn to God, so that your sins may be forgiven. Then you will know the kind of peace and strength God can give.

"Jesus is in heaven now. But the day will come when all things will be set right again. Then Jesus will return. For now, he wants you to come to God through himself. You are the sons and daughters of the prophets, the children of the people God chose. You have inherited the promises God made to them. That's why the good news that God has raised Jesus from the dead is coming to you first."

The people crowded around to hear Peter. But there were some Sadducees standing nearby, those who did not believe in the resurrection from the dead. It made them furious to hear anyone teaching that Jesus had been raised from the dead. With a nod to the temple guards, they began to move toward Peter and John. Then the guards broke into a run, pushed the startled crowds aside, and grabbed the two apostles.

"You're under arrest!" shouted the guard.

"Take them to prison and hold them overnight," ordered one of the priests. "Tomorrow they will answer to the Sanhedrin!"

But many of those who heard Peter speak in the temple that day believed in Jesus. Soon there were more than five thousand believers in Jerusalem!

Opposition from the Outside

"WHAT RIGHT DO you have to do this?" thundered Caiaphas, the high priest. "Whose name did you use? Whose power?"

Ever since he and John had been arrested the night before, Peter had been thinking about what he might say when he came up before the Sanhedrin. But he remembered what Jesus had said once. "They will drag you up in front of councils, but don't worry about what you will say. When the time comes, the Holy Spirit will speak through you." Even now, as he opened his mouth to answer Caiaphas, he could feel the power of the Holy Spirit.

"Are we being called before the Sanhedrin because we did a kindness for a poor cripple? I'll be glad to tell you how he was healed. It was done by the name of Jesus Christ of Nazareth, the one you crucified! But God has raised him from the dead, and his power has healed this man. Do you remember what David said in one of the psalms about the stone that was rejected by the builders but used by God for the foundation of the house? Jesus is the stone you rejected, but God has made him the foundation of his church. He is the only one who can save you."

The members of the council stared at Peter and John with unbelieving eyes. How did these common fishermen come to speak so well? And how did they know the Scriptures so well? Their only teacher had been Jesus of Nazareth! They wanted to give a sharp answer back, but they really could not think of anything to say. After all, there was the crippled man walking again, and who could argue with that? It made Caiaphas so frustrated that he shouted, "Get out! We'll decide what to do about you when we're alone!"

As soon as Peter and John were gone, Caiaphas turned to the others and asked, "What are we going to do with these men?"

"It's too late to do anything drastic," replied Annas. "The whole city has heard about it already."

"No one can doubt that a great miracle has happened," said Alexander, another member of the high priest's family. "But we can't have this teaching about Jesus spreading any further."

Caiaphas thought a moment, then said, "In that case, we'll warn them that if they do any more teaching in the name of this Jesus, it will be at their own risk. Call them back in." When Peter and John returned to the room he said, "We have decided to be lenient with you. We will not punish you in any way, because we feel that you acted in ignorance. However, we must warn you not to use the name of this Jesus anymore. He was a criminal, and Israel is well rid of him. If you continue to use his name, you will be guilty of his crimes. Do you understand?"

"We understand," John answered. "But that leaves us with a difficult decision. Shall we listen to you, or shall we listen to God? Judge for yourselves. How can we stop talking about the things we have seen and heard?"

"Be careful that you don't take the name of God in vain!" Caiaphas snapped. "We have warned you. Stop preaching in the name of Jesus, or your lives will be in danger."

"We have to obey God first, not men," Peter answered. Then he and John went back to the other disciples, leaving the members of the Sanhedrin frustrated and angry. But when the other believers heard about what had happened, they shouted, "Praise God!" And then one of them led the rest in prayer. "Lord, you have all power," he said. "You made heaven and earth. You spoke through our father David and said that the kings of the earth would rise up against you and against your chosen Messiah. Now those words have come true. Herod and Pontius Pilate, the leaders of Israel and the leaders of the Gentiles, have gotten together to oppose Jesus. You have heard their threats, Lord. Give us strength to speak out for you without being afraid. Give us the power to do many more signs and wonders in the name of Jesus, your holy servant. Amen."

Once again the house began to shake with the mighty wind of the Holy Spirit, just as it had on the day of Pentecost. They all went out and preached the Word of God, and they were not afraid.

Opposition from Within

BEGINNING IN JERUSALEM, the church was growing both in size and in the strength of the Lord. The power of the Holy Spirit had for the time being silenced those from outside who wanted to stop the spread of the gospel. The Spirit had joined the thousands of Christians in Jerusalem into a loving community. Every believer's house was open to all the others, and if people needed anything, they didn't even need to ask. No one said, "You can't have what belongs to me!" Instead, they all said, "What we have, the Lord has given to all of us."

A man named Joseph, a wealthy person from the island of Cyprus who owned a farm not far from Jerusalem, sold it and gave the money to the apostles to use. The apostles said to him, "Joseph, you have been a real encouragement to us. From now on, we will call you Barnabas, meaning 'son of encouragement.' "

This was the opening Satan used to try to break apart this new community from the inside. That very night, one of the couples in the group talked about what they had seen that day. "Ananias, did you see how happy Peter was today when Joseph brought him all that money?"

"I know, Sapphira," her husband answered. "It looks as if the people who bring money get all the attention these days."

"There's that piece of land we own outside of town. We could sell it and do what Joseph did."

"Sell it? Sapphira, that land is worth a lot of money. We can't afford to give all that away."

"Well, maybe we wouldn't have to give it *all* away. We can sell it and keep most of the money. We can take the rest to Peter, and everyone will see how generous we are."

"Do you think there's any way Peter would find out about it?" Ananias asked nervously.

"How would he find out?" his wife asked.

So the next day, the two of them arranged to sell the land. They kept most of the money, and Ananias brought the rest to Peter. "My wife and I have sold our land, Peter," he said. "Here is the money for you to use."

But the Holy Spirit had already told Peter what Ananias and Sapphira were up to. Instead of smiling and giving Ananias his blessing, Peter frowned at him and said, "Ananias, what made you think you could cheat the Holy Spirit? Did you really think God could be fooled?"

Ananias turned pale, and his hands began to tremble. "What are you talking about, Peter? I wouldn't lie to you. Here's the money."

"You didn't lie to me," Peter answered. "You tried to lie to God. The land was yours. No one made you sell it. You could have kept as much of the money as you needed. But you can't serve God and be out to glorify yourself." At these words Ananias fell down at Peter's feet and died.

"What a terrible way to have to see God's power," whispered one of the young believers standing nearby.

"God forgives those who turn away from their sins," Peter said to them, "but pretenders have no place among God's people." Then he added sadly, "Take Ananias out and bury him."

There was nothing strange to them in this request, for among the Jews it was the custom to bury a body as soon as possible after death. The young men wrapped the body, carried it out, and placed it in a tomb. So that's why Sapphira had not yet heard of her husband's death when she came into the same hall three hours later. She had waited a while so that no one would think she and Ananias were plotting anything. Then she could come in and see her husband in his new exalted position among the believers.

But when she came into the room, Ananias was nowhere to be seen. What in the world could have happened to him? Then she saw Peter, looking grim. He held out his hand with the money Ananias had given him in it. So her husband had been here after all.

"Tell me, Sapphira," Peter asked, "is this the amount you got for selling your land?"

"Yes, it is," she answered.

"So, you and your husband plotted this together!" he said angrily. "You decided to put the Holy Spirit of God to the test! What made you do it?" Sapphira was trapped in her own deceit. She had nothing to say. "Do you hear those footsteps?" Peter asked. "Those are the young men coming back from burying your husband. Now they will carry you out and bury you too!" And at that moment she collapsed at Peter's feet and died.

News of what had happened spread through the whole community. All

236

of the people stood in awe of God's power among them. Even when the powers of darkness tried to destroy the church from within, God was powerful against them, even to striking down those whom Satan tried to use.

God Frees the Prisoners

EVERY DAY THE believers in Jerusalem met in Solomon's Porch of the temple. There were so many of them now that no one could ignore them. But they were set apart, and the other Jews who came to the temple stayed far away from them—as if faith in Jesus were a disease that might be contagious! Yet every day more and more believers joined them.

The apostles were doing many great works. Once Jesus had said, "When I am gone, my followers will do greater works than I have done, because I will return to my Father." Now people would bring their sick friends and relatives out into the street, hoping that Peter or one of the other apostles would pass by. Even if only his shadow fell on them, they would be cured. And the people came not only from Jerusalem but also from the countryside around, bringing those who were sick and those who were controlled by evil spirits. All of them were made well.

But Jesus had also said, "If they hated me, they will hate you as well," and that saying also came true. The same Jewish leaders who had sent Jesus to his death were very angry about the things Jesus' followers were saying and doing. One day they became so furious that they had all twelve of the apostles arrested and thrown in jail with the common criminals.

But in the middle of the night an angel of the Lord came to them and opened the prison doors, even though they were locked tight. "Now go out into the city of Jerusalem," the angel said. "Go to the temple and tell the people about this new life in Jesus."

By the time they all got out of the jail, day was already dawning. So they set out for the temple, and when people began to arrive for the morning sacrifices, they began to teach them, just as John and Peter had before.

Meanwhile, the high priest was calling the Sanhedrin together, along with the whole Council of all the elders of Israel. They sent officers to the jail to bring the apostles in. But when the officers came back, they had only this to report: "We went to the jail, just as you said, and all the doors were locked tight, and the guard was posted outside. We asked him if he had seen anything during the night, and he said he hadn't. But when we went to the cell where these men were supposed to be, they weren't there."

"What do you mean, they weren't there?" demanded the high priest. "I sent them there myself. I watched them being marched away. They must be there!"

"I'm sorry, sir," said the captain of the officers apologetically, "but we did look everywhere for them. They are not in the prison."

"Then they must have escaped."

"But, sir, the doors were still locked, as I told you, and the guard was still standing outside."

"Confound it, man, I want to know where they are! I want to—wait a minute! What's going on here?" The high priest broke off in surprise as a captain from the temple guard hurried into the room and saluted. "Yes, yes, what is it?"

"Sir, those men you're looking for, the ones you had arrested yesterday? They are in the temple right now, teaching just as they were yesterday!"

"I told you they had escaped!" said the high priest triumphantly. "Go and bring them here. But be careful. Don't use too much force, or the people may stone you."

As it turned out, the guards did not have to use force at all. The apostles saw them coming and went along peacefully. But the high priest was anything but peaceful when he saw them. "I demand an explanation!" he shouted. "Not more than a week ago you stood in this very room, and I gave you strict instructions. You were not to teach anymore in the name of—in this name. And now look! You have filled the whole city with your teaching, and on top of that, you want to blame us for that man's death!"

"We would like to obey you, since you are the high priest of Israel," Peter said quietly, "but we must obey God first. The God of our fathers raised Jesus from the dead, after you had murdered him by nailing him on a cross. God has raised this man and set him at his own right hand as the Prince and the Savior who brings forgiveness of sins to Israel. We have seen Jesus alive and well, seen him with our own eyes. And God's Holy Spirit says the same thing."

Suddenly the whole room was a confusion of angry shouts. "Crucify them too!" someone shouted. "They are as bad as their master was!" said another. For a moment it looked as though they might drag the apostles out that very minute and stone them to death. But suddenly there was a new voice, louder and stronger than the others. "Quiet down!" it commanded. "Stop this noise! This is the Council of Israel, not a fish market. Quiet!" Heads turned to see who was speaking, and people stopped talking when they saw that it was Gamaliel, one of the most respected teachers among the Pharisees.

"Take those men out of here for a while," Gamaliel ordered. "I want to speak to this Council in private." When the apostles were gone, he turned back to the elders of Israel and said: "I must warn you that you nearly did something very foolish. Be careful what actions you take against these men. Don't you remember that fellow Theudas, who went around the countryside claiming to be a great leader? He had four hundred men following him at one time. But after he was killed, his followers were scattered and the whole thing came to nothing. And then there was that fellow Judas from Galilee, who stirred up a lot of people, but he died too, and his whole following disappeared.

"So let me give you a little advice. Leave these men alone. If you pay them too much attention, people will start to think they are important. If what they have to say is only human, the whole movement will end in nothing anyway. But if it comes from God, you can't stop them no matter what you do. You might end up fighting against God!"

The men on the Council thought this was good advice, so they called the apostles back in. "You disobeyed our orders," they said, "and you must be punished for that. And we must warn you again not to teach anymore in the name of this Jesus. Guards, take them out and whip them, and then let them go."

And that is exactly what happened. On the way home, although they were in great pain from the beating, the apostles sang songs and shouted thanks to God. "Remember what Jesus said about suffering?" Peter asked as they walked.

"Of course I do," said John. "I'll never forget it. He said, 'Happy are you when people beat you and say all kinds of evil things about you because of me, for your reward will be great.' And that's just what happened today."

So they went on their way, happy that God thought them worthy to suffer for the name of Jesus. Day after day, in the temple and at home, they never stopped telling the good news of Jesus Christ.

Servants of the Lord

THE DEATH OF Ananias and Sapphira did not end Satan's plots against the church. And it was money again that caused the next problem, but this time it involved many more of the believers. Many people had brought money to the apostles to be used for the care of the poor; but not everyone agreed with the way the money was being given out. Those who came from far countries, like Greece and Italy, complained that the poor and the widows from Judea were getting more money than the rest. The quarrel grew so fierce that it threatened to split up the community.

When the apostles heard about the problem, they took it right back to the whole body. "We don't have time to settle every argument that comes up," they said. "If we do, we won't have time to preach the Word of God. This is the time when some of you need to work to bring peace among the brothers and sisters. Now, this is what you should do. Look around among yourselves and find seven men whom everyone knows to be devoted to the Lord and filled with God's wisdom. Put them in charge of this money distribution, and we will be free to devote ourselves to prayer and preaching."

So the people chose seven men and brought them to the apostles. Among them were Stephen and Philip, men whom the Lord used to do great works. The apostles laid their hands on them and prayed for them, and appointed them to be *deacons*, a word which means "servants." "As servants of the Lord," the apostles said to them, "you must work hard to bring

brothers and sisters together and make sure that things are done in a way that doesn't divide the Lord's people." So the seven deacons settled the matter of how money was to be distributed to the poor and the widows, and the believers from every land once again lived together in harmony.

Once again, the Lord had saved his people from trouble arising within their own group, this time by appointing his servants to keep harmony among the brothers and sisters. So the good news continued to spread, and the number of believers continued to increase. There were even many priests from the temple who were beginning to believe in the Lord Jesus. And they all continued to serve the Lord together, praising him for the way he kept his promises.

THE CIRCLE GROWS WIDER

JESUS HAD SAID that Jerusalem was only the beginning. Very soon, events were to take place that would take the good news out of Jerusalem, on into Judea and Samaria, and even to the ends of the earth.

The Stoning of Stephen

STEPHEN WAS ONE of the deacons, whose task was to help keep peace within the community of believers. But he was also busy spreading the good news to those who had not heard. He went from one synagogue to another around Jerusalem, teaching as often as he was allowed. Many Jews who did not believe in Jesus tried to argue with him, but because of Stephen's wisdom, they always ended up sounding foolish. This made them so angry that they decided to get rid of him. They weren't able to discover anything he had done wrong, so they paid some worthless fellows off the street to bring false charges against him.

One day Stephen was teaching in a place called the "Synagogue of Free Men." He was trying to explain to the people that Jesus was the only one who could make them truly free. Suddenly the door of the synagogue burst open, and a troop of the temple guard seized Stephen and dragged him off to appear before the Sanhedrin.

"This man speaks against the temple and against the law," one of the false witnesses said. "His speeches are nothing but attacks on our religion."

"That's not all," said another. "We heard him say that Jesus of Nazareth will destroy this temple and change the customs Moses gave us."

Caiaphas, the high priest, looked at Stephen sternly and asked, "Are these accusations true?"

"My brothers, I will tell you what I have been teaching," Stephen said. He spoke up boldly, without any fear, because he was filled with the Holy Spirit. "When God called Abraham out of Ur, he didn't know where he was going. But God kept his promises. He gave him a son in his old age, Isaac, the father of Jacob, who became the father of all our people. This same God chose Moses to lead our people out of Egypt, when they were enslaved there."

Stephen's voice was stronger now, and his eyes sparkled, but there was no trace of anger in his voice. "This same Moses told the people of Israel, 'God will raise up a prophet from among you, a prophet like me.' He passed on the word of the Lord to the people, but they would not listen to him. They made a golden calf and brought sacrifices to it. They built the temple in this land and began to believe that they had God all to themselves. But the prophet Isaiah says, 'Heaven is God's throne, and the earth is his footstool. What kind of house can you build for God? He made everything with his own hand.'

"Don't you see what our own history tells us?" Stephen demanded. "The people of Israel have never listened to God! They have always resisted the Holy Spirit! Can you name a single prophet your ancestors did not persecute? They killed those who said God's holy one would come, and now in our own day you have betrayed and murdered the Redeemer himself. You are the men who received the law of God, and you are the ones who never kept it!"

There were screams and shouts in the room now. "Stop him! Don't listen to him! The man has blasphemed God!" But Stephen looked up toward heaven, and his whole face seemed to glow with joy. "Look!" he said. "The heavens are opened, and I can see Jesus standing at God's right hand!"

These words shot like arrows into the hearts of the crowd and made them furious. Some of them stuck their fingers in their ears and screamed, "I won't listen to another word! Shut him up! Kill him, kill him!" Roaring their fury, the mob rushed at Stephen and dragged him outside the city. They threw him to the ground and began to snatch up stones to kill him. But even in their fury they did not forget their laws. The "witnesses" who had testified that Stephen deserved to die would have to throw the first stones.

So the false witnesses stepped forward, took off their robes, and laid them at the feet of Saul, a Pharisee from the city of Tarsus, who approved of the execution. Then they picked up heavy stones to hurl at Stephen. But Stephen did not look away or try to run. Instead, he looked toward the heavens and said, "Lord Jesus, I am coming to you. Receive me now!" The first volley of stones caught him on the side of the head, and he crumpled to his knees, wounded and bleeding. Still he did not cry out against the men who were killing him. "Lord," he said, in a voice loud enough for all to hear, "forgive them for this sin." This only enraged the mob still further. The second volley of stones crushed Stephen's skull, and he fell to the earth—dead.

But the anger of the mob was still not satisfied. They stormed back into the city and were joined there by many others who hated Jesus. They attacked the houses of Christians all over the city, breaking down doors, smashing crockery and furniture, and dragging people out into the streets. Leading the mob was Saul of Tarsus. Mercilessly, he went from house to house, taking the temple guard with him to throw believers into prison. Many of them were beaten, and some were killed.

The city was in such an uproar that the Christians had to flee for their lives. Out into the countryside of Judea and Samaria they fled, taking refuge with friends, relatives, or anyone who would take them in. It seemed at first that Gamaliel's prediction was coming true. Jesus was dead, and his followers were scattered. But the church did not die, because it was God's own work. The power of the Holy Spirit was not stopped by the death of Stephen or by Saul's arrests. Wherever the scattered believers went, they took the good news with them.

One of those forced to leave Jerusalem was Philip, Stephen's friend and fellow deacon. He went into Samaria, the last place a Jew would have gone by choice, and preached about Jesus to the people there. The response was the same as it had been those first days in Jerusalem. Crowds came out to see the miracles Philip did and stayed to hear the message of the gospel. Crippled people walked again, blind people received their sight, and many were freed from the power of evil spirits. Hundreds of Samaritans believed in Jesus and became his disciples.

Saul did his best to destroy the church. But the Spirit of God used his persecution to spread the good news beyond Jerusalem, beyond Judea. Satan's efforts only served to help make the words of Jesus come true:

"You will be eyewitnesses to me in Jerusalem, and in Judea, and in Samaria, and to the far corners of the earth."

Simon the Magician

WHEN PHILIP CAME to Samaria, there was a magician there named Simon, who had the whole city in the palm of his hand. He made great claims for himself and did works of magic such as no one there had ever seen before. Many people had come out to consult him, and some of them said, "This man has great power from God."

When Philip came to Samaria, many people believed in Jesus. Some of those had been under the spell of Simon's magic for a long time; but when they believed Philip's message about the kingdom of God, they were baptized, and Simon found his followers drifting away. At length, Simon decided to find out what this was all about, and one day he went to hear Philip preach. He was astounded at what he heard and believed everything that Philip said. Simon was even baptized like the others, and he followed Philip everywhere, watching in amazement the miracles that were done through him.

Soon the apostles in Jerusalem heard that the Samaritans were believing the Word of God, so they sent Peter and John down to find out what was happening. When they arrived, they asked the new Christians, "Have you received the Holy Spirit?"

"No," they answered, "but we have been baptized in the name of Jesus." Then Peter and John prayed for them and laid their hands on them, and the Holy Spirit came upon them just as he had upon the believers in Jerusalem on the day of Pentecost. So God showed by his power that salvation in Jesus was truly given to everyone, no matter where they were born or what language they spoke. God was calling a new people to be his own.

But Simon the magician had eyes only for the power Peter and John had shown in the laying on of hands. He had to have that power for himself! So he came to Peter and John one day with a bag of money in his hand. "Give me that same power," he said, "so that when I lay my hands on people, they will receive the Holy Spirit. I will pay you well."

Peter turned on Simon, filled with fury! "May your money perish, and you with it! God's gift is not for sale! You will never have anything to do with the Holy Spirit as long as your heart is so wicked!" Simon stood in stunned silence, his face pale and his hands shaking. "There is only one hope for you," Peter went on. "Give up this wickedness of yours! Pray to the Lord that he will forgive you for your evil plans. I can see what you are like inside, envious of God's power and a prisoner of sin!"

Simon fell to his knees in front of Peter. "Oh please, will you pray for me too?" he begged. "Pray that this terrible thing will not happen to me!"

Then Peter and John showed Simon and the crowds around the wonderful power of God. After that they set out for Jerusalem, to bring the great news that the Word of God was spreading throughout Samaria. They stopped in many Samaritan villages themselves, preaching the message of Jesus, and many of the people believed.

Philip and the Ethiopian

FOR MANY MONTHS Philip had worked among the people of Samaria, bringing the good news of Jesus. But the gospel was not only for the Jews and the Samaritans. An angel of the Lord came to Philip and said, "Get up now and head south, down the road that leads from Jerusalem out to Gaza in the desert."

Philip obeyed at once, and set out on the desert road. It seemed very lonely on that road, especially after the crowds he had preached to in Samaria. Why on earth did the Lord send him out into this forsaken countryside?

Then in the distance Philip saw a plume of dust rising lazily into the air. Horses pulling a carriage! A beautiful carriage too, he saw as it drew closer, surrounded by servants. It was traveling slowly so that the tall, distinguished-looking black man traveling in it could read. He was in fact none other than the treasurer of Ethiopia, a country far to the south and west, beyond Egypt. He was one of the many from foreign nations who worshiped God and sometimes made pilgrimages to Jerusalem to worship.

It had been a long journey to Jerusalem, and he had stayed there for a long time, since he never expected to have another chance to go. Now he was on his way back to Ethiopia, carrying with him a priceless treasure, a scroll of the Jewish Scriptures. It was written in Greek, a language spoken by learned men all over the world. As the Ethiopian passed Philip slowly in his chariot, he was reading aloud from the book of the prophet Isaiah. The Holy Spirit said to Philip, "Go up to the chariot and speak to the man."

So Philip ran up beside the carriage and called out, "Do you understand what you are reading?"

The Ethopian looked up, surprised to hear a stranger's voice there in the desert. He ordered the carriage to halt, then turned to Philip and said, "How can I understand with no one to explain it to me?"

"I am a Jew," Philip answered, "and I have known the Scriptures since I was a small boy. Perhaps I can help."

"Then come up here beside me, by all means," the man said eagerly. "We can travel together, since we seem to be going the same way." Philip stepped up into the carriage, which again began its slow journey across the desert. "I was just reading this," the man explained, "when you spoke to me:

> He was led like a sheep to the slaughter.
> Just as a lamb is quiet before the one who shears him,
> So he did not open his mouth.
> He is humiliated, and there is no one to defend him.
> Who will ever talk about his descendants?
> Because his life on earth has been cut short.

"Now tell me, my friend, what does this mean? Is the prophet talking about himself or about someone else?"

"Not about himself," Philip answered. "He is talking about God's promised Savior, who would die like a sacrificial lamb to take away the sin of the world." Then Philip went on to open up the meaning of Scripture to him and to tell him that Jesus was the one the prophet was talking about.

The Ethiopian listened closely to every word. Everything he knew about himself, everything he had learned about the God of Israel, pointed to the truth of what Philip was saying. More than anything else, he wanted to be a citizen of God's kingdom. The Ethiopian gazed off into the distance for a moment, then suddenly pointed his finger in excitement. "Look over there! Stop the carriage!" As the carriage came to a halt, Philip's eyes followed his host's outstretched arm. He was pointing to a stream that ran through a rocky valley. "There is some water," he said. "Is there any reason why I shouldn't be baptized right now?"

"Not if that is what you really want," Philip answered. "Do you really want to follow Jesus?"

"I believe that he is the Son of God," the Ethiopian said. "What else can I do but serve him?"

So Philip led him down into the water. "Just as this water washes away the dust of the road," Philip said, "so the blood of Jesus Christ washes away your sins. The water will cover you. Going under the water is like dying; coming up from the water is like being raised from the dead, just as God raised Jesus from the dead. And you will rise from the water a new person, a follower of Christ. Now I baptize you in the name of the Father, and of the Son, and of the Holy Spirit."

Then they walked together toward the carriage, the Ethiopian dripping wet and bursting with joy. He turned to thank Philip, but there was no one there! He looked in every direction, but there was no sign of Philip. Then the Ethiopian broke into a smile. "It seems that Philip's job is finished," he thought, and he went on his way rejoicing, eager to tell everyone he met about the good news of Jesus Christ.

But Philip's work was not finished. The Lord had taken him away to the village of Azotus, where he brought the message of the gospel. And so he went from town to town on orders from the Holy Spirit, preaching the good news all the way to Caesarea.

The Conversion of Saul

SAUL WAS AN angry man. He had thought that the stoning of Stephen would put an end to this new community. But the believers were bolder than ever, and more and more people were listening to them! They had to be stopped! Whenever he heard of anyone listening to the message of Jesus, Saul rounded up the temple guard, raided the house, and dragged the Christians off to prison.

"This message is spreading all over Israel," he raged, striding angrily back and forth before the Sanhedrin. "We have driven them out of Jerusalem, but they just go to other towns and keep on saying the same sacrilegious things. I want permission to go down to Damascus and arrest everyone who is in this new Way."

"You are right, brother Saul," the Council agreed. "These men must be stopped. We will give you a letter to the synagogue at Damascus, telling them that we have given you the power to arrest any man or woman who lives according to the new Way."

So Saul got his men together and set out for Damascus. But as he traveled, he had time to think. Why did they do it? he wondered. Why did they go on talking about that man Jesus when they knew they could be thrown in jail? He could understand if they were preaching rebellion against the Romans. But they only talked about living a new kind of life rather than following the old tradition. And that was just the problem: the old ways were the only thing holding the people together now that they were under foreign rule; these Christians were a threat to the very life of the people of Israel. They had to be stamped out! Jesus was a dangerous rabble-rouser, that's all. Now that he was dead, why hadn't there been an end to it? Why did the news about him keep on going and growing? Why did his followers talk about him as if he were still alive? Was it possible that they were right and Saul was wrong? Saul shook his head in frustration. Nothing would distract him from his purpose.

Then suddenly the desert air around Saul blazed with light, a light so dazzling that it blotted out the sun. Saul cried out and threw up his arms in front of his eyes to shield them, but it was already too late. Blinded, he stumbled and fell to the ground. He heard his men crying out in fear and falling to the desert floor. Then he heard nothing.

Far away, through the darkness, Saul saw a small glow of light, which grew larger as it drew near him. Soon he saw that it was not a light but a man in shining clothes who came toward him and called his name: "Saul, Saul, why are you persecuting me?"

All at once, Saul was overtaken by a terrible fear: he was afraid of the answer, yet even more afraid not to ask. Saul said, "Sir, who are you?"

"I am Jesus, the one you are persecuting."

Something broke up inside Saul at those words. He could no longer resist. Jesus was the Messiah, the Son of God. The message of Jesus had been like a cattle prod, pushing him and jabbing him and telling him that he was going in the wrong direction. But he had been proud and stubborn, and he had wanted to silence the message and go on in his own way. Now he could no longer ignore Jesus: he was standing there in front of him, surrounded by the heavenly light that had blinded Saul. Jesus knew him through and through, knew how he had helped to kill Stephen, knew about the men and women he had thrown into jail, knew about his sins and his pride—and in these actions how Saul had persecuted the Son of God. What was left for him? In his agony he cried out, "Lord, what can I do?"

"I have chosen you, Saul," Jesus said. "You will be my servant. Get up on your feet now. Go on into the city. When you get there, someone will tell you what to do next."

As suddenly as he had come, Jesus faded from Saul's sight. Now there was nothing but darkness. He felt hands grasping his arms, lifting him to his feet. "Are you all right, Saul?" anxious voices asked. "What was that light? Was it lightning? We heard something that sounded like thunder, but there isn't a cloud in the sky. Are you all right?"

"I'm blind," Saul managed to answer. "You'll have to help me into the city." So the great Saul, who had come thundering and cursing out of Jerusalem, had to be led by the hand into Damascus—pale, trembling, and blind.

God Makes Saul His Messenger

IN DAMASCUS THERE lived a man who believed in Jesus by the name of Ananias. One night Jesus himself appeared to him in a vision. "Ananias!" he called.

"I'm here, Lord."

"I want you to go right away to Straight Street, to the house of a man named Judas. When you get there, ask for Saul of Tarsus. He is there now, praying."

"But Lord, he is your enemy!" Ananias objected. "I have heard terrible things about him. He has done nothing but harm to your people in Jerusalem. The only reason he came here to Damascus was to arrest everyone who believed in you. How can I go to him?"

"You must go," Jesus answered. "I have chosen him to be my messenger to the Gentiles. Don't worry, he won't harm you. But when he begins to serve me, he will learn what it is like to be persecuted for my sake. I will tell him about that myself. You go and do as I have told you."

Still shaking his head in amazement, Ananias set out for Straight Street, where he found the house of Judas. He announced himself to the servant who came to the door.

"There is a man named Ananias here to see you," the servant said to Saul.

Saul turned his blind eyes in the direction of the servant's voice. "I've been waiting for him," he said. "The Lord told me he would come."

From the doorway Ananias looked down on Saul, who was kneeling in prayer. So this was what had become of the persecutor of the Lord Jesus, he thought. Humbled—on his knees before God. Ananias could not help feeling a little thrill about that. He stepped closer to Saul, reached out his hands and placed them on Saul's head. "Saul, my brother," he said, "I have been sent here by the Lord Jesus, who appeared to you on the road. Receive your sight again, and be filled with the Holy Spirit."

Suddenly it was as if scales were falling from Saul's eyes and he could see again. Saul looked steadily at Ananias, waiting to hear what else the Lord had to say to him.

"God has chosen you," Ananias said to him. "He wants you to tell the truth about Jesus, that he is the Son of God and the Savior of the world. Tell it to Gentiles, to kings, and to Jewish people scattered everywhere. Get up and be baptized!" And Ananias baptized Saul then and there.

Meanwhile, the leaders of the synagogue in Damascus were waiting for Saul's arrival from Jerusalem. But what they saw and heard when he arrived set their minds reeling. When they discovered him, he was in the synagogue telling everyone that Jesus was the Son of God. "Isn't this the man who came here to arrest people who call on this name?" they whispered to one another. "What has happened to him?" Some of them spoke out against Saul, but he knew Scripture better than they did, and he showed them from the books of Moses and the prophets that Jesus was truly the Messiah, God's chosen Redeemer.

When the synagogue leaders found that they could not argue against Saul, some of them grew even angrier than before. They decided that they would have to kill him. They stationed men to watch the city gates day and night so that if Saul left Damascus they could ambush him on the road and kill him. But some Jews friendly to Christ's cause heard about their plot and told the other Christians about it. So one night some of the believers took Saul up to the top of the city wall, placed him in a large basket and lowered him to the ground outside with ropes. In this way Saul was finally able to leave Damascus and return to Jerusalem.

When he arrived there, however, he did not find a happy group of Christians waiting to meet him. "It's a trick," some of them said. "He is just trying to get inside the church so he can find out who we all are and then put us in jail." They were so afraid that they would not go near him. But one man, named Barnabas, knew what had happened to Saul on the road to Damascus. He found Saul and took him to meet the disciples who had known Jesus while he was on earth. Barnabas told them how Saul had met Jesus and how he had risked his life to tell about Jesus in the synagogue. From that time on, the other Christians accepted Saul as one who had seen the Lord in person.

Saul stayed in Jerusalem for some time, going freely from place to place in the city, telling people the good news. He did get into debates with some of the Greek-speaking Jews, and they became so angry that they tried to kill him. But once again the plot became known to some of the believers, and they hurried Saul off to Caesarea so that he could return to his home city of Tarsus.

Now that Saul's persecution had ended in his conversion, the church enjoyed a time of peace. The good news had spread throughout Judea, Galilee, and Samaria, just as Jesus had promised, and the church was growing both in size and in the knowledge of the Lord. The believers had seen opposition from the leaders of Israel, from among their own body, and from the angry persecutor, Saul. But the Holy Spirit had protected the church community from those attacks, and although many believers already had died for their faith, the church continued to grow. They were learning what Jesus had meant when he said that the Holy Spirit would be the great Comforter.

AND STILL THE
CIRCLE WIDENS

SAUL'S PERSECUTION DROVE the believers out of Jerusalem into the countryside of Judea and Samaria. Now the time had come for the gospel to reach out still further, not only to Jews but to Gentiles as well, to the ends of the earth.

The Word Goes Forth in Power

IT WAS PETER, the big fisherman, who made journey after journey into the towns of Judea and Samaria. One of those journeys brought him a big surprise. It began with a visit to the Christians at Lydda, a city inhabited by both Jews and Gentiles. There Peter found a man named Aeneas, who was paralyzed and had been bedridden for eight years. Peter was filled with the Holy Spirit, and he said, "Aeneas! Jesus Christ is making you well. Get up now and make your bed." And immediately Aeneas stood up, his legs whole and strong again. When the people of Lydda and the nearby villages heard what had happened, they also believed in the Lord Jesus.

But Peter could not stay long in Lydda. An urgent message came to him from the Christians in the seacoast town of Joppa. There was a woman there by the name of Dorcas (her Hebrew name was Tabitha), who was an example to the whole community for her love and generosity. Dorcas had spent a great deal of time sewing clothing for the poor. But she had suddenly fallen ill and died.

The believers in Joppa could not understand why this had happened. But one of them said, "The Lord does not mean it to end this way. He wants to show his great power."

"Then what shall we do?" asked another.

"Send a message to the apostle Peter, who is at Lydda. Ask him to come here at once."

When Peter got the message, he immediately left Lydda and went to Dorcas' house in Joppa. He made everyone else leave the house; then he knelt down and prayed. "O Lord," Peter said, "you are the one who raised Christ Jesus from the dead. I know that you want to show your power over death by giving this woman life again. Please, let the power of your Holy Spirit enable me to raise her up. I ask this only so that the name of your Son Jesus may be held in honor. Amen."

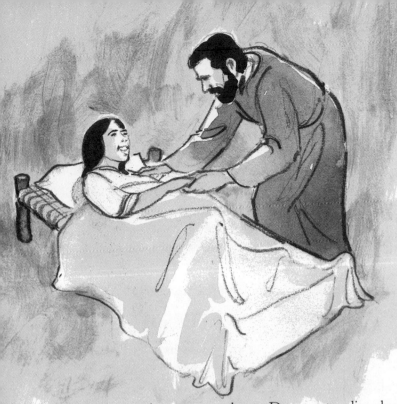

Then Peter stood up, turned to the dead woman, and said, "Tabitha, stand up!" She opened her eyes, and when she saw Peter, she sat up. He held out his hand to her and helped her to her feet. Then he called out, "Brothers and sisters! Come in here! Your sister Dorcas has been restored to you again." They came hurrying into the room and saw Dorcas standing before them alive and well. There were many tears shed that afternoon, tears of joy that Dorcas had been raised from death. They begged Peter to stay with them in Joppa for a while. So he stayed with a man named Simon, who was a tanner, a man who made leather from animal skins. All the Jews of the city wondered why Peter would stay there, because their tradition taught that the tanning occupation was unclean. But in Peter's choice of lodging the Lord was already showing that his messengers would take the gospel far beyond the Jewish people.

The Turning Point

THE CITY OF Caesarea lay on the coast of the Mediterranean Sea. Ships came from all parts of the world, bringing in goods from every nation. Often ships would come from Rome itself with messages from the emperor or visitors from the capital. The governor of Judea had his home in Caesarea so that he could greet all the officials who came to visit his province. Because it was such an important city, there were many Roman soldiers stationed there. One division of about a hundred soldiers was known as the "Italian Regiment," and its commander was a man named Cornelius.

During his years in Judea, Cornelius had come to admire the Jewish people. He began to read the books of Moses and the psalms of David, and he learned that there is only one God, who made heaven and earth. He gave up his many Roman gods and instead went to the synagogue every Sabbath day to worship the one true God. Soon his whole household came to love God too. And because of that love, Cornelius contributed a great deal of money to help the poor people of Judea.

One afternoon when Cornelius went into his room to pray, a very strange thing happened. He looked up from his prayer to see a strange man standing in the room with him, a man whose robe was so white that it almost seemed to shine with a light of its own. Cornelius had heard about such visitors, messengers from God called angels. But why would one come to visit him? Was God displeased with him?

Then the angel said his name. Trembling with fear, Cornelius could only answer, "What is it, sir?"

"Don't be afraid," the angel replied. "God has heard your prayers and has seen how generous you are to his people. Now you are to send some men to the town of Joppa. Have them ask for a man named Simon, also known as Peter; he is staying with Simon the tanner, who lives by the sea."

"But what shall I say—" Cornelius started to ask, but the angel was gone. Still trembling, he called for two of his servants. "I want you to go immediately to Joppa, to the home of a tanner named Simon. There I want you to ask for another man named Simon, who is also known as Peter."

The servants stood for a moment, waiting. "Well, go on now," Cornelius told them.

"But what shall we say to this man Simon Peter?" they asked.

Cornelius frowned a moment, then his face cleared. "He will know why I have sent you," he replied finally. "I don't really know myself though. I only know that an angel from God told me to send for this Simon Peter, so I am going to do it. Off you go to Joppa now, and bring him back quickly."

It was a good ten-hour walk to Joppa, but people were used to walking in those days. Cornelius' servants walked through the cool of the evening and on into the night. After stopping by the wayside to sleep for a few hours, they went on their journey and arrived at the gates of Joppa just before noon on the following day.

At that very moment, Peter was praying up on the flat roof of Simon's home. He was hungry, and he had asked that some food be prepared so that it would be ready when he came down again. While they were preparing it, Peter fell into a trance and saw a most amazing sight. It seemed that the sky itself was opening up, and something that looked like a big sheet of sailcloth was lowered down by the four corners. When it reached the ground, Peter saw that the sheet contained all kinds of animals, including snakes and birds. "What is going on here?" Peter wondered to himself. "It must be a vision from God."

Just then, Peter heard a voice. "Get up, Peter," the voice said. "Kill one of these animals and eat it."

"It's unthinkable!" Peter answered. "These animals aren't fit to eat. God's law says so! No forbidden animal has ever been part of a meal for me. No, I couldn't do that!"

"Do not call something unclean when God has made it pure," the voice said, and then the sheet was drawn back up into heaven.

Twice more the sheet came down from heaven, and each time the voice commanded him to kill an animal and eat it. "Nothing impure has ever entered my mouth," Peter protested again and again. But each time the voice said, "Do not call something unclean when God has made it pure."

Peter was still trying to figure out what the vision meant when he heard another voice, this time one that seemed to come from within. It was the Holy Spirit speaking, and he said: "There are two men downstairs looking for you. Don't hesitate to go down to them. I have sent them."

So Peter went down and found two men standing at the door, just as the Spirit had said. He could see at once that they were Gentiles, servants of a wealthy Roman by the look of them. "I am the man you are looking for," Peter said. "What brings you here?"

"We have been sent by Cornelius, an army captain from Caesarea," they answered. "He is a good man who worships God, and the Jewish people all think very highly of him. A messenger from God told him to send for you, so that he can hear what you have to say."

Then the meaning of his vision dawned on Peter. The image was of animals, but its meaning was about people. Until now the Gentiles had always been considered outside the Jews' fellowship, as if they were like the unclean animals Jews were forbidden to eat. But now God was telling him that they too must be invited to join God's people! Peter could hardly believe it. This was truly an astounding turn of events. "Come in," he said to the Roman servants, opening the door wider. "You will be our guests for the remainder of the day. Tomorrow I will go with you to Caesarea." So the two Roman messengers became guests of a Jew, who had been brought up to believe that no Gentile should enter his house.

In the House of Cornelius

THE FOLLOWING MORNING Peter took with him some of his Christian friends from Joppa, and together they made the long walk up to Caesarea. When they arrived, they found Cornelius waiting for them with all his relatives and friends. Cornelius was so pleased to see Peter that he welcomed him like a Roman prince and bowed down on the floor. Startled, Peter cried out, "Get up on your feet again! I'm not a god; you should not bow down to me. I have come as any other guest would to your home."

"I am honored that you should come into my house at all," Cornelius answered. He took Peter by the arm and led him toward the room where his family was gathered. "After all, you are a Jew, and few of your people will come to visit me."

"I don't have to tell you that we Jews don't consider it proper to be friends with Gentiles," Peter said. "But God has showed me that I may not treat any people as if they were impure or on the outside. That is why I came when you called me. But I would like to know why you have brought me here."

"Just three days ago, about this time of day," Cornelius said, "I was praying at home as I do every day. Suddenly a man in shining clothing appeared to me and said, 'Cornelius, your prayer has been heard.' He spoke to me just like that, and he called me by name. 'God has seen how generous you are to his people,' he said. 'Now send someone to Joppa to invite Simon Peter to come here. You will find him in the house of Simon the tanner.' So I sent for you, and you were good enough to come. That is all I know. We are just waiting now to hear whatever the Lord has told you to say."

Peter looked around at the room full of people and shook his head in amazement. "I am so slow to learn my lessons," he said. "But now I am beginning to see that it is really true that God does not play favorites. No matter what nation people come from, they are accepted by God if they worship him and obey him. So I am going to bring to you the same message God has given to the children of Israel." The Romans shifted in their seats a little, eager to hear Peter explain the word of the Lord.

"I imagine you have already heard about Jesus of Nazareth," Peter went on. "News of him has spread all over Judea. Most people have already heard about how he was baptized by John the Baptist, and how God's Holy Spirit came on him then." Peter noticed several people in the room nodding knowingly, so he went on more surely. "Jesus spent his lifetime going around Judea and Samaria doing good and healing those who were sick or under the power of the devil. God was with him. We saw with our own eyes the great things he did.

"The Jewish leaders killed him finally; they had the Romans crucify him. But God raised him back to life on the third day after his death and he appeared to us again. But this time he didn't go out in public. He only came to those of us whom God had chosen as messengers; we stand before you today as witnesses who ate and drank with him after he rose from the dead." Peter could see that his audience was taking in every word, and he began to be excited about what the Lord was doing in that house.

"Jesus commanded us to preach to the people and tell them what we know: that he is the one designated by God to be the judge of the living and the dead. I know that you have read Scripture. All of the prophets speak of him, saying that everyone who believes in him will have his sins forgiven."

Suddenly Peter stepped back in amazement. He had not even finished his message, yet people were beginning to stand up and praise God, some of them in languages they had never learned! Peter turned to his companions and said, "Listen to that! It's Pentecost all over again! God has poured out his Holy Spirit on these Gentiles!"

"It's amazing!" one of the Jewish Christians from Joppa said. "And they haven't even been baptized."

"Who could refuse that now?" Peter shouted over the growing noise of joy and thanksgiving in the room. "If God has poured out his Spirit on them, who could stop them from being baptized with water?"

And so Peter, his heart almost bursting with joy, led the new believers out to the nearest body of water, and they were all baptized. Then they returned to the house of Cornelius, and Peter stayed with them there for several days, teaching them more about Jesus. The believers from Joppa continued to be amazed that the Lord had brought his salvation even to the pagans.

The Wall Broken Down

BEFORE LONG, THE news reached Jerusalem: the gospel had been preached to the pagans, and they had received the Holy Spirit. Many of the believers were happy to hear this, but there were some of Jewish birth who were very upset. "What are you trying to do, behaving this way?" they scolded Peter when he arrived back in the city. "You went into the home of a man who had never been circumcised. You even ate with him!"

"A week ago, I would have said the same thing myself," Peter answered. "But let me tell you what happened to me." Then Peter told them about the vision of the animals let down from heaven in a sheet. "So when the messengers came from the house of Cornelius," Peter explained, "what could I do but go with them? The Holy Spirit was directing me. Here are six other believers from Joppa who went to the house of Cornelius. When we got there, he told us that an angel had visited him, telling him to send for me. So I told them the good news, and before I had even finished speaking, the Holy Spirit came upon them, just as he did on us at Pentecost. Then I remembered what the Lord had said: 'John baptized you with water, but you will be baptized with the Holy Spirit.' Now, listen to me. If God gave those Gentiles the same gift he gave us when we believed in Jesus, who are we to try to stand in God's way?"

When the Jerusalem Christians heard Peter's story, their concern turned to joy. "Then it's really true," they said. "God is also calling the Gentiles to repent and have new life!"

Within a few days they learned that Peter was not the only one who had brought the gospel to the Gentiles. When the Jewish believers were scattered by Saul's persecution, some went out telling the message only to the Jews. But there were some who went to Antioch, far to the north in Syria. There they preached the good news to the Gentiles as well, and many believed in Jesus. The believers in Jerusalem were ready for this news now that Peter had told them how God had broken down the wall that separated Jews and Gentiles. They sent Barnabas to Antioch to welcome these new believers into the whole community.

When Barnabas arrived, he was delighted with what he found. He encouraged the new believers to serve the Lord with their whole hearts; but he knew that these Gentiles would need more careful teaching, since they knew nothing of God's covenant through the ages. So he went to Tarsus to find Saul, because Saul had been trained in Greek schools and knew their ways of thinking, but as a Jew he was also close to God's covenant with his people. The two of them went back to Antioch and spent a whole year teaching the new believers. It was there in Antioch that people first called the believers "Christians." "Look at those Christ people!" they said, for that is what the word *Christian* means. Sometimes it was intended as ridicule, but the believers were happy to be called followers of Christ, because that was what Jesus had called them to be.

The believers in Antioch were learning what it meant to be part of the community of Christians. One day a prophet named Agabus came from Jerusalem. While he was in Antioch, speaking through the power of the Holy Spirit, he said that there was going to be a great famine. The believers in Antioch decided to help their brothers and sisters in Judea, people they had never met. They all gave as much as they could, and they sent the money with Barnabas and Saul. So the Lord was building all believers, both Jews and Gentiles, into one body of Christ.

Herod Opposes the Church

FOR SEVERAL YEARS—since the end of Saul's period of persecution—the church had enjoyed a time of peace. But that was about to come to an end. There was a new ruler in Jerusalem, a new King Herod, nephew of the Herod who killed John the Baptist and who mocked Jesus at his trial. This Herod wanted the support of the Jewish people and would do almost anything to get it. He kept very strictly to Jewish laws and customs and became a friend of the Pharisees.

Herod soon noticed how unpopular the followers of Jesus were with the Jewish leaders. So he began to arrest some Christians, and he found that his action pleased the religious authorities. They were happy to have a government authority doing their dirty work for them. Then Herod decided to make an example of one of the Christians, so he ordered that James, the brother of John, be beheaded. Thus God chose James to be the first of the apostles to lay down his life for the sake of Jesus Christ, the first of the apostles to see his Savior in glory.

The Pharisees were very pleased with Herod's action, and that made him bold to do even more. No one had greater authority or visibility among the Christians than did Simon Peter. So, early in the Passover holiday week,

Herod had Peter arrested and thrown into prison. "Be careful of him," warned some of Herod's friends on the Sanhedrin. "We arrested him once, but he escaped. Very mysterious—the whole business. He was closely guarded, but he got out anyway."

So Herod took no chances with Peter. He had two guards chained to him, one on each arm, so he could not even move without being noticed. Two more guards stood at the door of his cell, and another two at the outer door. The guards were changed often so that those on duty would be alert at all times. This time there would be no escape. As soon as Passover was over, Peter would be brought up for trial.

When they heard the news that Peter had been arrested, the Christians in Jerusalem were very concerned. With James dead and Peter in jail, what was happening to their leadership? So they came together in the house of Mary, the mother of John Mark, to pray for Peter and for the whole church.

The night before the trial, all was quiet in Peter's jail cell. Peter himself was sleeping peacefully, knowing that whether he lived or died, he belonged to the Lord. The soldiers chained to either side of him were also sleeping, certain that any move by their prisoner would awaken them at once. And all across the city prayers went up to God for Peter's safety.

It was nearly midnight when Peter woke up. Well—perhaps I'm not awake, he thought; perhaps I'm only dreaming that I'm awake. But what was it that woke me? Oh yes, it was the voice . . . and the light. It wasn't morning yet, but there was a light near the door of the cell. The light seemed to be coming from the robe of a man who stood there. The man came closer and tapped Peter on the side. "Hurry now! Get up!" the man said. Peter lifted his arm, and to his amazement his arm was free! He

looked down and saw the chains from his wrists lying opened on the stone floor of the prison. Peter still was not sure whether he was awake or dreaming, and he seemed unable to move.

"Put on your belt and your sandals," the angel commanded. So Peter did, and then he just stood there, wondering what would happen next. "Now put on your robe."

Peter did that too. "Now follow me." They walked past the first guards, through the door of the cell, past the second guards, and out into the night. They came at last to the great prison gate, but it swung open by itself. Out into the streets they walked, through a narrow alley to another street. And suddenly Peter was alone. When he saw the streets and the buildings, Peter knew it was not a vision after all. It was real! He was free! "It really was an angel," Peter said to himself. "So the Lord has rescued me from Herod's clutches."

Slowly he found his way through the dark streets to the house of John Mark's mother. There were lights in the house, and it looked like a number of people were inside. Peter stood for a moment at the gate of the house. "Won't they be surprised when they see me!" he thought. He could hardly wait to see their faces. He knocked softly on the door.

Inside, the servant girl Rhoda heard the knocking and gave a little gasp. "Who can that be at this hour of the night?" she thought. What if it's someone from the Sanhedrin? Or worse, what if Herod's henchmen have found out about this prayer meeting? Nervously, she went to the door; but she did not unbolt it yet. "Who's there?" she called.

"It's me—Peter!"

"What? Who?"

"Simon Peter! Quick, open the door. Don't you recognize my voice?"

"Oh, Peter!" she cried, and she was so excited that she turned and ran back into the house. "Listen, everyone!" she said, rushing into the room. "Peter is free from jail! He's standing outside right this minute!"

"Don't be silly," someone said. "There's no one outside."

"But there is," she insisted. "It's Peter, and he's standing outside the gate!"

"You must be out of your wits," said another crossly. "Nobody gets out of a Roman prison in the middle of the night."

"But I heard him. I recognized his voice."

"Perhaps it's his angel," someone else offered. "He's dead, and his guardian angel has come to tell us so."

"Can't you hear that knocking at the door?" Rhoda demanded. "Come with me, and I'll show you!" So they followed her to the door, and Rhoda pulled back the latch. The door creaked open on its hinges, and there in the moonlight stood Peter.

"Peter! You're alive!" they all cried out. He quickly motioned to them to keep quiet.

"Don't make so much noise," he said. "You'll wake up the neighborhood, and then we'll have Herod's troops down on us for sure."

"But what are you doing here? How did you get out?"

Peter explained how the angel had led him out of the prison. "Report this to the other brothers," he told them. "I have to leave right away so that Herod's men can't find me."

Then he was gone into the night, leaving the others praising God for the way he had freed Peter. They quickly spread the word to the whole church that Peter was free.

In the morning, the guards awoke to find the chains still on the floor between them, but there was no Peter. In a panic they searched the prison high and low, but there was no sign of him. Herod ordered his own soldiers to search the city, but they found nothing. In a rage, he ordered the guards arrested and killed. Once more, Satan's efforts to destroy the community of believers had come to nothing.

The Death of the Persecutor

HEROD HOPED TO win the friendship of the Jewish people by putting to death James and other leaders of the Christian church. But he soon had to face the consequences of his own evil deeds.

Herod ruled a large territory, reaching as far as the Roman cities of Tyre and Sidon on the seacoast. There came a time when Herod was angry with the people of Tyre and Sidon, so he decided to cut off their food supply as a punishment. The famine was still going on, and the people of Tyre and Sidon were desperate; so they sent a delegation to Caesarea to make peace with King Herod. They first won the friendship of Blastus, the king's chief steward, who decided to help them. "You know how vain Herod is," Blastus told them. "He likes to think he is as great as the Caesar, who calls himself a god. So if you want to win King Herod's favor, let him know that you think he also deserves to be called divine."

The day Herod chose to see the delegation from Tyre and Sidon was the day of a great feast given in honor of a victory won by Emperor Claudius. If the delegates would bow down to Herod in front of the great crowds that would be in the city that day, he might make his peace with them. So at the appointed time, Herod appeared in the hall where the celebration was to take place. He was beautifully dressed—in a robe woven entirely of silver thread. What a magnificent sight he was!

When Herod was seated on his throne, the delegation from Tyre and Sidon was brought before him. They bowed before him, and he received their show of respect. Then he stood and addressed the crowds. He had carefully rehearsed every word of his speech, and the people were duly impressed. As they cheered, one of the Sidonians shouted out, "He has the voice of a god!" Then the men from Tyre joined, "The voice of a god, not of a man!" Soon the whole crowd was shouting, "Hail to the divine King Herod!" Herod smiled and waved to them, and inside he was bursting with pride. To think that they thought so much of him!

But Herod should have known better. He pretended to serve the God of Israel, yet he allowed men to call him a god. At the moment of his greatest glory Herod was struck down by an angel of God, and he became terribly sick. His body was infested with worms, and he died a frightful death. The man who tried to use food to gain power became food for worms himself.

So those who opposed God came to nothing. But the Word of the Lord continued to spread, and more and more people believed in Jesus.

To Gentiles Far and Wide

AT THAT TIME, Barnabas was in Antioch with Saul, whom the Greek-speaking believers called Paul. But God had other plans for the two of them. One day, all the prophets and teachers among the Antioch Christians were together, praying and worshiping the Lord so heartily that they didn't even stop to eat. Suddenly the Holy Spirit spoke through one of the prophets and said, "Let me have Paul and Barnabas for the work I have called them to do."

It was a day of both sadness and joy for the church in Antioch. They loved Paul and Barnabas and hoped the two would stay there. But the Lord had called them to another work. So the other believers prayed with them and sent them on their mission with the Lord's blessing.

When they arrived on the island of Cyprus, they preached in every synagogue there, and word of them soon reached the ears of the Roman governor, Sergius Paulus. "Send for those two men," he said to a servant one day. "I want to hear this message they are preaching."

But there was one man in the court of Sergius Paulus who opposed the message of Jesus. He was a magician named Elymas, a Jew who claimed to be a prophet of God. But just like Simon the magician, he was a man whose power came from Satan. He was even more under the power of evil than Simon, however, and every time Barnabas or Paul would speak, Elymas would try to persuade the governor that they were wrong. God was very patient with Elymas, giving him every chance to listen to the good news about Jesus. But one day, as Paul stood talking with Sergius Paulus, Elymas once again opposed him. This time the Holy Spirit gave Paul a message of terrible judgment.

Paul pointed his finger at Elymas and shouted out, "You are a fraud, you son of Satan! You oppose everything that is right! Are you going to go on forever taking the Lord's straight path and trying to make it crooked? Now the Lord's judgment is upon you! God is going to strike you blind for a while, as blind in your eyes as you are in your soul!" Elymas was at once plunged into darkness, and he cried out as if in pain. He could not see even a glimmer of light, and had to be led by the hand from the court of Sergius Paulus.

When Sergius Paulus saw what had happened, he was amazed. But he was impressed even more by what Paul taught him. "Now I know that you are speaking the truth," he said. "I do believe in Jesus, the Son of God!" So the Roman governor found the light, but Elymas the magician was left in darkness. Once again, Satan's opposition to the gospel had been turned aside by the power of God.

Not Peace, but a Sword

PAUL AND BARNABAS sailed on from Cyprus and came to the town of Perga, on the seacoast far to the north of their homeland. Their assistant, John Mark, left them there and went back to Jerusalem. They continued northward, overland from town to town, until they came to another city with the same name as the one they had left, Antioch. There was a community of Jews there, so they went to the synagogue on the Sabbath day. The people of the town were very excited to have visitors, especially one who came from the holy city of Jerusalem and who had studied the Scriptures all of his life. So when it came time for someone to speak, they invited Paul to do so. He was glad for the chance to tell them of the great things God had done.

Paul stood up and looked at his audience. Most of the people were Jews, but there were also some Gentiles who had learned to serve God. "Men of Israel, and all of you who fear God," Paul began, "God chose Israel to be his special people when they were in Egypt. Then he led them out of that land and kept them alive for forty years in the wilderness. He drove out the people of Canaan and gave the land to Israel. He gave them judges, and then he gave them a king. When David came to the throne, God said, 'Here is a man who will do my will.'

"God promised that he would send Israel a savior through the family of David. Now that man has come, and his name is Jesus. John the Baptist came ahead of him to prepare the way. But the people in Jerusalem refused to listen to Jesus, even though they hear the Scriptures read in the synagogue every Sabbath. They turned him over to Pilate and had him killed, but on the third day God raised him from the dead. Many of his followers saw him in the days that followed."

Some in the audience were beginning to shift nervously in their seats, and some were frowning, but many were leaning forward to hear every word. "We have come," Paul went on, "to tell you the good news that God's promises to our forefathers have come true. You must understand, my brothers, that God is bringing the forgiveness of sins through Jesus."

When Paul had finished speaking, people began to crowd around him. "Will you come back next week and tell us more?" they asked. "Please, we really want to know about Jesus."

"Yes, of course we'll come," Paul answered. But some of the listeners could not wait a week, and they followed Paul and Barnabas to where they were staying. All that week people came and went from the house, and Paul and Barnabas told them the good news of the kingdom of God. Soon the word had spread throughout the whole area.

On the following Sabbath, the synagogue was packed. Almost the whole city had turned out, Jews and Gentiles alike, and the streets around the synagogue were filled with people. When the synagogue leaders saw the crowds, they were very angry with Paul. "Who does he think he is, inviting all those Gentiles to come here?" they demanded. "They have no right to hear about the kingdom. We are the people God has chosen."

When Paul heard what they were saying, he spoke to them sternly. "I came to you first, because you are the sons of Jacob. Apparently you think you are too good for the message. All right, then. If you are going to turn your backs on eternal life, then we are going to turn our backs on you. From now on we are going to preach to the Gentiles."

A cheer went up from the Greeks and Romans who stood in the street. That day, hundreds of the Gentiles believed in Jesus, and their sins were forgiven. For several weeks Paul and Barnabas went on preaching. Meanwhile, the Jews who did not believe in Jesus were spreading rumors about them, and some even threatened to kill Paul. So the apostles left and went to the town of Iconium, but the same thing happened there. Many people listened to them gladly, but there were others who became so angry that they wanted to kill Paul and Barnabas. The apostles had to flee for their lives.

At last the apostles began to learn what Jesus meant when he said, "I did not come to bring peace, but a sword." The good news of the kingdom divided people into two groups, those who heard the message and loved God, and those who wouldn't listen. But even though the apostles were forced to go on to other towns, the Christians they left behind continued to tell the good news of Jesus.

The Gospel Confirmed by Miracles

CONTINUING ON THEIR journey, Paul and Barnabas came to the city called Lystra. Because it had no synagogue, Paul preached in the streets; and a great crowd stood around him, listening eagerly to what this stranger had to say. On the ground close to Paul sat a man who could not walk. He had been crippled since birth and had never known what it was like to stand on his own legs.

As Paul spoke, the crippled man caught his attention. He remembered how Jesus had helped all those who had come to him. Seeing that the crippled man had faith, Paul looked him straight in the eye and said in a loud voice, "Stand up on your feet!"

Before he could think what he was doing, the startled man sprang to his feet. Then his eyes opened wide, and he looked down at his legs in amazement. He took one step forward, then another. A murmur of excitement began to run through the crowd. "These can't be humans," someone said. "They must be gods!"

"The great god Jupiter has come to earth," the rumor raced on.

"And what about the one who does the talking, the one who calls himself Paul?" someone else said. "He must be Mercury, the god of speech."

The stories spread through the city like wildfire and came to the ears of the priest of the temple of Jupiter. When he heard the news, he quickly took a fat ox, hung a wreath of flowers around its neck and led it toward the city gate, where he planned to offer a sacrifice to this messenger of Jupiter. But when Paul looked up and saw the priest coming through the crowd leading the ox, he suddenly realized what was happening. He and Barnabas snatched off their robes and tore them in two. They rushed into

the crowd shouting, "Stop it! Stop it! What do you think you are doing? We aren't gods! We're only humans, just like you!"

"No, no!" the crowd shouted back. "You must be gods come to earth as men."

"But we came here to tell you about the living God!" Paul protested. "He is the one who made the world and everything in it. We serve him, the only true God. Please, listen to us!" The people around them began to quiet down so that they could hear what Paul was saying. "God has let you do these things in the past, but he was always telling you about himself. He gave you the rain and good harvests; he gave you food and happiness. Now he is telling you to worship him and to turn away from false gods. We are only men, but we have come to give you this message from God."

Many in the crowd still wanted to offer a sacrifice to Paul and Barnabas, but the apostles kept on arguing with them until they finally persuaded them to stop. For some of the Jews, this pagan exhibition was too much to take. So when Jewish leaders from Antioch and Iconium came to Lystra and tried to arouse the crowds against Paul and Barnabas, there were some who were only too willing to listen. The leaders now saw their chance to get rid of Paul once and for all. "You see what these men do?" they asked. "They go around causing trouble everywhere. Look how they have put your whole city in an uproar."

Now some of the Gentile leaders chimed in. "Did you see how they insulted the priest of Jupiter?" they demanded. "What right do they have to come here pretending to be gods?" Soon those who opposed Paul had gathered an angry mob. Shouting and waving their fists, they rushed through the streets to find Paul. He was preaching to a group of people in the street when the mob spied him. Rough hands reached out to grab Paul, and then dragged him through the streets, out through the gates and into the fields beyond the city. In their anger, the crowd picked up stones and began to hurl them at Paul. Thick and fast the stones flew, until Paul fell to the ground, bruised and bleeding. Only when they were sure he was dead did the mob break up and return to the city, satisfied that they had rid their town of a great threat.

Anxiously, the other Christians gathered around the body of Paul. But as they watched, he lifted himself on one elbow, then slowly rose to his feet. A shout of joy went up from the circle of believers. "God be praised! He's alive!" they cried. And together they returned to the city, singing and praising the Lord.

"You must not be afraid," Paul told them that night. "Remember what Jesus said to those who followed him. If we are like him, then the world will hate us just as much as it hated him. The way to the kingdom of God lies through many troubles. So be strong in the Lord, and never let your faith grow weak. Remember, he promised always to be with us."

The Council in Jerusalem

As PAUL AND Barnabas retraced their journey, they came back to some of the cities where they had preached the gospel. They found the believers learning more about the Lord and living their new lives of love and service to one another. In every place they found some whom the Lord was bringing up as leaders in the local community. They laid hands on these people and appointed them to be shepherds in God's flock.

At last they came to Antioch in Syria, the place where their journey had begun. They shared with the other believers the great things God had done, how many Gentiles had come to know the Lord. There was great rejoicing in the community of believers there, and Paul and Barnabas stayed with them for a long time.

But there were some teachers who came up from Jerusalem to Antioch who said to the Gentile believers, "According to the law of Moses, you cannot be saved unless you are circumcised." Paul and Barnabas argued fiercely with them about this, but they would not change their teaching. It was confusing and upsetting to the believers in Antioch, who could not decide whom to believe. One of them finally said, "We must send a delegation to Jerusalem to consult with the apostles and elders there." So the group was chosen, Paul and Barnabas among them, and they set off for Jerusalem. They found communities of believers in every town where they stayed on the way, and they told them all about how the Gentiles were receiving the Lord. This news brought great joy in every place. There was the same rejoicing in Jerusalem, and they were welcomed by the apostles and the elders.

When they heard the news of what the Lord was doing among the Gentiles, some of the Pharisees who had become Christians stood up and said, "We cannot overlook the law. God called all those who would obey him to carry the mark of his covenant in their bodies. Throughout all the Scriptures, it says that anyone from another nation who wishes to belong to the Lord has to first be circumcised, and to obey the whole law of Moses."

"No, all that has changed," said one of the elders. "God has brought a new day, and he is speaking now to all peoples, not only to us who are children of Israel. These signs were meant for us, not for everybody."

The debate went on for a long time. Finally Peter stood up and said, "I have listened to everything you have said. Now I think I should speak, because as you know, I was the one God first chose to bring the good news to the Gentiles, so that they could also hear it and believe. When I first went to the house of Cornelius, God showed that he accepted the Gentiles by sending his Holy Spirit, just as he did to us at the beginning. He did not make a difference between us and them. He forgave them because they believed, before anybody had a chance to speak about circumcision or law observances or any of that stuff. We ourselves were never able to keep all the commandments of law, nor were our ancestors! Why do you want to put the load on the backs of these people if we couldn't even carry it? No, we are saved in the same way as they are—not by obeying the law but by the grace of Jesus Christ."

Then the whole group sat in silence as Paul and Barnabas reported to them all the miracles God had done through them while they were bringing the gospel to the Gentiles. Finally James, one of the leaders of the believers in Jerusalem, stood and said, "Brother Simon has just told us how the Lord is choosing a new people for himself, even from among the Gentiles. What he has said is in agreement with the words of the prophets, such as these words of Amos:

> I will return after those days
> And will rebuild the House of David;

I will set it up again from its ruins.
Then the rest of mankind will come to me,
All the Gentiles whom I have called.
So says the Lord, who long ago made this known.

"So we should not cause any difficulties for the Gentiles who are turning to the Lord. Instead, let us write them and ask that they not eat meat that has been sacrificed to idols, or any meat with the blood still in it, that they not marry anyone closely related to them, and that they keep themselves from sexual sins. Most Gentiles already know that the law of Moses forbids these practices, because this law has been read in every synagogue of every city for generations. If Gentile Christians keep to these rules, then outsiders will clearly see that they have changed their pagan ways. And Jewish and Gentile Christians will be able to live and worship together in peace, without anyone being offended by what the other does."

All the apostles and elders, and the whole community in Jerusalem, agreed that this was the right thing to do. They sent a letter back to Antioch with Paul and Barnabas, and to make sure there was no doubt about the decision, they sent along two men from Jerusalem—Judas and Silas—to give them the same message in person. There were only a few who objected, people Paul later talked about in a letter he wrote to the believers in Galatia: "They pretended to be fellow believers," he said, "and wormed their way into the community as spies. They found out about our freedom in Christ, and wanted to make us slaves again."

When the believers in Antioch read the letter from the apostles and elders, and heard the words of Judas and Silas, they were filled with joy. God had truly broken down the wall that separated Jews and Gentiles and had brought them together into one community of believers. Paul and Barnabas and the others stayed there for a long time, preaching and teaching the word of the Lord.

THE CIRCLE CONTINUES TO GROW

FROM THAT FIRST stone thrown into the water at Jerusalem, the ripples had spread outward into Judea, into Samaria, and on into the country of the Gentiles. But the heart of the Gentile world, Greece and Italy, had not yet been reached with the gospel. God had further work for Paul to do.

A New Journey Begins

PAUL SAID TO Barnabas one day, "We should go back to the other places where we preached the good news and find out how the believers are getting along." Barnabas agreed and wanted to take John Mark with them; but Paul said, "He quit once and went back to Jerusalem. We shouldn't take him along this time." They argued about it so much that they finally went separate ways. Barnabas sailed with John Mark for Cyprus; Paul set out with Silas by land north and west, toward Derbe and Lystra, and on toward the other Antioch.

In Lystra, Paul met a young believer named Timothy, the son of a Jewish mother and a Greek father. In the eyes of the Jews, therefore, Timothy was a Jew; but because his father was Greek, Timothy had never been circumcised. Paul knew that this would offend many of the Jews if Timothy were to speak to them about the good news of the kingdom. Even though Paul did not want to force Gentiles to obey Jewish rules on circumcision, he asked Timothy to be circumcised—to make it possible for Timothy to be accepted as a preacher in Jewish synagogues. Timothy agreed, and after allowing a few days for his body to heal, he went with Paul through the towns, announcing the good news and encouraging the believers. When they came to the province of Asia Minor, they found that there was no freedom to preach the message, so they traveled on and at last came to Troas, on the coast of the Adriatic Sea, across the water from Greece.

The Call from Macedonia

"HELP US, PAUL!" The voice seemed to come from a great distance. Paul stirred in his sleep, then breathed quietly again.

"Help us, Paul!" came the voice a second time. Through the darkness Paul seemed to see a man dressed in the clothing of someone from Macedonia, a region in northern Greece. The man faded for a moment, as if he were only a cloud, then became clear again. He raised his hand and beckoned to Paul. "Come over to Macedonia and help us. Please, come and help us." The voice was fading now, but Paul could still hear the final words: "Help us."

Paul sat bolt upright in the chilly darkness. He was wide awake now, and there was no one in the room. He felt out of touch, not sure where he was. Then he remembered. He was in Troas, on the seacoast, on a journey with Silas and Timothy. He had been dreaming, but it was no ordinary dream. It was a vision from the Lord, and the message was clear. He had to travel across the sea to Macedonia. People there were also hungry for the good news of the kingdom of God.

Early the next morning, Paul was at the docks, searching for a ship that could take him and his friends to Macedonia. It took only a few hours to find the right ship, and within days they were on their way to Philippi, the main Roman town in Macedonia. The journey across the sea took less than a week, and Philippi was only a day's journey inland from the port of Neapolis.

There were so few Jews in Philippi that they had no synagogue. Instead, they met each Sabbath by the river outside the city. Paul went to the river on the first Sabbath after his arrival and found that only a few women had come to pray. One of them was Lydia, a Greek widow who sold purple cloth. The purple dye came from small shellfish, and it took so many of them to dye a piece of cloth that only rich people could afford to buy it. Lydia herself was a wealthy woman—and a busy one. She had heard about God from the Jewish people, and she loved him with all her heart.

Lydia listened eagerly as Paul spoke to them about Jesus, the Son of God. "Now I know that God has saved me," she said when Paul was finished. "I want to follow Jesus myself. So do the rest of my family. Please baptize us right here in the river." So Paul baptized Lydia and her whole family.

"You will need a place to stay while you tell others about Jesus," Lydia said when they came up out of the water. "Will you stay with me and my family?" She must have seen the hesitant look on Paul's face, so she insisted, "Since I am a fellow believer, accept my hospitality."

"I didn't hesitate because you are Greek," Paul reassured her. "Usually I earn my way as a tentmaker when I travel, so that I won't be a burden to anyone. But since you insist, I will accept your hospitality." So Paul stayed at the home of Lydia the cloth merchant, and he preached the good news of the kingdom of God in that whole region of Macedonia.

The Lord Is Stronger than Evil

THERE WERE PEOPLE of many nationalities in Philippi, and everyone seemed to have his own god. There were only a few who served the God who made heaven and earth, and only Lydia's family had come to know Jesus Christ. Some people served their gods out of fear of what might happen if they didn't, others only because their parents had taught them to. There were still others who knew that they were dealing with evil spirits but didn't care as long as they could make a profit.

Wherever a crowd gathered, there were merchants selling little idols and sacrifices for the gods. There were magicians and fortunetellers and people who said they could read the will of the gods. They all followed the crowds, selling their wares. These days, the crowds all seemed to be following the visitor from Palestine, Paul of Tarsus, who spoke of the love of God and said many things that were strange to the ears of Philippians.

Where Paul went, the crowds went; and where the crowds went, the fortunetellers and the idol sellers went along. There was one fortuneteller in particular who began to bother Paul, Silas, and Timothy. She was a slave girl, owned by some men of the city. But that was not the worst of it, because she was also the slave of an evil spirit that told her things that had not yet happened. Her owners made quite a bit of money from her fortunetelling, but they could not control what she was going to say.

Every day, when the girl's owners took her out among the crowds following the apostle Paul, she would cry out, "These men serve the Most High God! They are telling you the way to be saved!" Paul was annoyed, but he did not want to cause trouble in the city, so he said nothing. Nevertheless, he became more and more irritated as the same thing happened day after day. He knew that Satan was only trying to take attention away from Jesus' message and make people think Paul was just another of the many religion-sellers who walked the streets of Philippi. Just as in the case of Simon and Elymas, the magicians, it seemed that Satan was sending out his forces to oppose the good news when it came into a new territory.

But Paul would not allow the devil to go on taking the credit for the message of the gospel. One Sabbath morning he could not stand it any longer. The girl cried out again, "These men serve the Most High God!" This time Paul turned sharply to her and spoke directly to the evil spirit. "I command you in the name of Jesus Christ to come out of her!"

273

The girl's body jerked once, and then she shook her head as if she were shaking away a bad dream. She looked up at the people around her, and the wild look was gone from her eyes. Her owners saw at once that she had changed. But they didn't think for a minute about the girl's well-being, now that she was free from the evil spirit. They could only think of all that money they would never see now that she could no longer tell people's fortunes. They wanted only one thing: revenge.

"We don't have to put up with this!" one of the owners shouted. He turned to the people standing nearby. "That Jew just ruined our business. He's a troublemaker if there ever was one. He attacks our gods, and if we don't watch out, he'll tear down our whole way of life. We should get rid of those Jews now!"

Within a few minutes the words of the two men had whipped the crowd into a frenzy. They swept through the streets of the city searching for Paul and Silas. When they found them, they grabbed the apostles roughly and dragged them into the center of the city, where the Roman troops were stationed. "These Jews were causing an uproar in the city," they shouted to the officer in charge. "They were teaching things we Romans shouldn't even think of doing!"

"So, you Jews are at it again, are you?" snarled the officer. "Preaching rebellion against Rome, no doubt. When are you people going to realize that the only power worth worrying about is the power of Rome? We'll see what a few days in prison can teach you. Not even your God can help you there! Guard, take them and teach them a lesson with the whip first."

The soldiers grabbed Paul and Silas and pushed them toward the walls of the garrison, where they raised the prisoners' hands and tied them to two pillars. With a quick jerk, the soldiers ripped the prisoners' robes off, exposing their bare backs. The whip whistled through the air and snapped against Paul's back. Again and again the whip flew, and each time Paul winced in pain. Then it was Silas' turn, and when his back was as raw and bleeding as Paul's the two men were thrown into a deep dungeon. "Guard them well," the officer said to the jailer. "Whipping isn't enough for scum like these."

The Jailer Hears the Gospel

FOR THE JAILER at Philippi, chaining men to the iron rings that protruded from the stone floor and walls of the cell was all in a day's work. It was not his business to ask why men were being jailed. His only job was to guard them well. If he wondered why Paul and Silas did not resist being shackled, he certainly did not show it. The door of the cell shut with a clang that echoed down the stone corridor, and the jailer went on with his rounds.

The moans and cries that filled the dungeons during the day died away as night wore on and even the prisoners fell into a fitful sleep. After making sure that the guards were properly posted, the jailer himself lay down to get a few hours' sleep. But tonight there was a new sound echoing up from the depths of the dungeon, a sound the jailer had never before heard from men in chains: the sound of singing.

Down in their cell Paul and Silas had spent their time in prayer. Now they were raising their voices in song—a song of the new community of believers in Jesus Christ:

Though he was in the form of God,
*   He did not cling to that high place,*
But he came down, became a slave,
*   Was born among the human race.*

And when he had become a man,
*   He suffered even greater loss:*
He did God's will and suffered death,
*   Even death upon a cross.*

So God has raised him up on high,
*   And placed him at his own right hand.*
And given him the highest name,
*   So none before him now can stand;*

But every knee in earth and heaven
*   Most bow before the eternal Word,*
And every tongue must worship God
*   And say that Jesus Christ is Lord!*

The other prisoners could hardly believe their ears. There they were, damp and cold and miserable, feeling sorry for themselves and wishing they were free, when suddenly they heard the voices of Paul and Silas singing praises to God. How could anyone be that happy in a Roman prison? But happy they were; there was no doubt about that. It lifted the spirits of the other prisoners to hear the singing, and at midnight they were still listening to the voices of Paul and Silas.

Then all at once there was another sound, a deep rumbling that seemed to come from the heart of the earth itself, a rumbling that grew louder and louder until it drowned out the songs. Still louder it grew, and then the earth beneath the prison began to shake. The dozing jailer was startled awake as the floor began to tremble. Stronger and stronger the earthquake grew, shaking the pillars of the prison until it seemed that the room would collapse and kill them all. The jailer screamed with fear and threw his arms over his head. But the stones did not fall, and slowly the rumbling died away.

275

As soon as the floor had stopped shaking, the jailer rushed out into the corridors to see what damage had been done. He was horrified at what he saw. The gates to the inner prison were standing wide open, and many of the stones in the walls were so loose that the iron chains had fallen out onto the floor. "They've all escaped," he thought. "The army will kill me for this. I would rather die by my own hand than be tortured to death." Overcome by fear, he drew his sword to kill himself.

"Wait!" came a voice from inside the prison. Startled, he turned toward the sound. It came from the blackness of the dungeon below. "Don't harm yourself," the voice said. "Nobody has escaped."

"Bring a light!" cried the frightened jailer. Seizing the torch from the trembling hand of his servant, the jailer hurried down the steps. There he saw Paul and Silas and the other prisoners walking around free, their chains dangling where they had pulled out of the walls. His knees gave way at the sight, and fell down in front of the two apostles, thanking them for keeping the prisoners there. When at last he rose to his feet, he took Paul and Silas by the hand and led them out through the gates, leaving orders for the other prisoners to be locked up again.

The jailer's mind was racing. He had heard the prayers and songs of the apostles earlier in the evening. They had called on their God to save them from prison. This God must have sent the earthquake to free them. But if he could do that, what would he do to the man who held them prisoner? The jailer was still trembling with fear, but now it was fear of what God might do to him. He turned to Paul and Silas and asked in a quivering voice, "Men, how can I escape the anger of your God? How can I be saved?"

"If you believe in the Lord Jesus Christ," Paul answered, "you and your whole household will be saved."

"But who is he?" the jailer asked. "Please, come home with me and tell me about your God and about this Jesus you speak of." So he led them to his own house and took care of the wounds on their backs, while they told him and his family about Jesus.

For the jailer and his family, it was as if a lantern had been lit in the darkness. They had never heard of a God of love, and they received the good news with joy. Then and there, Paul and Silas took water and baptized the jailer and his whole family.

"Now we must have something to eat," the jailer said. So Paul and Silas sat down with the jailer and his family, and together they celebrated their new-found faith in God. But when dawn came, the three men went back to the prison.

Within hours, messengers came from the judges of the city. The jailer went out to meet them and came back smiling. "They have sent orders for you to be set free," he told Paul and Silas. "You were right. God has saved me from the anger of the Roman army. You can go now."

"Not so fast," Paul answered. "I have a message to send back to those judges. They beat us in public and threw us in jail without a trial, even though we are Roman citizens. Now they want to smuggle us out in secret. Nothing doing! Let them come to the prison themselves and get us, so the whole city will know that we have done nothing wrong."

The smile disappeared from the jailer's face. For a moment the old fear started to come back. Then he remembered what God had done for him, and he took heart. He gave the message to the soldiers, and they went back to the judges.

When the judges heard that Paul and Silas were Roman citizens, they got very nervous. "What if the emperor should hear about this?" they asked. "Roman citizens are entitled to a fair trial! We'll have to do whatever they ask to keep them from reporting us!" So they came to the prison and said to Paul and Silas, "We admit we made a mistake. Please don't say anything about this. We will get in trouble if you report us. We will bring you out of prison ourselves, but please leave the city at once and don't make trouble for us."

"We accept your apology," Paul and Silas answered. "But we have business to take care of in the city." And they went at once to Lydia's house and told the Christians there everything that had happened to them. "Welcome the jailer and his family as the Lord's own people," they said. "And never forget what great things God can do." Then they left the city, leaving behind them in Philippi a growing community of believers.

Paul Speaks in Athens

WHEREVER PAUL AND Silas went with the good news, there were always some to oppose them. At Thessalonica they preached in the synagogue for three Sabbath days in a row. But when they saw that Greeks were received by the Christians, some of the Jews who had rejected the message became very angry. They got together a crowd of loafers and crooks from the city street and set the whole city in an uproar. They attacked the house of a Christian named Jason, hoping to find Paul and Silas there. When they couldn't find those two, they dragged Jason off to the authorities. "This man is breaking the law," they exclaimed. He is harboring all these Christians, who are against the emperor. They say that some fellow named Jesus is the real king."

Paul and Silas had to leave under cover of night because there was such a riot in the city. They went to Berea, where the people in the synagogue listened eagerly to the good news. They studied Scripture every day to see whether what Paul and Silas said was really true. Many of them believed in the Lord Jesus. But as soon as some of the Greeks believed too, some of those same Thessalonian Jews came down and stirred up the mobs against the Christians. Once again Paul had to escape, but Silas and Timothy stayed behind in Berea.

The men who helped Paul escape were on their way to Athens, one of the most beautiful cities of the world. For hundreds of years, great thinkers had been coming to Athens. The favorite pastime of the city was not sports, although they did have wrestling matches; it was not going to plays, although there was a great theater there; and it was not reading the newspaper, for there were no printing presses in those days. In Athens the favorite pastime was talking about great ideas—such as love, truth, beauty, and justice. Some of the greatest minds in the world had spoken on those subjects in Athens.

Paul was an educated man, and he was acquainted with the ideas of the great Greek thinkers. He also knew what they were missing. They were trying to shape their lives around themselves and their own ideas and abilities. The whole Roman world was influenced by these ideas—ideas that did not recognize God as Creator and Savior. That was why Paul had come to Athens, one of the centers of that world. Here he would declare that Jesus Christ was the Lord of the whole creation, Lord of all of human life.

On the highest hill of the city stood the beautiful public buildings of Athens. Their white marble columns rose gracefully into the air, and people gathered on the cool porches beneath the columns to talk and hear the latest ideas. But the square was also dotted with statues, beautiful statues of the many gods the Greeks worshiped. The sight of these idols made Paul very sad. For all their great learning, the people of Athens did not know the Lord.

Paul could not remain silent. In the synagogue he talked about Jesus with the Jews and Gentiles who served the Lord, and in the public square he debated with anyone who would talk with him. Word began to get around the city that there was a new teacher in town, one who came with some strange ideas. Some of those who talked with Paul came away asking each other, "What do you suppose that ignorant show-off is really trying to say?"

"I don't know," someone said. "The best I can make of it is that he's

spreading propaganda about some foreign gods.''

"Well, he had some pretty good ideas," said another. "But when he got to the part about someone being raised from the dead, he lost me completely."

"Still, I think more people ought to get to hear him, don't you? It could be interesting for a while."

"Why not? Let's ask the High Council to call him in to explain his ideas."

So a few days later Paul found himself standing in front of the High Council of Athens. "We would like to hear about this new teaching you have brought to our city," they said. "Some of the things you say sound very strange, and we would like to know what they mean." The crowd standing nearby stirred, hoping for the excitement of a great debate.

"I have noticed that you Athenians are very religious," Paul answered. "Everywhere I go in the city, I see places of worship. I even found one altar that was marked 'To an Unknown God.' I was glad to see that, because that is the God I am going to tell you about." A buzz of interest went through the crowd. The people always wanted to hear about the unknown.

"This God I am telling you about," Paul went on, "is the one who made the world and everything in it. He is Lord of heaven and earth.

279

Therefore, he does not need temples made by men, because the whole universe is his temple. He does not need anything we can give him, because everything already belongs to him. He does not even need to have animals sacrificed to him, because he gives life to every living thing." Paul's listeners were amazed. Most of them had never heard of a God who created anything. The gods they knew were more like immortal people, forever changing and unreliable. It was not easy to believe in such gods, and they were always searching for truer answers to their questions.

"Long ago," Paul said to them, "God created one man, and all the nations of the world are descended from him. God decided where the peoples of the earth would live. He spread them out over the whole world so that they could see the world he had made—and perhaps reach out and find him. You yourselves are reaching out for God, and he is not very far from any of us. One of your own poets said it very well:

> We live and move and are in him;
> We are his children.

"If we are his children, we shouldn't imagine that he looks like any statue we can make, no matter how beautiful it may be. I tell you, God has let us all get away with a great deal in the past. But now he is sending a message out into the whole world. 'Turn from your evil ways,' he said. 'The day is coming when I will judge the whole world through a man I have chosen.' That man is named Jesus. And God proved that Jesus is the one he chose by raising him from death."

At these words, some of those in the crowd turned to leave. "Raised from death, indeed!" they scoffed. "Everyone knows that death is the end of everything. Forget this fellow. He's wasting our time!"

But there were others who came up to Paul and said, "Will you come back tomorrow? We would like to hear more about this." A few believed in Jesus, including one of the members of the High Council, a man named Dionysius. So God's church continued to grow, as both Jews and Greeks received the good news.

Growing Conflict

PAUL WAS A Jew, but he had learned the ideas of the Greek thinkers. He was able to live in two worlds, speaking with the Jews in the synagogue and with the Greeks in the public square, persuading them that Jesus was the Savior of the world. But it seemed that the more the gospel was received, the greater the opposition became—particularly among Paul's own people, the Jews. It was after Paul left Athens and came to Corinth that the conflict again came out into the open.

Paul was staying in Corinth with a tentmaker named Aquila and his wife Priscilla. He worked alongside them, making tents and earning his own living. Silas and Timothy had also come down from Macedonia to join him. Every Sabbath Paul went to the synagogue, where he spent long hours going through Scripture with the people who met there, showing them God's promise that he would send the Redeemer. But the Jews of Corinth did not want to hear the good news. They argued bitterly with him, and even insulted him. Finally one Sabbath, Paul became completely fed up with them. Angrily he stood up, tore off his robe, and shook it out in their faces. "Your own words will come back on your heads to condemn you, like the dust from this robe," he cried. "Your judgment will be your own fault. No one can say I didn't try. But I'm not going to waste my time with you any more. From now on, I am going to take the good news to the Gentiles." With that, he turned on his heel and stalked out of the synagogue.

"I'm finished with these people!" Paul said to Aquila when he arrived back at the house.

Aquila looked at him with alarm. "What's wrong, Paul?"

"I'm not preaching at the synagogue any longer," Paul answered. "The time has come to show that the message of Jesus is not just for us Jews. From now on, I'm going to preach at the house of Titus Justus, right next door to the synagogue."

"But Paul," Aquila protested, "if you do that, none of our people will listen to you—not if you preach in a Gentile home."

"They don't listen to me now," Paul replied. "None of our people will change their minds about me, even if I were to move in with a Gentile family. Those who know Jesus will still know him, and those who have rejected him will still reject him. They have had their chance. Now it is time for the whole Gentile world to hear the good news."

For a year and a half Paul taught at the house of Titus Justus. Many people of Corinth, both Jews and Gentiles, came to know Christ through him. But Paul still had moments when he wondered whether he had done the right thing. In answer to Paul's unspoken questions, the Lord came to him one night in a vision and said, "Don't be afraid, Paul. Don't let them silence you. I will be with you, so go right on speaking. I will not let anyone in Corinth harm you. And there are many in this city who belong to me."

So Paul settled down there for eighteen months, preaching and teaching the word of God.

However, the Lord's promise *was* put to the test. Jews from all the cities in the region, that is, those who would not listen to the good news, got together and took Paul to court. Gallio, the new Roman governor, listened while they accused Paul.

"This fellow goes around spreading all kinds of strange ideas," they said. "He keeps stirring up our people and getting them to do things that are against our law."

Paul was about to defend himself when the governor spoke up. "Get out of here!" he said. "I thought you were going to accuse this man of some kind of crime or serious misdemeanor. But now I find out this is all bickering about some business in your Jewish religious law. I do not intend to try to decide on those things. Don't waste my time!" And his guards moved them firmly toward the door.

Outside there was an angry mob waiting to see Paul punished by the Romans. When Paul did come out, however, he was escorted safely away by Roman soldiers. When they saw the object of their rage getting away, they were beside themselves with rage. They pounced on Sosthenes, one of the synagogue leaders, and began to beat him up.

"Do you want us to stop them?" one of the guards asked Gallio.

"No," the governor answered. "Let these Jews fight it out among themselves."

So Paul was left in peace, just as the Lord had promised. Once again, just as in those early days when Peter and the other apostles were brought up before the Sanhedrin, those who wanted to silence the good news of the kingdom were themselves silenced. The message continued to spread, and the community of believers went on growing.

Paul in Ephesus

WHEN PAUL FINALLY left Corinth, Aquila and Priscilla went with him as far as the city of Ephesus. Ephesus was a large and prosperous city, the capital of one of the Roman provinces. There was a synagogue there, but most of the people of the city were Greeks who served the goddess Diana. Pilgrims came from all over the Roman world to visit the shrine of the goddess. They often took home with them little gold or silver models of the great statue of Diana. This tourist trade brought a great deal of money into Ephesus, and kept its goldsmiths and silversmiths very prosperous.

As usual, Paul first went to the Jewish synagogue and got into discussions with the leaders about the Messiah. He could stay only a few days, however, and even though many of them begged him to stay longer, he replied, "If it is God's will, I will come back to you." But Aquila and Priscilla did remain behind in the city, teaching many of the Jewish people the way of the Lord. One of them was a man named Apollos, who spoke enthusiastically in the synagogue about Jesus. But he knew only about the baptism of John the Baptist and had not heard the whole of the good news. Aquila and Priscilla took him home with them and taught him more fully. After that, Apollos became one of the greatest of missionaries to the Jewish people.

Apollos had gone on to Corinth by the time Paul returned to Ephesus on a later journey. As Paul preached in the city, he met some disciples who had heard something about Jesus but did not seem to understand many things. "Did you receive the Holy Spirit when you believed?" Paul asked them.

"No, we hadn't even heard that there is a Holy Spirit," they answered.

"Well, then, how were you baptized?"

"We were baptized by followers of John the Baptist," they replied.

"Then let me explain," Paul said to them. "You see, John baptized people who were turning away from their sins. But he told them to believe in the one who would follow him—Jesus." And he went on to tell them how the Messiah was crucified and was raised from death on the third day.

"Then if Jesus is the one who has brought salvation," one of the men said, "shouldn't we be baptized in his name rather than John's?" And all the others agreed.

So Paul called for water to be brought, and he baptized them there in the name of the Lord Jesus. When Paul laid his hands on them, the Holy Spirit came upon them just as he had come upon the Christians in Jerusalem at the feast of Pentecost. They began to speak in languages they had never learned, and all of them were telling the good news.

For three months Paul went to the synagogue every day and discussed questions about the kingdom of God. Some believed in Jesus, but there were others, as usual, who wanted to shut Paul up. They made such a disturbance that Paul finally said, "I won't trouble you any longer. From now on we will use the public square." And for the next two years Paul and his followers could be found every day in a hall that was set aside for lecture and debates. The Greeks loved talking and debating so much that they had built a perfect place for the preaching of the good news!

During those two years the Lord showed his power through the works of Paul. So strong was that power that many people were healed of their diseases, some of them only by being touched by scarves or handkerchiefs that Paul had touched. Evil spirits were also driven out of many, showing that the God of heaven and earth was more powerful than the powers of darkness.

The news of what Paul was doing reached some traveling Jewish preachers who were in town, men who used spells and incantations to try to drive out evil spirits. When they heard about Paul, they decided to use the name of Jesus as one of their spells. The seven sons of Sceva, a Jewish high priest, tried to use the name of Jesus in this way, but things did not work out as they had planned. One of them said to a man who was under the control of an evil spirit, "I command you to depart, in the name of Jesus whom Paul preaches." But the man with the evil spirit glared back at them and said, "I know who Jesus is, and I know who Paul is, but who are you?" He sprang at them, kicking and scratching, tearing off their clothing, and battering them against the walls. Naked and bruised, all seven of them fled from the house.

When news of Sceva's sons spread through the town, people began to realize that the name of Jesus was not something to be toyed with. Many believed in Jesus and came to Paul to confess that they had practiced black magic. They brought their secret books, books filled with devil stories and spells, and burned them in the public square. So the word of the Lord continued to spread with great power, and many people joined the body of Christ—the church.

The Riot in Ephesus

As THE NAME of Jesus spread in the city of Ephesus, the powers of evil gathered to oppose him. The worship of false gods was big business in Ephesus, and many of the craftsmen and businessmen of the town depended for their income on the pilgrims who came to worship at the temple of Diana. People who were converted to believe in Jesus would stop going to the pagan temple; thus the good news was beginning to cut into the tourist trade. The merchants were becoming very upset. Finally, a silversmith named Demetrius decided to hold a meeting of all those who made their living in the silver and gold idol trade.

"You all know what this fellow Paul has been doing," Demetrius said to them. "He goes around saying that the gods we make with our hands are not really gods at all. Now men, you know that our business depends on these gods. Paul has persuaded a large number of people, not only in Ephesus but throughout Asia. If this continues, we could be in real trouble. We could all lose our jobs! And what about our temple? Diana has been good to us. She has made us all prosperous. Are we going to stand by and let this Jew turn people away from her?"

"No!" the angry crowd shouted back. "Great is Diana of Ephesus! Down with the blasphemer! Great is Diana of Ephesus!" The meeting nearly became a riot, and news of it spread through the city. Workers who had lost their jobs, workers who were afraid they would lose their jobs, idol makers whose business was bad, and people who had nothing better to do—all joined the chanting crowds streaming into the public amphitheater. One group of angry workers recognized Gaius and Aristarchus, two friends of Paul, seized them, and dragged them into the theater.

When Paul heard what was happening, he wanted to go to the theater himself. But his friends urged him not to go, because it would be too dangerous. As they were discussing the matter, a message arrived from some of Paul's friends in the local government. "Paul, whatever you do, stay away from that mob in the theater," it said. "We could not guarantee your safety if you were to go there."

Meanwhile, inside the amphitheater the crowd was close to rioting. Some people were shouting one thing, some were shouting another. Most of them did not even know why they were there. One of the Jewish businessmen tried to say something to the crowd, but as soon as they saw that he was Jew, they began to chant, "Great is Diana of Ephesus! Great is Diana of Ephesus!" For two hours the crowd continued the chant, while the city officials tried to decide what to do.

Finally, the city clerk succeeded in quieting the mob. When the shouting died away at last, he said, "Fellow Ephesians, everyone knows about our temple and the sacred image of Diana that fell from the sky. No one can doubt these things. So please, calm down and don't do anything rash! These men you have brought here have not broken our laws. They have not robbed the temple or insulted our goddess. If Demetrius and his workers want to make any charges, we have courts for that. But these things should be done according to the law. Otherwise, we might be accused of rioting. There is no excuse for this uproar. Now go back to your homes and shops. And whatever you do, stay calm!"

So the Lord saved Paul and the Ephesian Christians from the anger of those who served false gods. As in every city Paul visited, the power of the Lord was shown to be greater than all the power Satan could muster. And the church in Ephesus continued to grow day by day. It was just as the apostle John wrote in his first letter to the churches: "You are of God, my children, and you have conquered the false prophets. The one who is in you is greater than any in the world."

Paul's Farewell

WHEN PAUL FINALLY left Ephesus, he went northward into Macedonia, then down into Greece, preaching the good news and encouraging the Christians there. After several months, he returned to the region around Ephesus and came to the town of Miletus. He was determined to go to Jerusalem, and he wanted to arrive before Pentecost, if possible. So he sent a message to the elders of the church in Ephesus and its vicinity, and they all came to meet him at Miletus. There Paul said farewell to them, knowing that he would never return.

"None of you will ever see me again," Paul said to the elders when they were all gathered. He saw the looks of disappointment and confusion that came over their faces, but he went on. "The Holy Spirit has shown me that I must go to Jerusalem. The Spirit has also warned me that trouble and time in prison lie ahead of me. But that doesn't matter, as long as I can finish the work the Lord Jesus gave me to do.

"I have been preaching the kingdom of God among you for a long time. In spite of the plots of some of the Jews, I have never stopped teaching you—in public and in private. So I will not take the blame if any of you fails to listen to the message, because I have never held back from telling the whole story of what God is doing in Christ.

"Now I am leaving the work in your hands. Watch over the flock of God, the church Jesus died for. Be on your guard against vicious wolves that will come in and try to scatter the sheep. Even some from your own group will try to lead people away after themselves, and not after Christ. So be on guard, and remember how I have taught you all for the past three years.

"I am leaving you in God's care. His grace will keep you strong. Be like me, and don't long for anyone's money. I have set you an example of hard work. You must help the weak, not take advantage of them. Remember the words of the Lord Jesus himself: 'There is more happiness in giving than in receiving.'"

Then they knelt down and prayed together. There were many tears as the other Christians hugged Paul for the last time and watched him board his ship. They stayed at dockside talking with him until at last the tide began to flow out of the harbor, carrying the ship away from the shore and out onto the open sea. They knew that they were witnessing the end of an era. Paul the apostle had done his work among them, preaching the good news and teaching them, strengthening them in the faith. Now they were ready to carry on the work of the Lord, and Paul had passed the task on to them, for the growth of the church had only begun.

TO THE ENDS OF THE EARTH

FOR PAUL, THE farewell at Miletus was an end and a beginning. His days as an evangelist, planting the seed of the good news and nurturing the growth of the church in new places, were coming to an end. Ahead of him lay a new kind of conflict, a conflict with powers and authorities at the very centers of the Jewish and Roman worlds—in Jerusalem and in Rome.

Full Circle: Paul Returns to Jerusalem

IT WAS A long journey to Jerusalem, and Paul was weary when the weeks of travel finally came to an end. But he went at once to the leaders of the church and told them the wonderful things God was doing among the Gentiles. They praised the Lord for what had happened, but they also had a problem they wanted to discuss with him. "There are rumors going around about you, Paul," they said. "People are saying that you teach the Jewish people who live among the Gentiles to give up circumcising their children and to abandon the law of Moses. Won't you please prove to them that this is not true?"

"You know what I have taught you about the law," Paul answered. "The law was our teacher, to lead us to Christ. Now that Jesus has come, the commandments about circumcision and sacrifices and feasts no longer have the same meaning. But I respect those who still keep the law, and I would never tell anyone to break it. What can I do to stop these stories?"

"There are four young men here who need to go up to the temple to fulfill a vow they have made," answered the elders. "Will you go along with them and pay for the animals for their sacrifices? That way, all the people will see that the stories they have heard are not true, but instead that you treat the law of Moses with respect. As for the Gentiles who have believed on the Lord, we have already sent them a letter asking them to keep themselves from sexual sins, and not to eat meat with the blood still in it or meat that has been sacrificed to idols—out of respect for the Jews who live in all the cities of the Gentiles."

So the next day Paul went with the four men to the temple, where they presented themselves to the priest and began a period of seven days in which they would purify themselves. At the end of a week they would return to the temple to bring the sacrifices Paul had paid for.

In the days that followed, Paul was watched everywhere he went. Although there were many in Jerusalem who followed Jesus, there were many more who hated Paul for what he taught. The most hostile were the Jews from Asia, where Paul had spent so much time preaching. They had come to Jerusalem for the feast of Pentecost, and they often saw Paul walking through the city streets with Trophimus, a Gentile believer from Ephesus. "You see," they snarled to one another, "he pals around with that unclean Gentile. The next thing you know, he'll be bringing Gentiles into the temple! What a disgrace!"

When the seven days had passed, Paul again went to the temple to be with the four young Jews when they brought their sacrifices. When the Asian Jews saw Paul walking in the temple court, they were outraged. "There he is!" one of them said. "He must have brought that Gentile friend of his with him." Another ran up to Paul and grabbed him by the

arm. "Israelites! Help!" he shouted. "This is the man who has been misleading our people and twisting our law!"

"He even brought a Gentile into the temple!" shouted a third. "He has defiled the temple!"

The temple court was thronged with worshipers that day. When they heard the shouts, they ran to where Paul and his accusers were standing. What they heard made them furious. The crowd became an angry mob that dragged Paul outside the temple court and began beating him. The riot spread through the streets, and the Roman commander thought the city was in revolution. His troops rushed from their garrison toward the temple, where the center of the violence seemed to be. As soon as they saw the Romans coming, the crowd broke up and stopped beating Paul. Some of them ran for home, but most of them stood their ground, their fists clenched in anger.

"Arrest that man!" shouted the commander, pointing at Paul. "Chain him up and take him to jail!" Then he turned to the crowds. "What is the meaning of this?" he demanded. "Who is this man, and what has he done?" But the crowd was so confused that they could not give him a straight answer. Some shouted one thing and some shouted another, but most of them just shouted, "Kill him! Kill the blasphemer!" They crowded in so close around the Roman soldiers, trying to get at Paul, that the Romans had to carry Paul up the steps of the fort.

When they reached the top of the stairs, Paul spoke to the commander. "May I say something to you?" he asked in Greek.

The commander's eyebrows shot up in surprise. "You speak Greek?

289

Then you aren't that Egyptian fellow who led a revolt a few months ago?"

"No, I am a Jew," Paul answered. "I was born in Tarsus in Cilicia, and I am a citizen of that city. Please let me speak to the people."

"If they are your people," the commander said, "then you may speak to them." So Paul stood on the platform at the top of the stairs and signaled to the crowd for quiet. He was ready to tell them his story.

Paul Defends Himself

"BROTHERS AND FATHERS, listen to me!" Paul said in Hebrew. When the crowd in the street outside the Roman garrison heard that he was speaking their language, they began to quiet down. "I am a Jew from Tarsus," Paul continued, "but I was brought up here in Jerusalem. I studied in Gamaliel's school. I learned the law of Moses and was just as devoted to it as you are. The people whom you hate, the people of the Way, I also used to hate. I arrested many of them and threw them into prison. The Sanhedrin can tell you that this is the truth, because they gave me letters allowing me to go to Damascus so I could arrest more of these people."

Then Paul told them what had happened to him on the way to Damascus: how he saw a dazzling light; how he heard the voice of Jesus calling to him; how he went on into Damascus, a blind man; how Ananias came to him, cured his blindness and told him about Jesus; and how he believed in Jesus and was baptized.

"Then I came back to Jerusalem," Paul said, "and while I was praying in the temple, the Lord appeared to me again. He said, 'Hurry and leave Jerusalem, because the people here will not listen to you.' 'Lord,' I said, 'they know that I used to arrest everyone who believed in you. When Stephen was killed, I gave my approval and stood by, guarding the clothes of those who murdered him. Surely they will believe me.' But the Lord said, 'Leave Jerusalem, because I am going to send you to the Gentiles.'"

Up to that point, the people had listened attentively to Paul. But as soon as he said that the Lord had sent him to the Gentiles, they again began to scream, "Kill him! He isn't fit to live!" They could not stand the thought that God would have anything to do with anyone but a Jew. They screamed and shouted and waved their robes in the air, all the while throwing so much dirt at Paul that the air was filled with a choking dust.

"The whole city is going to be in revolt if this keeps up," said the Roman commander. "We have to find out what this is all about, and we have to find out fast. Tie him up and whip him, and then we'll see if we can find out why these people want to kill him."

The soldiers dragged Paul into the garrison, yanked off his robe, and began to tie him to the whipping post. "Is this the way you treat a Roman citizen?" Paul asked one of the soldiers. "I haven't been accused of anything yet."

Startled, the captain ordered his men to wait. He went quickly to the commander of the garrison and asked, "What are you doing? This man is a Roman citizen!"

The commander immediately came down to the whipping post.

"Is this true?" he asked Paul nervously.

"Yes, it is true."

This was bad news. The Romans could treat conquered people however they pleased, but a Roman citizen had rights. Well, thought the commander, perhaps Paul was a second-class citizen. "I also am a Roman citizen," he said. "It cost me a great deal of money."

"I did not buy my citizenship," Paul answered. "I was born a citizen."

This was even worse. It meant that Paul outranked the Roman commander. If the case came to court, the judge would take Paul's word first. "I apologize for treating you so roughly," the commander stammered. "I only arrested you for your own good. That crowd would have killed you. You will have to stay here tonight. But tomorrow we will get to the bottom of this!"

Paul Before the Council

THE ROMAN COMMANDER still did not know why the Jews were so angry with Paul, but he knew it had something to do with their religion. Therefore, he decided to bring Paul before the Jewish Council, the Sanhedrin. Perhaps they could find out what the trouble was.

The very next day, the commander ordered a meeting of the Sanhedrin. Rome did not often use its power so openly in Jerusalem. The members of the Council were insulted, but they had no choice but to come. When they had gathered, Paul—untied now—was led before them. He was not afraid of these men, because he knew that he was in God's good care. Undaunted, he faced them and began to speak.

"My brothers," he said, "I have a clear conscience about the way I have lived my life before God to this very day."

Ananias the high priest, who was already angry because he was forced to hear this man, now became furious. A clear conscience before God? How could the fellow say such a thing? "Slap his lying mouth," he ordered those standing around Paul.

"God will slap you, you hypocrite!" Paul snapped. "You sit here to judge me by the law, but you break the law by ordering them to strike me!"

"How dare you insult God's high priest!" the men exclaimed.

Paul was surprised. He had not recognized the high priest without his formal robes. "I am sorry, my brothers, but I did not know that he was the high priest," Paul said. "Otherwise, I would never have said that. I know that the law says, 'You shall not speak evil of a ruler of your people.'"

In the silence that followed, Paul looked around at the members of the Council. He knew many of them by name, and he knew that some were Pharisees and some were Sadducees. The Sadducees did not believe in spirits or angels or the resurrection of the dead, but the Pharisees believed in all those things. So Paul said, "My brothers, I am a Pharisee, the son of a Pharisee; and the reason I am on trial today is because I believe in the resurrection of the dead."

The Council chamber was instantly in an uproar. The Pharisees and the Sadducees almost flew at one another. "Away with this man!" shouted the Sadducees.

"No! He's not guilty," said one of the Pharisees. "He's right—there is a resurrection of the dead!"

"Nonsense! The dead won't rise again! This fellow is a fraud!"

"Wait!" said another of the Pharisees. "Perhaps a spirit did talk to him, or an angel!"

"They don't exist! Take him away!"

The Pharisees had Paul by one arm, and the Sadducees had him by the other; and the Roman commander was afraid they would tear him to pieces. His soldiers waded into the fray and rescued Paul, carrying him back to the fort.

That night, Paul lay on his bed wondering whether he had accomplished anything at all. Was it worth all that shouting and fighting? Would anyone listen to him? Discouraged and depressed, he fell asleep. But that very night the Lord came to him in a vision and said, "Keep up your courage, Paul! Just as you have testified for me in Jerusalem, so you must also witness in Rome." After that, Paul slept peacefully through the night.

A Plot Against Paul's Life

PAUL'S ENEMIES HAD not given up yet. The morning after the meeting with the Sanhedrin, they got together to hatch their plot. "Yesterday's meeting was a disaster," one of them said. "We must not let our own differences get in the way of our plans."

"But how can we be sure that we will work together?" another asked.

"We must take a vow," the first suggested. "We must vow that we will not eat or drink until Paul is dead."

So these men, more than forty of them altogether, vowed that they would not eat or drink until they had killed Paul. Then they went to the Sanhedrin and told them what they had done. "All you have to do is cooperate with us," they said. "Send a message to the Roman commander that you need more information from this man. Ask that he be brought here to the Council chamber. When he comes, we will be waiting for him." And the council agreed.

There was only one problem with their plan. It is difficult enough for two people to keep a secret; for forty people to keep one is almost impossible. Some of them just had to tell their friends how clever they were to think of a way to get rid of Paul. Two men were talking about the plot in the noisy market square, sure that no one would be able to hear them above all the clamor. They scarcely noticed the young man so busily eating a pomegranate and spitting the seeds onto the cobblestones. But when the young man heard the two mention the name of Paul, he was suddenly all ears. Could they mean his uncle Paul?

Within an hour Paul's sister's son was visiting him in prison, telling him what he had overheard in the marketplace. When he had finished his story, Paul called for one of the guards. "Will you take my nephew to the commander, please?" he asked. "I think he will be interested in what the lad has to say."

The guard was only too happy to do as Paul asked. After all, Paul was almost a privileged guest, being a Roman citizen and all. So he took Paul's nephew to the commanding officer. "The prisoner Paul asked me to bring this young man to you," he said. "It seems he has some information for you."

The commander motioned to the young man and led him to a quiet corner. "Now, what did you have to tell me?" he asked.

"I heard two men plotting in the marketplace today," the nephew said.

"The Jewish Council has decided to ask you to bring Paul to them tomorrow. They are going to pretend that they want more information from him. Please don't listen to them! There will be more than forty men hiding and waiting to kill him. They have taken a vow that they won't eat or drink anything until Paul is dead."

"All right, I'll take care of it," the commander said. "But don't you tell anyone that you've told me. We don't want them to find out that their plot has failed."

As soon as Paul's nephew was gone, the commander called in two of his officers. "It seems that we have a problem on our hands," he said. "Someone wants to assassinate our prisoner. I want you to get together a company of two hundred infantrymen, a company of two hundred spearmen, and a squadron of seventy mounted cavalry. I want this to look like a troop movement, not the transfer of a prisoner. Make sure there's an extra horse for Paul to ride, and get the prisoner safely to Governor Felix in Caesarea. You'll leave at nine o'clock tonight. By the time you're ready, I'll have a letter waiting for you to take to the governor."

The officers saluted and went out, and the commander sat down to write his letter. "Greetings to Governor Felix from Commander Claudius Lysias," he wrote. "This man was taken by the Jews, who tried to kill him. But I found out that he is a Roman citizen, so I sent my men to rescue him. I took him to their Council to discover what the accusation was, but I found that the whole matter has something to do with Jewish laws. He has done nothing to deserve imprisonment. But in the meantime I learned that there is a plot against his life, so I thought it best to send him to you. I will tell the Jewish authorities that they may go to Caesarea and make their accusations."

That night, under cover of darkness, Paul was moved to Caesarea. It was morning when they arrived at the palace of the governor. When Felix had read the letter from Claudius, he asked Paul, "What province are you from?"

"From Cilicia," Paul answered.

"Hmm. Very well," the governor said. "I will hear you out when your accusers arrive. For the time being, you will stay in my headquarters under guard—for your own protection."

The Governor Hears Paul's Case

FIVE DAYS LATER, Ananias the high priest and several other Jewish leaders arrived in Caesarea to make their charges against Paul. Governor Felix immediately sent for Paul, because as a Roman citizen he was entitled to hear everything that was said against him. It was not the high priest who spoke, however, but a lawyer named Tertullus.

"Your Excellency," Tertullus began, "your wisdom and statesmanship have brought peace to our province. You have also made important reforms, for which we are very grateful."

"I am well acquainted with Jewish gratitude," Felix said. "Get on with it."

"Yes, well, I do not wish to take up too much of your time, so I will be brief," Tertullus went on.

"Good," said the governor.

"Paul is a dangerous man, Your Excellency. He has started riots among the Jews in all parts of the world, just as he did in Jerusalem. He is a leader of a group known as the Nazarenes. When he tried to pollute our temple, we arrested him. We would have tried him by our own law if Commander Lysias had not come and taken him. If you question the prisoner, you will discover that what we have said is true." And all the others agreed that this was the charge against Paul.

"Paul, you may speak in your own defense," said Governor Felix.

"I know that you have been governor for twelve years, and so have some knowledge of our people," Paul began. "You should be aware that I came to Jerusalem only twelve days ago. I did not speak in any of the synagogues or argue with anyone or stir up any trouble. There is no proof of the accusations they have made. But I do admit to this: I worship the God of Israel by following the Way, which they say is a false sect. But I still believe everything written in the law and the prophets. Just like these men, I believe that all people, both bad and good, will be raised from the dead. Therefore, I always do my best to live with a clear conscience before God.

"I was in the temple when some Jews from Asia seized me," Paul went on. "There was no mob with me, and there was no riot. Actually, those who seized me should be the ones making accusations here. The only crime these men can testify to is what I said to the Sanhedrin—that I was accused because I believe in the resurrection of the dead."

Felix saw that Paul was not guilty of a crime, but he did not want to

295

anger the Jewish leaders by letting him go. So he decided to delay. "We must wait for the commander Lysias to arrive," he said. "Then I will decide this case. This hearing is closed."

Paul remained under guard, but his friends were allowed to visit him. Felix himself had heard quite a bit about the new Way, as people called it, and he thought it would be interesting to hear more. So after a few days, he called Paul to talk with him and his wife Drusilla, who was Jewish. Paul spoke about faith in the Lord Jesus, about right living and about the day of judgment that is coming. As Paul talked, Felix grew more and more nervous. He knew that his own life was not what it ought to be. But rather than listen to the Lord's message, Felix decided to shut it out. "That's enough for now," he said quickly. "I'll send for you again when I have the time."

Still, Felix did not set Paul free. He hoped that Paul would pay him a bribe to gain his freedom. But Paul knew that the Lord had a reason for his imprisonment, so he refused to take this easy way out. Felix sent for Paul often and talked with him, but he was more interested in receiving a bribe than in receiving God's gift of life in Christ Jesus. Soon his chance to hear the good news was completely gone. After two years, he was called back to Rome, and Porcius Festus became governor. Because he wanted the emperor to hear good reports about him from the Jewish leaders, Felix left Paul in prison.

Paul Appears Before Festus and Agrippa

THE NEW GOVERNOR, Porcius Festus, first went to Jerusalem to meet the Jewish leaders. They immediately told him about Paul and asked that the prisoner be brought to Jerusalem. Once again they were plotting to have Paul killed. But Festus replied, "I am going to Caesarea. Come back there with me, and you can make your charges."

A week or so later, Festus went back to Caesarea with the Jewish leaders from Jerusalem, and the next day he called for a hearing with them and the prisoner. The Council members made the same old accusations against Paul, but they were unable to prove any of them. "I have done nothing wrong," Paul said. "I have not broken the law of Moses or the law of Rome."

Festus knew Paul's words were true. But he was the new governor, and he wanted the Jewish leaders to think well of him. Perhaps he could please them with a trial in Jerusalem. "Would you be willing to go to Jerusalem," he asked Paul, "and be tried on these charges there?"

"The emperor's court is here in Caesarea," Paul answered, "and this is where I should be tried. I have done no wrong to the Jews, you know that. If I have committed some other crime, I will not try to escape the penalty.

But if their charges are false, I should not be handed over to them. I appeal to the emperor."

"Can he do that?" Festus asked his advisors after calling them aside for a private conference.

"Your Excellency, the man is a Roman citizen," they replied. "He has the right to appeal his case directly to the emperor."

"What's the matter with the fellow, doesn't he think he will get justice from me?" Festus asked. Paul's action irritated him. What would Caesar think when such a small matter was brought before him?

"It is not necessary for him to give a reason for his appeal, as you well know, Your Excellency. The case is now out of your hands."

Festus returned to his court and sat again in his seat of judgment. He looked at Paul and said, "You have appealed to the emperor. Very well, you shall go to the emperor. I will have nothing more to do with this case." And the Jewish leaders had to go back to Jerusalem disappointed.

But the Lord still had work for Paul to do in Caesarea. He was kept there for several months, waiting for all the arrangements to be made for his trip to Rome. While he was waiting, Governor Festus had some visitors: King Agrippa and his sister Bernice came to welcome the governor and congratulate him on his appointment. Agrippa was not much of a king, really; he ruled a small region in the northern part of Palestine. But Festus wanted to keep all the Jewish leaders happy. Besides, his visitors were the brother and sister of Drusilla, the wife of the former governor. So Festus made them welcome, and they stayed for several days.

To keep the conversation going one evening, Festus told Agrippa and Bernice about Paul. "A most interesting case," he said. "When I went to Jerusalem, the Jewish leaders brought charges against him. I told them, of course, that under Roman law they would have to make their charges to his face. I thought they would accuse him of murder or something serious. But as it turned out, they only had some arguments with him about their own religion and about a man named Jesus, who is dead, although this Paul claims that the man is alive. Well, I couldn't make heads or tails out of that, so I asked Paul if he would be willing to go to Jerusalem for a trial. But what do you suppose he did? He appealed to the emperor! So now I have to keep him under guard until he goes to Rome. I don't think the man is guilty of anything, but I have to write something to the emperor. I thought perhaps that since you are Jewish, you might be able to help me understand this case."

"I would like to hear what the man has to say," Agrippa answered.

It was busy in the palace the next morning. Everyone of any rank had been invited, from military officers to city officials. King Agrippa and his sister entered with great pomp and ceremony, dressed in their royal robes. Then Festus sent for Paul.

"King Agrippa," he said when the prisoner had arrived, "you see before you a man whom the Jewish people in Jerusalem say is a great criminal. They clamor for his death. But I could not find him guilty of any crime. Now he has appealed to the emperor, and I have decided to send him. But I have nothing very definite to say to the emperor about him. So I have brought him before this distinguished audience—and especially before you, King Agrippa—so that you may advise me as to what I should write. I can hardly send him to Rome without stating the charges against him." Then Festus turned to Paul and said, "You may speak for yourself."

"King Agrippa," Paul began, "I feel fortunate that you are here to hear me today, because you know Jewish customs and Jewish arguments well. So allow me to explain myself. The Jewish leaders have known me since I was a boy. They know, if they would only admit it, that I have always been a Pharisee, a member of the strictest sect of our religion. But today I am on trial because of my hope in the resurrection of the dead, the promise God made to our fathers." Here Paul looked at his whole audience. "Why do you find it so hard to believe that God can raise the dead? I myself am a witness to the fact that Jesus of Nazareth has arisen.

"There was a time when I did everything I could against Jesus of Nazareth. The same Council that now accuses me once gave me authority to arrest those who followed Jesus and to throw them into prison. When these people of God were tried and sentenced to death, I voted against them. I even hunted them down in foreign cities.

"I was on my way to Damascus to arrest more followers of Jesus when I was surrounded by a light brighter than the sun. My companions and I all fell to the ground. Then I heard a voice speaking to me in Hebrew and saying, 'Saul! Why are you persecuting me? You only hurt yourself by resisting me.' 'Who are you, Lord?' I asked. And the Lord said to me, 'I am Jesus, whom you are persecuting. Now stand up. I have come to make you my servant. You will tell others about me. I will even send you to the gentiles. Open their eyes, so that they may turn from darkness to the light, and from Satan's power to God. By believing in me, they will have their sins forgiven and will become part of God's own people.' ''

Paul paused for the effect of this to sink in. Then he said, "I obeyed this heavenly vision, King Agrippa. I brought the good news to many Jews and then to the Gentiles. Because I preached God's message to the Gentiles, I was seized in the temple by some Jews and brought here. But God has helped me and has allowed me to stand here today, telling what I know to the great and the small. My message is nothing but what Moses and the prophets said would happen—how the Christ would suffer and die and be the first one to be raised from the dead, so that the light of salvation could shine on both Jews and Gentiles."

Suddenly Governor Festus shouted out: "You've gone mad, Paul! Your great learning has driven you mad."

"I am not mad, Your Excellency!" Paul answered. "I am speaking the sober truth. King Agrippa, you know about these things. Jesus did not live and die in some faraway corner of the world. Do you believe what the prophets said, King Agrippa? I know you do!"

Agrippa was shaken to his very roots. This was a challenge he could not avoid. But he was not ready to take a stand for Jesus. He tried to laugh off the message of salvation. "You think you can make a Christian out of me in such a short time, Paul?" he said.

"Whether it's a short or long time," Paul answered, "I wish to God that you and everyone here might become what I am—except for these chains."

But Festus and Agrippa had heard enough. They had wealth and power, and there was no room left in their lives for Jesus of Nazareth. The crowd filed out of the court room, leaving Paul alone with his guards. Only the Lord knew whether his message had gotten through to anyone.

"The man may be a fanatic, but he has not committed a crime," Agrippa said when they had left the court room.

"I agree with my brother," Bernice said. "He has done nothing that deserves death or imprisonment."

"I know," Festus said disgustedly. How could he explain to the emperor that he was sending an innocent man to Rome for trial? There was no comfort for Festus when King Agrippa said, "If only he had not appealed to the emperor, you could have set him free. What a pity!"

But Paul had no regrets. He had the Lord's word that he would proclaim the good news in Rome itself. The Roman ship that came to pick up a prisoner would be carrying out the will of God.

Shipwreck

JULIUS, THE CAPTAIN of the emperor's regiment, looked over the bunch of prisoners he was to take to Rome. The usual crew of thieves and murderers, most of them headed for the galleys no doubt. But Paul, this Jewish fellow, was different. "No need to keep him chained," Governor Festus had said. "He won't try to escape. He actually seems glad to be going." And so he was. He seemed to be a scholar of some sort, and certainly not a criminal.

The Lord gave Paul companionship on the long voyage: two Christian friends were on board as passengers. When the ship stopped at Sidon, Captain Julius allowed Paul to go ashore with them. There they met brothers and sisters of the church with whom they could pray and talk about the Lord. When it was time for Paul to leave, his friends saw to it that he had everything he needed. The Lord was watching over his messenger.

In Myra, a large port city, they changed to another ship, which was on its way from Egypt to Italy. But now the wind had changed, and it was slow going along the coast. They could not take the shortest route, but had to sail south and then westward again along the sheltered side of the island of Crete. It was still tough going, and after a long and difficult voyage they finally managed to make port at Fair Havens on the southern coast of the island.

They stayed at Fair Havens for several weeks, waiting for the weather to change; but the wind still blew out of the west. Winter, the most dangerous season of the year for a voyage, was coming, and Captain Julius had to decide whether to stay in Fair Havens or to risk continuing the voyage. Paul was filled with the Holy Spirit, and he advised Julius: "It will be a dangerous voyage. If we go on, there will be a great deal of loss to the ship and the cargo. We will lose some men too. We should stay here for the winter."

"Nonsense!" said the ship's captain. "Fair Havens is no place to spend the winter. The harbor is open to the weather. The ship might sink at anchor. We should sail to Phoenix, farther along the coast, and stay there for the winter."

"I appreciate your advice, Paul," Julius said, "but the captain is a seafaring man. He knows the weather in these parts. If he says he can get us to Phoenix, then I think we should go."

They sailed from Fair Havens under a light breeze. For a few days it seemed as though the ship's captain were right. Then suddenly a strong northeaster blew down and caught the ship on the open sea. The ship bobbed and lurched like a cork on the water. Bracing himself against the shrieking gale, the helmsman tried to keep the ship on course, but it was no

use. "Captain, we'll just have to let her run with the wind," he shouted, and swung the ship around so that the wind blew from the stern. Now they could only hope that there were no rocks or sand bars ahead.

The wind blew them alongside the island of Cauda, though it was too dangerous to attempt a landing. But the island gave them a little shelter from the wind, enough so that they could pull the ship's boat aboard and prevent it from being smashed against the stern. Then the storm broke on them with renewed fury, carrying them toward the coast of Africa. "At this rate, we'll run aground and be smashed to pieces," the captain shouted over the noise of the gale. "Drop the sail! We'll let the wind carry us!"

The crew knew they were in a desperate spot. With no sail, they had no way of steering the ship away from any island or sand bar that might lie in their path. They lashed together some heavy beams from the cargo hold and made a sort of raft, which they pushed overboard and tied to the stern rail with some stout rope. They hoped the raft would serve as a sea anchor to slow the ship and keep them from running aground.

Waves now washed over the deck, and the ship took on so much water that she began to founder. In desperation, the crew began throwing cargo overboard to lighten the ship. On the following day, they threw overboard everything that could be moved, everything but the food they needed to survive. But the ship pitched and rolled so violently that they could not eat anyway. And still the storm continued. The skies were so black that they could hardly tell day from night. Some of the crew began to pray to their gods, but after days of weathering the storm, they gave up even that hope and despaired of their lives. Exhausted from lack of food and sleep, the sailors and passengers could only wait for death.

Day after day the storm raged on. The sailors lost track of time because of the darkness, and they grew weak from lack of food. But just when they were most desperate, Paul got up and began to speak to them. He was the only one on board who had not given up hope. "Listen to me, men!" he shouted so that he could be heard above the storm. "If you had listened to me before we left Crete, we wouldn't be in this spot now."

"True enough," one of the men said. "But it's too late now."

"No, it's not too late," Paul answered. "You didn't listen to me before, but listen to me now. Don't give up! No one is going to die. Only the ship will be lost. Last night an angel came to me from my God, the God I belong to and worship. The angel said, 'Don't be afraid, Paul. You must appear before the emperor. In his mercy to you, God will save the lives of all those on board.'"

Paul was so confident that the men began to take hope. Their gods had failed them, but here was a man who still had faith in his God. Perhaps he was a prophet. After all, he had warned them not to set sail. Yet it was pretty hard to believe. "How is this going to happen?" asked one of the crew.

"God will make the storm blow us ashore on an island," Paul answered. "The ship will be broken up, but all of us will be saved. I trust God to do just as he promised."

That night was the fourteenth night since the storm had struck. About midnight there was a change in the sound of the storm. Above the noise of the wind they could hear the booming of great breakers crashing against rocks. "Take a sounding!" the captain ordered. The crew threw over the sounding line and read the depth at twenty fathoms. There had to be land nearby. A few minutes later they took another sounding: only fifteen fathoms this time. The sea bed was rising fast, and the sound of the breakers was getting closer. They were going to be dashed against the rocks!

The crew quickly dropped four anchors from the stern of the ship, hoping that those would hold the ship off the rocks until daylight. But still the ship drifted closer and closer to the rocky shore. Then the captain saw that some of the men were cutting loose the ship's boat. "What are you doing there?" he demanded.

"We need the bow anchors, Captain," one of them answered. "We can't throw them over because they might damage the ship. We'll have to row them out in the boat and drop them."

But Paul saw right through that scheme: he knew they were trying to abandon ship. He said to Captain Julius, "If the sailors don't stay on board, there is no hope for anyone to be saved."

Julius knew that Paul's God was their only hope now. "Cut those ropes!" he shouted to his men. The soldiers ran to the side and cut the ropes the sailors were using to lower the ship's boat. The boat dropped into the water, bobbed wildly on the waves for a moment, then nosed under a giant wave and disappeared.

Just before dawn, Paul urged the men to eat something. "You haven't eaten anything for days," he said. "But you're going to need your strength. I promise that you won't be hurt. You won't even lose a hair from your head. But you must eat." Then Paul took a loaf of bread, raised his hand toward heaven, and thanked God for the food. When they saw Paul's faith, they took courage and began to eat. When they had finished, they threw all the rest of the food on board into the sea to lighten the ship.

At daybreak they saw land, but the sailors did not recognize the coast. There was a small bay, and the captain decided to make a run for the beach. "Cut away the anchor lines!" he ordered. "Cut loose the rudder! Make some sail!" The sailors scrambled to raise the forward sail, the helmsman took the rudder, and the soldiers cut the lines holding the anchors. The ship leaped toward the beach. Then, with a shuddering crunch, the ship ran aground on a sand bar. The bow stuck fast, but the stern was whipped back and forth by the waves. "The ship is breaking up!" the captain shouted. "Abandon ship!"

"Kill the prisoners!" said one of the soldiers. "We don't want them to escape!"

"No!" their captain ordered. He didn't want to see Paul die now, after he had brought them through the storm. "If you can swim, jump overboard now and swim for shore. If you can't, grab one of the boards or pieces of wood in the water and kick like mad!" And so, swimming through the water or floating on pieces of the broken ship, every man aboard—all 276 of them—came safely to land. The Lord had kept his promise. His messenger Paul would yet proclaim the good news in Rome.

On the Island of Malta

FROM ALL SIDES the people of the island rushed to help the shipwrecked men. The men learned that they were on Malta, which was quite close to Italy. So all that time, the storm had been blowing them in the right direction! A helmsman could not have done better.

The storm was dying down at last, but a cold rain was still falling. So the Maltese people built a fire on the beach as they welcomed the strangers. The men from the ship helped gather wood for the fire, and Paul joined in by carrying an armful of driftwood. Just as he was throwing

it onto the fire, a snake slithered out of the wood and bit Paul's hand. The snake did not let go, and Paul stood there with the snake dangling from his hand. The native people looked at Paul, horrified. "He must be a criminal," one of them said. "He escaped from the sea, but the gods will not allow him to live."

Paul did not even look worried. He believed God's promise that he would go to Rome. No snake on Malta could kill him! So he shook the snake off into the fire and went on about his business as if nothing had happened. The people of the island watched him in astonishment. Surely his hand would swell up any minute, and he would go into convulsions and die. But nothing happened. Paul went right on gathering wood. After keeping an eye on him for quite a while, the Maltese began muttering among themselves: "He has defied Fate! He must be a god!"

Not far from the beach were the house and lands of Publius, the most important man on the island. He was wealthy enough to provide hospitality for the crew while he found places for them to stay on the island for the winter. Paul found his friend Luke (the doctor who had been one of Jesus' followers), who was a passenger aboard the shipwrecked vessel, and they stayed in Publius' house for three days. They soon learned that Publius' father had been sick in bed with a fever for some time. Paul went at once to his room, placed his hands on him, and prayed. And immediately the man got up, dressed, and came to the table for something to eat.

Publius was astounded at what Paul had done. Word soon spread throughout the island, and many sick people were brought to him. He healed them all, and many believed in Jesus because of the miracles Paul did. So everywhere Paul went, God used him to bring the good news about Jesus.

Paul in Rome

AFTER THREE MONTHS on the island of Malta, the group set sail for Rome aboard another ship that had spent the winter there. The people of the island brought gifts to Paul and Luke so that they would have everything they needed for the voyage. By this time, the Christians in Rome knew that Paul had been in Malta, and they knew what ship he would be arriving on. Many of them came out of the city to greet him, and he was overjoyed to see them. The Roman authorities allowed him to have a house of his own, but they kept him under guard.

Since he was under house arrest and not free to go to the synagogue, Paul asked the local Jewish leaders to meet him at his house. "Fellow Israelites," he said to them when they were assembled, "I have done nothing against our people or our law. Nevertheless, I was taken prisoner in Jerusalem and handed over to the Romans. They could not find me guilty of any crime, and would have released me, but the Jewish leaders opposed this. So I was forced to appeal to the emperor. But I do not want you to think that I am going to make any accusations against my own people. That's why I wanted to talk with you. The only reason I am wearing these chains is because I share the hope of Israel."

"We have not heard anything from Jerusalem about you," they answered. "No one has made any accusations. But we would like to hear what you have to say. We have heard many people speak against this group you belong to, the ones they call the people of the Way. May we come back and hear you out?"

So they agreed on a day, and leaders came from every synagogue in Rome on that day. They came early in the morning and stayed all through the day and into the evening as Paul spoke to them about the kingdom of God. He quoted from the law of Moses and from the prophets to show them that Jesus really was the Messiah who had come to die for the sins of the world. Some of them believed in Jesus, but others did not.

"You see," said Paul, "the words of the prophet Isaiah have come true this very day. Remember his words:

> Go and tell this people,
> You will listen, but you will not understand;
>   you will look, but you will see nothing.
> Because their minds have become dull,
>   and they have closed their eyes and ears.
> Otherwise, they would see and hear
>   and they would turn to me, says the Lord,
>   and I would heal them.

"You have heard the message," Paul went on, "and you have rejected it. Now the message of salvation will be taken to the Gentiles. They will listen." With this speech, God's prophecy was fulfilled: Paul would preach the gospel in Rome, the capital of the empire.

Paul used his time well while he was under arrest. He often visited with the Christians in Rome, and he wrote many letters to other churches. Some of these letters were so important that they became part of the New Testament. But the Romans could not keep Paul in prison indefinitely. After about two years they released him, and he spent the next three or four years continuing his preaching, as well as caring for the groups of believers in all the cities he had visited before. During this time he visited Crete again, along with a man named Titus, whom he left there to care for the growing churches. Paul also had time to train Timothy, and, leaving Timothy in charge of the church in Ephesus, he crossed over to Macedonia, the northern part of Greece.

By this time, however, the Romans had decided that the message of Jesus was dangerous. After all, Christians claimed that all power and authority belonged to Jesus Christ; the Romans said that the emperor was the only all-powerful god. Faith in God and faith in Rome were bound to crash head-on. When they did, Paul was arrested and taken back to Rome. This time he lived in a Roman dungeon instead of his own house. When he knew that he was soon going to die for his faith in Jesus, Paul wrote to Timothy, his friend and pupil: "I have fought the good fight, I have finished the race, and I have kept the faith. Now the crown of victory is waiting for me. On that day the Lord, the righteous judge, will award it to me—and to all those who eagerly wait for him to appear."

VII.
The Revelation
to John

What's Happening

THE WORLD WE live in today is filled with doubt and confusion. Terrorists strike, wars flare up, people are kidnapped and held hostage, inner city streets are scenes of daily violence. About half of the world's population goes to bed hungry every night. People are confused, wondering whether there is any real meaning to life, whether there is any real hope. Even those who believe in Jesus Christ often feel helpless and hopeless in the face of such a world.

We are not the first Christians to feel this way. Just fifty years after Jesus' death and resurrection, the church was experiencing a period of great persecution. Roman emperors, trying to keep their pagan world secure, turned in hatred and anger on those who believed in Christ and had them arrested. They sent many to an early death chained to oars in the bottom of Roman ships. They forced others to work as slaves in Roman mines. Still others were killed by gladiators or by animals in Roman arenas as entertainment for the people. Where was the promise of the Lord's return? Where was the hope of the new earth? Why was it taking so long? What was happening?

One by one, the original followers of Jesus died and went to be with him, including Paul, who gave his life as a martyr for the gospel of the Lord Jesus Christ. Only the apostle John was still alive and preaching, but he too had been arrested. He had been sentenced to exile rather than death, banished to the island of Patmos, north of Crete in the islands of the Aegean Sea. It was a bitter lot for John, for he could neither preach nor take care of the churches.

There on Patmos the Lord gave John a series of visions, in which he showed him the meaning of the things that were taking place and would take place, and reminded him that God was still the sovereign Lord of all. The Lord gave these visions, this revelation, to John in order to encourage the whole church, to show God's people that he had not forgotten them. "This is the Revelation God gave to Jesus Christ," John wrote, "so that his servants might know what is happening. He made it known by sending his angel to his servant John."

What John wrote down were visions. In them, nothing is exactly what it seems to be; everything is a symbol for something else. For this reason, the language John uses is often difficult to understand. John says that he saw Jesus as "a lamb that had been killed, a lamb with seven horns and seven eyes." We would think that a seven-eyed, seven-horned dead lamb would look rather horrible. But John does not want us to think that this is what the Lord Jesus looks like. The lamb was dead because Jesus died for our sins. It had seven horns and seven eyes because seven is a number that stands for something being finished—just as we are told in the Genesis story that God created the world in seven days. Symbols of this kind were used through the whole book of the Revelation. They were a kind of code: Christians of John's day would understand them, but other people would find them a mystery.

John sent his message to the seven churches of Asia, not because there were only seven but because the number seven stands for the whole of God's people scattered throughout the world. "John wishes you grace and peace," he began, "from the one who was, the one who is, the one who is to come. This comes from Jesus Christ, the one whose word can always be trusted, the one who was the first-born of all those who will rise from death, the one who rules all the kings of the earth. He loves us and has washed away our sins with his own blood, and has made us a royal nation of priests to serve his God and Father. May all glory be to him, forever and ever!

"Look! He is coming among the clouds.
　　Everyone will see him,
　　even those who killed him.
All peoples of the earth shall mourn over him.
　　This will surely come to pass!
'I am the Alpha and the Omega,' says the Lord God,
　　the one who was, who is, and who is to come,
　　the Almighty One."

With this greeting on behalf of Jesus, John set the stage for the great visions to come.

The Royal Shepherd

"WRITE DOWN WHAT you see," said the voice, "and send the book to the churches in the seven cities of Asia."

In his vision John looked around to see who was talking to him. There before him he saw seven golden lampstands. Walking among the lampstands was what seemed to be a person wearing a long robe. His hair was as white as snow, and his eyes were as bright as fire. His feet were like polished brass, and his voice roared like a waterfall. In his right hand were seven stars, and in his mouth was a doubled-edged sword. His face was so bright that John fell down at the man's feet.

"Don't be afraid," said the voice. "I am the first and the last. I am the one who lives. I was dead, but I am alive again forever. I have power over death. Write down the things you see. These seven lampstands are the seven churches, and the seven stars are their guardians."

Then Christ, the royal shepherd, showed his care for his flock by giving

John a message for each of the seven churches. Jesus knew each church well—its strengths and weaknesses, hopes and fears—and to each he gave a message of his own personal care. Some he warned, some he praised, some he scolded, some he encouraged, but to each he was the shepherd who was still watching over them, even in times of great distress.

To Ephesus he said, "I know how you have worked, and how you have endured. You cannot stand wicked people. You are patient and do not become discouraged. But you no longer love me as you did at first. Repent, and do as you did at first, or I will remove your lampstand from its place."

To Smyrna he said, "I know what trials you have gone through. I know how much you have suffered from those who persecute you. But do not fear the suffering that is yet to come. The devil will send some of you to

310

prison to test you. Remain faithful even if you have to die, and I will crown you with life."

For his people in Pergamum and Thyatira, Jesus had both encouragement and warning, but for his people in Sardis his warning was much stronger. "People say that you are alive, but I know how dead you are! Wake up! Build on what you have left. If you do not repent, I will come in judgment on you like a thief who sneaks in when no one is looking. But there are a few of you who have never strayed away from me. You will walk with me in white robes of joy and victory."

Jesus also had words of encouragement for a weak and struggling church in Philadelphia. "You do not have much strength," he said, "but you have kept my commandments and have not denied me. I will keep you safe through the sufferings that are coming. Remember, I am coming soon. Hold on to what you have, and don't let anyone rob you of your crown."

The last of the seven churches was in Laodicea. "I wish you were hot or cold," Jesus said to his people there. "But because you are lukewarm, I will spit you out. You say, 'I am so rich that I don't need anything more.' You don't know how poor you are, how blind and naked! Listen to me! If you want to be rich, get the gold from me that has been refined in the fire. Remember that you need the white robes that only I can give you. Your eyes are closed, and only I can give you the ointment that will make you see again. Repent! I am knocking at your door. Open it, and I will come in and dine with you. Let all those with ears to hear listen to the Spirit's word to the churches."

With these words Jesus spoke both correction and encouragement to his people in all the world, so that they would be able to face the difficult times that lay ahead of them.

He's Got the Whole World in His Hand

AFTER THE VISION of the seven letters, John once more heard the same voice, loud as a trumpet blast, saying, "Come up here, and I will show you what is going to happen." Then John's eyes were opened and he saw the throne of God, shining like a precious stone and covered with a rainbow. There were twenty-four other thrones around it, and on each throne sat an elder in white robes wearing a golden crown. Twelve of them stood for the twelve tribes of Israel, and twelve for the twelve apostles.

Surrounding the throne of God were four creatures, each with six wings, and they were singing:

> Holy, holy, holy
>   is the Lord God almighty,
> who was, and who is,
>   and who is to come.

311

Then the twenty-four elders knelt down in front of the throne, took the crowns from their heads, and threw them down at the foot of the throne. As they knelt they said:

O Lord our God, you are worthy
  to receive glory and honor and power,
For you have created all things;
  by your will they came into being!

John saw a scroll in the right hand of the one who sat on the throne, and the scroll was sealed with seven seals. It was the book of God's will—his purposes in everything that was happening. A loud voice cried out, "Who is worthy to take the scroll and break its seals?" But there was no

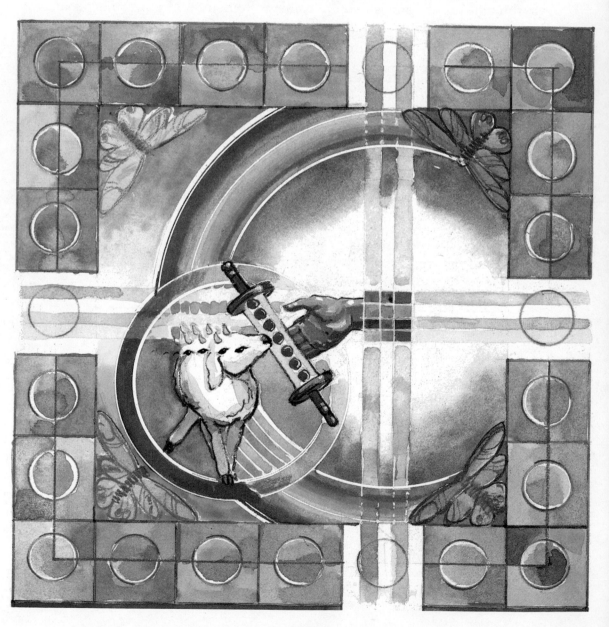

answer from heaven or earth. John bowed his head and wept when he saw that there was no one to open the scroll. Was there no answer? Could no one know the meaning of the terrible things happening on the earth?

Then one of the twenty-four elders said to him, "Don't cry any more. Look! The Lion from Judah's tribe, the son of David, has won the victory. He can open the scroll." John looked up and saw beside the throne a lamb that had been killed, but which was alive again. The lamb had seven horns and seven eyes, which stood for the seven spirits of God sent out into the whole earth. The lamb took the scroll from the hand of the one on the throne. John's heart leaped up within him when he saw this. The Lamb of God held the key to all the secrets! No matter what happened, no matter how terrible things might be, everything was in his hand!

Then John heard the voices of the elders rising in a song of praise to Jesus, a song no one had ever sung before. The twenty-four elders, the church from the Old Testament time and from the New Testament time, bowed down in front of the Lamb. Each of them carried a harp and a golden bowl full of incense, the prayers of the Lord's people. The prayers came out of the suffering and pain that surrounded the church in a world full of sin; but when they were poured out, they were like the incense burned on the altars in Israel, rising up in a sweet smell of praise to the Lord. And the elders sang this song:

> You are worthy to take the scroll,
>   and to open its seals.
> With your blood you bought for God
>   people from every tribe and nation.
> You have made of them a kingdom,
>   and priests to serve our God,
>   and they shall rule on earth.

Then there came a sound such as no one had ever heard before, the voices of thousands and millions of angels, who stood around the throne and sang:

> Worthy is the lamb that was slain
>   to receive power and riches,
>   and wisdom and strength,
>   and honor and glory and praise.

Then every creature in heaven and on earth joined their voices in the singing:

> To him who sits upon the throne,
>   and to the Lamb,
>   be praise and honor, glory and might,
>   forever and ever!

We Are Protected

THE LAMB TOOK the sealed book of God's will from the hand of the one who sat on the throne and began to break the seals. Then John began to see that, as God's will unfolds, terrible and frightening things come also. The persecutions and sufferings of the past, the present, and the future are part of the way God's will is worked out. When the Lamb broke the first seal, John saw a white horse ride out of heaven with a rider wearing a crown and carrying a bow and arrow; and the rider went forth to conquer. When the Lamb broke the second seal, a red horse rode out bearing a rider with a large sword; he brought war on the earth. The third seal was broken, and a black horse rode out carrying a rider with a pair of scales in his hand; he brought famine on the earth. Then the fourth seal was broken, and a deathly pale horse rode out; its rider's name was Death, and Hades followed close behind. In one quarter of the earth, people died of war and famine and disease.

Then the Lamb opened the fifth seal, and suddenly John heard the sound of voices shouting. There, under the altar, were those who had died for their faith in the Lord. They were saying, "How long will it be, O faithful and true God, before you judge our case and punish those who murdered us?" Then each of them was given a white robe, and they were told to rest a while longer, until the number of the martyrs had been completed; for there were others who would yet die for their faith.

When the Lamb opened the sixth seal, there was a terrible earthquake. The sun was blotted out, and the stars fell down like overripe fruit. The sky disappeared, and the mountains were shaken down. The mighty men of the earth, the rich and the powerful, tried to hide in caves in the mountains. They cried out, "O mountains, fall on us and hide us from the eyes of the one who sits on the throne, and from the anger of the Lamb! The great day of their anger has come, and who can stand against it?"

Then John saw twelve thousand people from each of the twelve tribes of Israel, and God's mark was on their foreheads. He looked again and saw an enormous throng of people from every race and nation on earth, dressed in white robes and holding palm branches in their hands. "Salvation comes from our God, who sits on the throne," they said, "and from the Lamb." Then the angels and the twenty-four elders and the four six-winged creatures bowed down and said, "Amen! Praise and glory, wisdom and thanksgiving, honor, power, and might belong to our God forever and ever. Amen!"

"Who are these people," one of the elders asked, "and where do they come from?"

"I don't know," John answered. "Please tell me."

"These are the people who have come through the persecution," he

answered. "They have washed their robes white in the blood of the Lamb.

> This has brought them before God's throne;
>> they stand and serve him day and night in his temple;
>> the one who sits on the throne will shelter them.
> Never again will they know hunger or thirst,
>> nor shall the sun burn them in its heat,
>> for the Lamb on the throne has become their shepherd.
> He will lead them to life-giving springs,
>> and God will wipe away every tear from their eyes."

John stood in awe at these words, understanding at last the thing that he and the whole church through the ages needed to hear: that God's people are secure and protected through all that time might bring, for they are sealed forever as God's own.

The Seventh Seal

WHEN THE LAMB opened the seventh seal, there was silence in heaven for about half an hour. At last, seven angels stepped forward, each of them carrying a trumpet. The first trumpet blew, and a third of the grass and trees on the earth were burned up. The second angel blew his trumpet, and a third of the sea turned to blood, and a third of the ships on the sea and a third of the creatures in it were destroyed. When the third trumpet sounded, a star fell from heaven, and a third of the waters of the earth turned bitter and poisonous; a great many people died of the water. At the blast of the fourth trumpet, the sun and the moon grew dim, and a third of the stars went out.

Then the fifth angel blew his trumpet, and clouds of locusts flew out of the pit where Satan and his angels were tied up. Their bite was fiery, like the sting of a scorpion, and they tormented those who did not have God's sign on their foreheads. They king of the locusts was Apollyon, the Destroyer.

After this the sixth trumpet blew, and plagues were let loose on earth. A third of all humans were killed by the plagues, but those who remained did not turn away from their worship of idols, their robbery and murders, their witchcraft and immorality. Then a strong angel flew down to earth and stood with his right foot on the sea and his left foot on the land. "There will be no more delay!" he cried. "When the seventh trumpet blows, God will accomplish his secret plan, which he announced to his servants, the prophets."

Then the seventh angel blew his trumpet, and John heard mighty voices from heaven that cried out:

> The kingdom of the world
>   has become the kingdom of our Lord
>   and of his Christ,
> And he will reign forever and ever.

At the sound of these voices, the twenty-four elders fell on their faces before God and said:

> We praise you, Lord God Almighty,
>   who is and who was.

You have taken your great power,
   and you have begun to rule.
The heathen were filled with anger,
   but now the day of your anger has come,
   your moment to judge the dead;
The time to reward your servants the prophets,
   and all those who reverence you,
   both the great and the small;
The time to destroy
   those who destroy the earth!

John looked again and saw God's temple in heaven. The temple was opening, and John could see the ark of God's covenant! So he saw that through all the terrible judgments that had come to the earth, God's people still had cause to praise him. The Lord had won the victory; he had kept his promises, and soon he would make his home with them!

The Heart of the Matter

THE SEVEN SEALS had been opened, the seven trumpets blown. Then John saw a vision that captured in its images the whole story of salvation. In the sky he saw a woman dressed with the sun, with the moon under her feet. On her head was a crown of twelve stars. The woman stood for God's own people, and she appeared as the center of the universe because saving his people is the center of all God's purposes.

The woman was pregnant—about to give birth to her child. Suddenly John saw, standing in front of her, a huge red dragon with seven heads and ten horns. On each head was a crown of one of the kingdoms of the world. The dragon's tail swept a third of the stars out of the sky and threw them down to earth. He was armed with all the power of a world in rebellion against God, and he was waiting to devour the child as soon as it was born! Then the woman gave birth to her child, a son who would rule all the nations. The monster reached out with its claws to seize the child, but God snatched the boy away to his throne.

Suddenly John saw the meaning of the vision. The dragon was Satan, the one who deceived Adam and Eve in the garden of Eden. The whole world had come under the power of sin, and Satan intended to keep the world in his grasp. But God promised to set the world free through his Redeemer, who would be born to his people Israel. Satan knew this, and all along he tried to kill the child before he could be born. He prompted Cain to murder Abel; he sent Joseph's brothers to kill him; he goaded Pharoah to destroy Moses and the people of Israel; he tried to kill David, and he

317

persecuted the prophets. And when, in spite of all this, the Lord Jesus was
born in Bethlehem, Satan prompted King Herod to send his men to kill all
the babies born in that city. But though Satan pursued Jesus and finally
managed to have him killed on a Roman cross, the Redeemer rose from
the dead and was taken to be at the right hand of God on his throne.

Then John saw war in heaven. Michael, the commander of God's
angels, led his armies against the dragon and his angels. The dragon was
defeated and was thrown down to the earth. Then a loud voice said:

Now has God's salvation come,
    the reign of God and his chosen one.
For the great accuser has been cast out,
    who accused our brothers before God day and night.
They defeated him by the blood of the Lamb
    and by the message they proclaimed;
    their love for life did not make them afraid to die.
Rejoice, you heavens,
    and all you that dwell there!
But how terrible for you, O earth,
    for the devil has come down upon you.
He is filled with rage,
    for he knows that his time is short.

But the story was not over yet. When the dragon saw that he had been thrown to earth, he set out to kill the woman who had given birth to the child. Realizing that he could not kill the Redeemer, Satan now tried to destroy God's people. But God gave the woman wings to fly to a place of hiding in the desert. There he protected her against the attacks of the enemy. Then the dragon opened his mouth, and a flood of water spewed out to drown her—all the forces that Satan could muster to try to wipe out the life of the believers. But the earth opened up and swallowed the water, just as all of Satan's plans and schemes were swallowed up in God's plans, his control of the forces of creation and history. Furious that the woman had escaped, the dragon went off to fight against the rest of the woman's children, all those who obeyed God's commandments and stayed true to Jesus.

The dragon had the forces of might and war and earthly power at his command. In his vision John saw these powers as a beast that rose up from the sea. The peoples of the earth bowed down before it, except those whose names were written in the book of the living, which belonged to the Lamb who was killed. There was also a second beast, one that rose up from the earth. It did great wonders, all in the name of the first beast. All the people had to have a mark on their foreheads, and the mark was the name of the beast. Without that mark, no one was allowed to buy or sell anything. So John saw that there were two kingdoms, the kingdom of Christ and the kingdom of Antichrist, and that all the people on earth were marked on the forehead, either with the name of God or with the name of the beast.

John saw that it would be a bitter fight between those who loved the Lord and those who followed the beasts—the servants of the dragon. He also saw that there was no middle ground. All those who were not marked out by God would be marked by Satan. All those who did not willingly

319

serve the Lord would be forced to serve the power of darkness. But those who were marked with the seal of the Lord were protected forever. Nothing Satan could do, none of the powers he could muster, could harm those who belonged to the Lord Jesus. Even if they were killed, they would live forever with the Lord.

When John looked up from the vision of the dragon and the beasts—the forces of evil let loose in the world—it nearly took his breath away. For he saw the Lamb of God, the Lord Jesus himself, standing on Mount Zion. A great throng of people was gathered around him, so many that John could not count them. This was the church that had come through the times of darkness. They had never denied Christ and had never given in to the powers of evil. Now Christ had won the victory! He had kept them safe through all the times of persecution, because he had written his name on their foreheads. The throngs of men and women and children who were gathered around Jesus began to play their harps and sing a song no one had ever sung before. The sound of their song was as loud as a roaring waterfall, praising the name of Jesus.

Judgment

"HONOR GOD!" CAME a voice in John's vision. It was the voice of an angel who was flying through the heavens with a message of good news to all people on earth. "Praise the greatness of God," he cried. "The time has come for the Lord to judge mankind. Worship the one who made heaven and earth, the sea and the fountains of water."

A second angel came after him, crying out, "She has fallen! The great city Babylon has fallen! She made the peoples of the earth drunk with the wine of her wickedness. But she has fallen." And behind the second angel came a third, and his message was this: "Whoever has the name of the beast written on his forehead will drink the wine of the anger of God. The smoke of the fire that burns them will go up forever, and there will be no end to the punishment of those who carry the name of the beast."

Then John saw that the power of the dragon Satan and the power of all the forces that served him were nothing compared to the power of the Lord. The great city of man—which had been built to oppose the coming of the city of God—would fall into ruin, and those who served the beast would be punished. "Write this in your book," said the voice of the Spirit from heaven. "Happy are those who die in the service of the Lord. Yes, they will rest from their hard work, because the results of their work go with them."

In his vision John looked and saw one who looked like the Son of man, sitting on a white cloud, wearing a golden crown, and carrying a sharp sickle in his hand. An angel flew down and cried out, "Use your sickle and reap the harvest, because the earth is ripe!" So the one sitting on the cloud swung his sickle, and the harvest of the earth was reaped. There was no more time to plow or plant. The time had come for all people to reap the fruit of the seed they had sown. The fruit of evil seed was destruction, but the fruit of the seed of righteousness was eternal life.

Then the anger of the Lord, which the angels had announced, was poured out on the earth. Seven angels poured out seven bowls of God's judgment. The waters of the sea turned to blood, just as the waters of Egypt had done in the days of Moses. The creatures of the oceans died, and the rivers became unfit to drink; but those who served the kingdom of darkness would not turn away from their sins. Instead, they turned on God and cursed him. The demons that served the beast and the dragon brought the kings of the earth together for battle in the valley of Armageddon.

"Come," said an angel to John in the vision. "Come, and I will show you the famous prostitute. All the kings of the earth became drunk with her, and they will all be destroyed together." Immediately, John was carried into the desert. There he saw a woman dressed in rich robes, covered with diamonds and jewels. In her hand was a cup that held all the filthy and obscene things of the world. Her name was written on her forehead: "Babylon, mother of all the prostitutions and corruptions of the world." She was drunk with the blood of those who bore witness to Jesus.

John was astonished at the sight. Who could this woman be? Then an angel came to him and said, "The woman you see is the great city that rules the kings of the earth." John knew that city: it was Rome, the city that stood for everything people did in their proud hatred against God. Rome conquered the world and trampled justice underfoot. Her emperors called themselves gods and made people bow down and worship them. Rome was the great prostitute that caused all the nations of the world to serve false gods and to break faith with the Lord. But so was Babylon, the city that had conquered Israel and Judah. And so was old Jerusalem, the city God had chosen, but which had turned against him. And that godless city, that great prostitute, would continue to show itself in other times and other empires, all of which would stand against the Lord and against his people. But in the end the city of man would be destroyed, and the city of God would come.

"Babylon has fallen!" cried an angel flying down out of heaven. "The nations grew drunk with her, the kings of the earth deserted God for her, the businessmen of the world grew rich from her luxury. Now the kings will cry over her, and the businessmen will weep and say, 'How terrible! How awful! She was rich, but now all her wealth and glamor are gone. In a single hour she has been brought down!' The ships that carried goods to her ports will stand a long way off, and their captains and the crews will

cry, 'How terrible! How awful! She made us all rich, and now she is gone!'
But be glad, God's people! For God has condemned the great city Babylon
for what she did to you.''

Then John saw a white horse ride out of heaven, and its rider was
called "Faithful and True." His eyes blazed with fire, and he wore many
crowns on his head. His robe had been dipped in blood, and he was also
called the "Word of God." The armies of heaven rode behind him, and in
his mouth he carried a sharp sword of justice. On his robe was written
another name: "King of kings and Lord of lords."

The beast and all the kings that followed him, and all their armies,
came out to fight against the one who rode the white horse. But the beast
was taken prisoner and thrown into the fiery lake that was made for the

punishment of Satan and his angels. So all the powers that served the dragon Satan were destroyed forever. An angel flew down from heaven, and in his hand was the key to the pit. He seized the dragon, the old serpent Satan, and chained him up. Then the angel threw the dragon into the pit, locked it and sealed it. Satan had been overthrown for good. The day of deliverance had come!

Now John heard the roar of a great song coming from the heights of heaven. There was a great crowd assembled, and they sang:

> *Hallelujah!*
> *Salvation, glory and power belong to our God,*
> > *for his judgments are true and just.*
> *He has condemned the famous prostitute*
> > *who made the earth filthy with her sins.*
> *She shed the blood of his servants,*
> > *but now he has avenged them.*
> *Hallelujah!*

John looked, and in his vision he saw the twenty-four elders and the four six-winged creatures fall on their faces before God. The whole church, all those who served God from the beginning of the world to the end, and the whole creation joined together in a shout as mighty as thunder, as powerful as the roaring surf. And they cried:

> *Hallelujah!*
> *The Lord is king!*
> > *Our God, the Almighty one, reigns!*
> *Let us rejoice and be glad;*
> > *Let us give glory to God!*
> *For the wedding day of the Lamb has come.*
> > *His bride is prepared for the wedding.*
> *The dress she has been given to wear*
> > *Is the white linen of righteous lives.*

John looked back up to heaven, and he saw a great throne, white and shining. The earth and the heavens had disappeared, and only God's throne was left. All the graves had opened, and all those who had died stood before the throne. The books of their lives were opened, and they were judged according to what they had done. Another book was opened as well, the book of the living, in which were the names of all those who loved and served the Lord. Then Satan and the powers that served him, and all those who belonged to the world of death—even death itself—were thrown into the fiery lake. The fulfillment of all things had come at last, and Jesus Christ was shown to all to be the victor, the King of kings and the Lord of lords.

All Things New

ONCE MORE JOHN looked in his vision, and this time he saw a new heaven and a new earth. Everything that belonged to the old world, the world touched by sin and death, had disappeared. And he saw the holy city of God, the new Jerusalem, coming down out of heaven from God, just as a bride would come to meet her bridegroom. A voice cried out from the throne and said, "Now God shall dwell with mankind. They shall be his people, and he shall be their God. He will wipe away every tear from their eyes. There will be no more death, no more mourning or crying or pain. All the old things have disappeared."

Then the one who sits on the throne said, "Look! I am already making everything new, even now!" John was stunned by the power of those words, and joy washed over him like a great wave. So that was what his visions had meant! The voice came to him again and said, "Write all these things down, because these words are true. They are already being fulfilled! I am the beginning and the ending, the first and the last. Everything is in my hand, and everything is fulfilling my purposes. To those who are thirsty I will give water, free for the taking, from the fountain of the water of life. Those who win the victory will receive all these gifts from me. I will be their God, and they will be my children. As for those who turn against me, those who follow the ways of evil and sorcery and idolatry, they will be cast into the fire lake, and their death will last forever."

Again an angel flew down to John and said, "Come with me, and I will show you the Bride, the wife of the Lamb!" And the angel showed him Jerusalem, the Holy City, which was coming down out of heaven from God, shining with God's glory. There was no temple in the city, because the Lord himself is the temple. The city had twelve gates, one for each of the tribes of Israel, and its foundation was built of twelve rows of stones, one for each of the twelve apostles of the church. This was the city God had been building from the very beginning, the city God was building when John saw his vision, the city he is still building.

"I saw no temple in the city," John said, "because the Lord himself is the temple. It did not need the light of the sun or the moon, because the glory of God was shining on it, and the Lamb of God was the lamp of the city. The peoples of the earth will walk in the light of that city, and kings will bring their wealth into it. Its gates will never close, because there will be no night there. Nothing that is sinful or impure will enter that city. Only those whose names are written in the Lamb's book of the living will come in. They will see the face of God, and his name will be written on their foreheads. They will need no lamps, for the Lord God will be their light, and they will reign as kings forever and ever."

One last time the angel came to John. "These words are true," he said.

"They can be trusted. The Lord God, who spoke to the prophets, has sent me to show his servants what must happen very soon."

Then John heard the voice of Jesus saying, "Listen! I am coming soon! Happy are those who listen to the prophecy of this book. I am coming soon, and I will bring my rewards with me. I will give to each one according to what he has done. I am the first and the last, the beginning and the end. Happy are those who have washed their robes so that they may enter through the gates of the city. I, Jesus, have sent my angel to announce these things to the churches. I am the source and the son of David's line; I am the bright Morning Star!"

The last vision faded, and John once more saw only the island of Patmos. He was still in exile, and the church was still suffering under the

325

armies of Rome. But now John knew what God was doing in all that was happening. Joy had replaced sadness, and hope had replaced despair, because John now knew that even when things looked worst, when the powers of darkness pressed close around, God still had the whole world in his hand. His kingdom was truly coming: the new Jerusalem was still coming down out of heaven from God, and Jesus Christ was still making all things new.

John began to write, and he wrote down everything that he had seen and heard. When he had finished, the joy that he felt welled up within him, and he wrote: "The Spirit and the Bride say, 'Come!' Let those who hear these words answer, 'Come!' Let all those who are thirsty come and accept the gift of life-giving water. The one who spoke all these words says, 'Yes, I am coming soon!' Amen! Come, Lord Jesus!"

* * * * * *

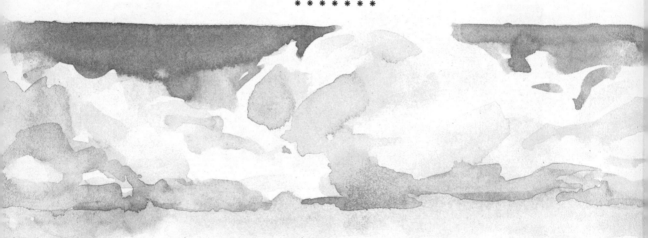

We are still living in the days of the revelation God gave through John. We are waiting for the Lord's return, for the great day when the heavens will open with a loud noise and the Lord will appear in the clouds in his great glory, with thousands of his angels. But the day will come like a thief in the night, when we least expect it. For that reason, Jesus warned all his disciples, and us too, when he was still on earth: "Watch, therefore, for you will not know on what day your Lord will come."

The church has been through many dark days since the days of John, and we know that even worse times may still be ahead for us. At those times it may seem to some that the Lord is not coming at all, and unbelievers will say, "That day will never come." But the Lord promised us in a letter from the apostle Peter: "Do not ignore this fact, my brothers, that with the Lord a day is the same as a thousand years. He has not forgotten his promises. He is hurrying toward us. He himself has said so."

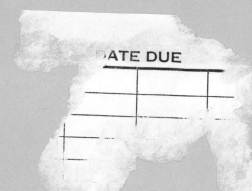